IGNATIUS OF ANTIOCH

The Letters

ST VLADIMIR'S SEMINARY PRESS
Popular Patristics Series
Number 49

The Popular Patristics Series published by St Vladimir's Seminary Press provides readable and accurate translations of a wide range of early Christian literature to a wide audience—students of Christian history to lay Christians reading for spiritual benefit. Recognized scholars in their fields provide short but comprehensive and clear introductions to the material. The texts include classics of Christian literature, thematic volumes, collections of homilies, letters on spiritual counsel, and poetical works from a variety of geographical contexts and historical backgrounds. The mission of the series is to mine the riches of the early Church and to make these treasures available to all.

Series Editor
JOHN BEHR

Associate Editor
AUGUSTINE CASIDAY

IGNATIUS OF ANTIOCH

The Letters

Translated by

ALISTAIR STEWART

ST VLADIMIR'S SEMINARY PRESS
YONKERS, NEW YORK
2013

Library of Congress Control Number: 20133945206

ST VLADIMIR'S SEMINARY PRESS
575 Scarsdale Road, Yonkers, NY 10707
1-800-204-2665
www.svspress.com

ISBN 978–088141–464–6
ISSN 1555–5755

PRINTED IN THE UNITED STATES OF AMERICA

For Patrick
with love

At peace

4th July 2010

Table of Contents

Foreword

To undertake a presentation of Ignatius' letters alongside the interpolated and expanded version of the collection which was undertaken in the fourth century, has been something of an indulgence, allowing me to engage my twin interests of second-century Christianity and the formation of the church order tradition. It has also enabled me to achieve a long-held ambition to reach a better understanding of the controversies of the fourth century than I had previously held. I hope that the volume is as useful to its audience as it has been to its translator.

In this light I must express my gratitude, once again, to all at St Vladimir's Seminary Press for allowing me to work with them once again. Fr John Behr has continued a friend and Fr Benedict Churchill has a superb critical eye for errors and omissions. I am also grateful, as always, to Fr Allen Brent who has always been an enlightening dialogue partner, especially as regards Ignatius, and to Jim Smith and Sara Parvis for sharing their deep knowledge and understanding of the fourth century with me, though I doubt they will agree with my conclusions. I began the work during a spell of residence at Codrington College, Barbados, and I thank Fr Ian Rock and all at the College once again for their hospitality. I continued the work whilst on the staff of Sherborne Abbey, and I thank Fr Eric Woods and all at the Abbey for their support. I conclude the work as I prepare to take up a pastoral ministry once again.

I wished to undertake this work not simply to deepen my own learning but also to commemorate my son Patrick. My other children have books in this series dedicated to them. Patrick will never see his. Yet he is at peace. This is an offering of love from his broken-hearted father.

Pray, reader, that in the day of resurrection I may hold my son in my arms.

Upton cum Chalvey
On the feast of the Theophany, 2013

On Ignatius of Antioch

All we know of Ignatius is what he tells is in his letters, namely that he is a Christian from Antioch in Syria who has been condemned to be executed in the circus, to be destroyed by wild animals. So he tells the Ephesians: "Intercede for the church which is in Syria, whence I am taken to Rome in chains."[1] He also tells us that he was a bishop. "God has made the bishop from Syria worthy of being found at the setting of the sun, after being sent from where it rises."[2] However, there is no indication of the year in which this occurs, an issue to which we will turn below.

More immediately we must stress that although Ignatius was a bishop this does not mean that he is "bishop of Syria" or "bishop of Antioch." A great deal has been written on the manner in which Ignatius supports the ministry of a single bishop, a system called "monepiscopate." It has been alleged that he introduced this system of church governance to places beyond Antioch. However, this depends on the idea that previously the churches had been under collective governance, which is not the case.[3] Rather he was the leader of a congregation within Antioch and, like other congregational leaders, designated *episkopos*, a word now translated as "bishop," though "supervisor" might be an equally valid translation.

With his guards, he travels as a prisoner to Rome in the summer.[4] He seems to go through Philadelphia, as he mentions a time when he was among the Philadelphian Christians.[5] He reaches Smyrna on

[1] Ign. *Eph*. 21.2.
[2] Ign. *Rom*. 2:2.
[3] As I argue at length, not only with regard to Antioch but more generally, in my *The Original Bishops* (Grand Rapids: Baker Academic, forthcoming 2014).
[4] Ign. *Rom*. 10.3 gives the date on which he leaves Asia by boat from Troas.
[5] Ign. *Phld*. 7.1.

11

the coast of Asia and stays here for a while. Subsequently he goes
northward to Troas before sailing to Philippi.[6] Here we lose touch
with him, though we may assume that he was eventually brought to
Rome and met martyrdom in the arena. Given that he was being sent
to Rome in the summer months, in which sailing would take place,
this would seem a very peculiar route; we will attempt to explain it
below. However, his stay in Smyrna allows him to receive bishops
from nearby cities (Ephesus, Magnesia, and Tralles) and also write
letters to the churches in each of these cities, as well as one to the
Roman churches. Subsequently, from Troas, he writes two letters to
Christian communities he had previously visited, Philadelphia and
Smyrna, as well as one to Polycarp, a bishop in Smyrna.

This is his theme:

> I am writing to all the churches and I am directing everyone
> that I am willingly dying for God, unless you prevent me. I
> beseech you, do not become an unseasonable kindness for
> me. Leave me to be bread for the beasts, through which I may
> be able to attain to God. I am God's wheat and through the
> beasts' teeth I shall be found to be pure bread for Christ.[7]

As martyr in waiting Ignatius is first of all concerned that
nothing, such as an attempt by Christians in Rome to save his life,
should prevent his martyrdom from taking place. This may seem
extreme to us, but we must understand that Ignatius sees himself as
an imitator of Paul, and of Paul as an imitator of Christ. As such he
sees his own offering of his life as an offering joined to that of Christ
himself. This is the means by which he gains unity with God through
Christ, namely by literally participating in his death. Thus Ignatius
is enunciating a theology of martyrdom understood within forming
Judaism. In 4 Maccabees, Eleazar, in being put to death, states: "Be
merciful to your people, and let our punishment suffice for them.

[6]Ign. *Pol.* 8.1.
[7]Ign. *Rom.* 4.1.

Make my blood their purification, and take my life as a ransom for theirs."[8] Here he is using the same word that Ignatius employs. But apart from imitating Christ, Ignatius is a self-conscious imitator of Paul. Thus he prays that he might be found in the footsteps of Paul and, also in writing the Ephesians, in describing himself as an expiation, immediately quotes Paul: "My spirit is an expiation on the cross, which is an offense to those who do not believe, but to us is salvation and eternal life. Where is the wise one? Where is the debater? Where is the boasting of those who are termed understanding?"[9] Although we hear of peace at Antioch, which may in turn imply that there was conflict among Christians in the city, and although Ignatius may have seen his sacrifice as a scapegoat as the means by which this peace came about, we should not necessarily link the two phenomena by making Ignatius, and his claim to be a bishop, the cause of the conflict.[10] Ignatius sees his forthcoming death as sealing the peace which the Antiochene Christians had found in the same way that a sacrifice offered together by disparate parties might bring those parties together.[11] As such we may see him enunciating an understanding found not only within forming Judaism but within the Hellenistic world known to him.

However, there are other themes within his letters. For apart from asking the Roman church not to intervene to prevent his martyrdom, Ignatius uses the opportunity presented by the visits from representatives in the churches and his stays in Philadelphia and Smyrna to raise a number of issues which affect the lives of Christians. In particular he is aware that there are teachers going through

[8] 4 Macc 6.28–29.

[9] Ign. *Eph.* 18 following 1 Cor 1.20.

[10] So, as representative of a long tradition of interpretation, Allen Brent, *Ignatius of Antioch, a Martyr Bishop and the Origin of Episcopacy* (London: Continuum, 2007), 45–49. Cf. Thomas A. Robinson, *Ignatius of Antioch and the Parting of the Ways: Early Jewish-Christian Relations* (Peabody, MA: Hendrickson, 2009), 165–77.

[11] Thus see the discussion below of ambassadors. We may also note the inscription SEG 38.1462, which describes the manner in which villages surrounding the city of Oinoanda were to participate in a common sacrifice and join in the sacrificial procession in the feast of the *Demosthenea*.

Asia teaching a form of Christianity alien to that which he, as martyr in waiting, represented.

First he warns of the dangers of Docetism. Docetism is the belief that Jesus was human only in appearance, and was in reality some form of disembodied ghost or phantom. Ignatius insists on the reality of the earthly Jesus and on the reality of his sufferings. As he says, if Jesus suffered only in appearance, then his own imprisonment was likewise only an appearance.[12] Secondly he warns of the danger of Jewish practices in Christianity, pointing to aspects of keeping the Jewish law, and especially of observing the Jewish Sabbath, as spiritually perilous. It is indeed possible that these are the same people being addressed, rather than two distinct groups.

But beyond the immediate danger of false teaching, Ignatius is opposed to the general trend within Christianity to adopt a scholastic outlook, as opposed to a domestic basis for the church. It is this which leads to what is often recognized as his most prominent theme, the importance of unity and concord in a Christian assembly centred on a bishop.[13]

The reason that Ignatius opposes a scholastic form of Christianity emphasizing the role of the bishop is that the role of the bishop was originally, and remained at the time, domestic and economic. Thus when he directs Polycarp in the performance of his episcopal duties we may note that he is told to look after widows, orphans, and the dispossessed, even to regulate the marriage of Christians (in order, we suggest, to ensure that marriages were not contracted in order to keep funds within a family and to concentrate wealth). As such it is important that the bishop should continue to exercise this domestic role, ensuring that everyone is fed at the eucharistic meal. For this reason he opposes the development by which the bishop was becoming a teacher.

Beyond this, we may suggest, should a bishop become a teacher, then he comes to attract financial support. This would divert support

[12]Ign. *Smyrn.* 2–3.
[13]Ign. *Trall.* 2, *Smyrn.* 8.

from those very persons in need who, he sees, should be the objects of the bishop's attention. This is bound up to the common idea in the ancient world of patronage, a social system by which persons would lend social support to others in return for economic benefits. For Ignatius, the true bishop is God; the bishop on earth is the broker of the benefits of Christ. In social theory a broker is a person who regulates access to patronage. Thus by diverting the focus of patronage away from the needy, for whom the bishop is the broker of financial support, and onto himself, the scholastic bishop, as opposed to a household bishop, undoes the fundamental episcopal duty. So it is that Ignatius defends the reported silence of Onesimus, the Ephesian bishop, and employs extensive household imagery in this letter.

Thus for Ignatius a community gathered around its bishop is a community representing the worship of heaven but is also a community representing the mercies of God to all. The Docetic vision of Christ destroys this, because, as Ignatius sees, these people cannot keep a Eucharist, cannot hold an agapē meal in integrity, because they have no true belief in the unity of flesh and spirit in Christ. For this reason they likewise have no idea of the unity of flesh and spirit sacramentally expressed, as they cannot see the unity of flesh and spirit in people more generally. But quite apart from that, the exaltation of teachers, also a mark of those who teach Jewish ways to Christians (if they are not, indeed, the same people) means that there are alternative foci of patronage apart from the Christian community more generally.

This leaves open the question of when Ignatius is writing. Conventionally Ignatius has been dated, following Eusebius, to the reign of the Roman Emperor Trajan. This dating has often been disputed, and there are numerous attempts to assign his work to a later period in the second century, and to claim that the work of Ignatius is a forgery from that period, as well as numerous defenses of the conventional date.[14] However, there is something of a false dichotomy between an authentic Trajanic Ignatius and the later

---

[14]See on these, most fully, Brent, *Ignatius*, 95–143.

creation of a pseudepigrapher. On this basis, and on the basis of a web of other evidence, I have argued elsewhere that Ignatius is writing in the summer of 134, and that he is travelling in the entourage of the emperor Hadrian, who at the time was returning from Syria to Rome overland, having been engaged in fighting in the Bar Kosiba revolt in Palestine.[15] As such, I suggest, the letters are indeed authentic, but that they date from a later period in the second century than is generally reckoned, though not as late as some modern critics would suggest.

The date of Ignatius is relevant for a number of reasons. In the first instance it informs us of the progress of the forms of Christianity known, generally, as "gnostic." For if a Hadrianic date is accepted, it is in turn possible to see the opponents of Ignatius as followers of the gnostic teacher Basilides.[16]

Secondly such a date gives a context for Ignatius' statements about the distinction between Judaism and Christianity. The revolt under Bar Kosiba led to the alienation of Christians of Jewish heritage and practice from other Jews, as Christians of Jewish heritage failed to support the rebellion.

Finally it enables us to see the extent to which the offices of bishop and deacon, together with a presbytery, have formed within Christian circles. One of the reasons for the suspicion cast on a Trajanic Ignatius is the doubt that the monepiscopate might have developed by that time. However, as already suggested, this is a doubt based on the false premise that leadership by a single bishop had developed out of collective leadership. Indeed, I argue in *The Original Bishops* that the ecclesial governance known to Ignatius had not changed from that of the first generations; even this, however, is a positive historical result as it demonstrates that the change which would in turn take place, namely a movement to a system where

[15]In *The Original Bishops*. This Jewish uprising in Palestine is also known as the "Bar Kochba" revolt. It was led by Simon bar Kosiba, who was given the name "bar Kochba" ("son of the star").

[16]Placed at the time of Hadrian by Eusebius' *Chronicle* and Jerome's *On Illustrious Men* 21.

bishops had charge of a number of congregations, with subordinate officers (as opposed to having charge of single congregations) had not occurred yet, even in the 130s. Truly to understand what Ignatius means when he speaks of congregations gathered around a bishop, however, we need to understand his imagery. It is often the case in ancient documents that the very things which made them comprehensible to ancient contemporaries are those which make them incomprehensible to today's readers. This is because a writer would assume knowledge of the social setting which he shared with his readers, and which we, in turn, do not share. Ignatius refers to the gathering of Christians for worship employing cultic imagery which would readily have been recognized by his first hearers, but which is entirely foreign to us.

To understand this cultic imagery, we may first observe that in every letter Ignatius describes himself as God-carrier. This same image of carrying is prominent in one passage of the letter to the Ephesians, when the Ephesian Christians are described as "God-carriers and temple-carriers, Christ-carriers, carriers of holy things, entirely decorated with the commandments of Jesus Christ."[17] This is a reference to the common practice of religious processions in the time of Ignatius, in which images of the gods were carried in procession as part of the cult. As an example we may note a procession of Isis described by Apuleius:

> The principal Priests which were apparelled with white surplesses hanging downe to the ground, bare the relikes of the puissant goddesse. One carried in his hand a light, not unlike to those which we used in our houses, saving that in the middle thereof appeared a bole which rendred a more bright flame. The second attired like the other bare in his hand an Altar, which the goddesse her selfe named the succor of nations. The third held a tree of palme with leaves of gold, and the verge of Mercurie. The fourth shewed out a token of

17 Ign. *Eph.* 9.

ʼ by his left hand, which was deformed in every place, signifiing thereby more equitie then by the right hand. The same Priest carried a round vessell of gold, in forme of a cap. The fifth bare a van, wrought with springs of gold, and another carried a vessell for wine: By and by after the goddesse followed a foot as men do, and specially Mercurie, the messenger of the goddesse infernall and supernall, with his face sometime blacke, sometime faire, lifting up the head of the dogges Annubis, and bearing in his left hand, his verge, and in his right hand, the branches of a palme tree, after whom followed a cow with an upright gate, representing the figure of the great goddesse, and he that guided her, marched on with much gravity. Another carried after the secrets of their religion, closed in a coffer. There was one that bare on his stomacke a figure of his god, not formed like any beast, bird, savage thing or humane shape, but made by a new invention, whereby was signified that such a religion should not be discovered or revealed to any person. There was a vessel wrought with a round bottome, haveing on the one side, pictures figured like unto the manner of the Egyptians, and on the other side was an eare, whereupon stood the Serpent Aspis, holding out his scaly necke.[18]

A similar cultic setting governs the references which will be found to Ignatius' suggestions that ambassadors be appointed from the various Asian cities to go to Antioch to celebrate the peace which had come about in that church. In the same way cultic ambassadors would be sent from various of the Asian cities to others to join in cultic celebrations, in particular in celebrations aimed at celebrating the achievement of peace between the cities. For although they were all part of a single Roman Empire, the cities retained a degree of independence and looked back to the days at which they were independent city states. This state of peace was described as *homonoia*,

[18]Apuleius, *Metamorphoses* 11.10, translated by William Adlington in 1566.

translated as "concord," a term which is found frequently in Ignatius' writing. Thus we may note the following inscription:

> We have received your letter and we have listened attentively to the ambassadors Andromenes and Philotheus. Wherefore you do well even conducting yourselves according to custom and celebrating the customary sacrifices to the king and queen in the appropriate seasons. And we have sent to you the copy of the decree on these matters that was despatched to us. . . . with the ambassadors Andromenes and Philotheus, instructing them to make this proclamation to you. . . . They shall also have the right to joint participation when they are present for the sacred acts . . . they shall be invited whenever the city sacrifices to Concord . . .[19]

Such an independence, leading to peaceful relations with other cities, was joined to the idea that peace had been brought about through the Roman Empire.

Other images from the city cults appear within Ignatius' writing. Thus when he writes to the Magnesians of the bishop "seated first," we may suggest that this is the same image used of tutelary deities of the Asian cities. Thus note the following introduction to an inscription:

> Demeter and Kore, the goddesses who are seated first in the city . . .[20]

We may describe Ignatius' attitude as "contra-cultural," in that he adopts the norms of the prevailing and surrounding culture and inverts them in such a way that they come to have reference to Christ and his church. If we are right about the circumstances of his removal to Rome, namely that he is part of an imperial procession,

[19]Inscription SEG 39.14260.
[20]Inscription *Syll3* 694.

we may see him as even more a contra-cultural figure, a chained figure in an imperial procession, a small part of a larger event, claiming to be the centre, as he is the carrier of the true God in the procession of an emperor already divinized by his non-Christian subjects. Small wonder that Ignatius says, "It is better for me to die in Jesus Christ than to reign over the ends of the earth."[21] However, it is in the Eucharist that the church fundamentally manifests itself, and it is in that context that Ignatius speaks to the Ephesians, encouraging them to come together as image carriers and temple-carriers in a tight gathering of harmony, which will expel evil from their midst.

Ignatius' references to the civic cults are not made simply to commend his insights to his hearers, but are central to his understanding of the church as a society centred on the bishop, as this society is brought into being when the Eucharist is celebrated, just as the civic cults constructed the city-states themselves. In this light we may note the image of the church as a chorus, participating in the eucharistic meal, not only in *Ephesians* 4, but also in *Romans*, where the Roman Christians are to form a chorus in the arena during the sacrificial death of Ignatius himself. This may readily be paralleled from contemporary Hellenistic political rhetoric:

> When the rulers and presidents are prudent and wise and the rest of the community are administered lawfully and moderately, according to their judgement, one should call such a city a real city, moderate and wise and under law's rule, because of their administrators, so we might call a choir musical when its conducting head is musical and its remaining members follow him together and utter no sound contrary to the melody . . .[22]

Ignatius' concentration on the figure of the bishop is not therefore simply a concern for good order. It is also motivated by a

---

[21]Ign. *Rom.* 6.1.
[22]Dio Chrysostom *Oration* 36.21.

concern that the goods of the church be fairly distributed; for this reason, in writing to the church in Smyrna, he upbraids the Docetists and points out that, by celebrating neither Eucharist nor agapē, they are showing their lack of concern for the widow and the orphan.[23] Rather it is the Eucharist, with the bishop as the host, which manifests the church. The presbyters, whom we may understand as those who offer the patronage managed by the bishop, are around the bishop as a "spiritual crown,"[24] just as the elders seen in the vision of John on Patmos surround the throne.[25] The unity of flesh and spirit, of which Ignatius speaks so much, indicates that spiritual acts, in particular the eucharistic gathering, are also means of economic support for the poor.

It is a tight, eucharistic, gathering, moreover, which is the means by which the church is preserved from heresy, rather than by a deposit of teaching and teaching activity. As Ignatius says:

> Seek, therefore, to come together more closely to give thanks to God and to glorify him. For when you are each together closely the powers of Satan are cast down and his destructive power is brought low by your agreement in the faith.[26]

In the same way that the harmony of citizens preserves the *polis*, so the harmonious gathering of Christians preserves the church. Ignatius has grounds to discuss this, as it is clear that the communion of Christians at Antioch was at best fractured. The evidence for this assertion is found, once again, in Ignatius' own letters as he informs us that the church at Antioch is at peace, implying that such peace had not always been known in the church.

[23]Ign. *Smyrn.* 7.
[24]Ign. *Magn.* 13.
[25]Rev 4.4.
[26]Ign. *Eph.* 13.1. This translation embodies the important observation of Taras Khomych, "The Notion of *Puknôs* as a Distinctive Characteristic of Liturgical Celebrations in the Letters of St Ignatius of Antioch," in F.M. Young et al., eds, *StPatr* 40 (Leuven: Peeters, 2006), 441–6, regarding the translation of this passage.

There have been various attempts to understand this statement, which is often linked to Ignatius' espousal of episcopal governance, with the understanding that this was controversial. Thus the peace is seen as either the triumph of the monepiscopal party or else the result of the removal of Ignatius himself. However, this is to fail to recognize what has to be the fundamental division within Antiochene Christianity, namely the division between Jewish and Gentile Christians over matters of table fellowship, a division which had been present since the time at which Paul and Peter had the discussion recorded in Galatians. If peace has come about then this must be the division which has been healed. Again, we may note, this is a breach which is eucharistically represented, since concerns of table fellowship would prevent law-observant Jews from participating in a single Eucharist with Gentiles, in particular those who were not law-observant. It would also mean that the eucharistic president, the bishop, could not be a Gentile should Jews participate. As noted above, Ignatius believes that his offering of himself has brought this peace about, in the same way that Christ's offering united Jew and Gentile. This discovery of unity between Christians of Jewish and non-Jewish heritage may well have come about at precisely this time, through the Bar Kosiba revolt; as has already been noted, the messianic claims of Bar Kosiba alienated those Jews who believed in Jesus Christ, and so they were forced to find fellowship with Gentile Christians, and to define themselves principally with reference to their Christian beliefs rather than their law-observant Jewish practices.

Not only does the Eucharist manifest the church, and preserve the church from heresy by modelling the agreement of Christians, the celebration manifests the nature of God. The bishop is described as a type of God the Father, and this may be seen in his position, seated first, at the Eucharist. The deacons are a type of Jesus Christ, insofar as their role in the eucharistic meal was the distribution of the eucharistic gifts, performing the will of the bishop. Thus the celebration of the church, mirroring the civic cults, mirrors the harmony of the church and the conformity of the church with the life of its Lord.

At the centre of Ignatius' thought, therefore, is the eucharistic gathering. Ignatius does not derive a theology from the Eucharist, but rather sees the Eucharist representing what his hearers will already recognize, the expression of the love of God in Jesus Christ.

IGNATIUS OF ANTIOCH

A Note on the Greek text:

The text of Ignatius reproduced here is that edited by J.B. Lightfoot, *The Apostolic Fathers* 2.1 (London: MacMillan, 1889 [1994]), and for Ps-Ignatius, vol. 2.3 (1889), texts now in the public domain. I have consulted also other editions, noted in the "Further Reading" section at the end of this volume. Throughout, I have noted major divergences between the readings I have employed and those in the Lightfoot text; I have not noted minor ones, nor have I called attention to distinctions of punctuation. In consequence, the careful reader may note that at various points, the translation is not fully in accordance with the Greek on the facing page.

Ephesians

Having been visited by Onesimus, an Ephesian bishop, Ignatius responds to the needs of the church by warning them strongly against false teachers who seem to have appeared in Ephesus. Here his political imagery of unity is particularly strong, seeing the unity of the Ephesian Christians as a defense against the devil represented by the false teachers. However, also noteworthy is the household imagery which Ignatius employs, which may be seen as a response to the scholasticization of Onesimus' Ephesian church. Onesimus himself had been criticized by those within the church for his silence; presumably there was an expectation that the bishop should be teaching, which was not shared by the bishop himself.

ΠΡΟΣ ΕΦΕΣΙΟΥΣ ΙΓΝΑΤΙΟΣ

Ἰγνάτιος, ὁ καὶ Θεοφόρος, τῇ εὐλογημένῃ ἐν μεγέθει θεοῦ πατρὸς πληρώματι, τῇ προωρισμένῃ πρὸ αἰώνων εἶναι διὰ παντὸς εἰς δόξαν παράμονον, ἄτρεπτον ἡνωμένην καὶ ἐκλελεγμένην ἐν πάθει ἀληθινῷ, ἐν θελήματι τοῦ πατρὸς καὶ Ἰησοῦ Χριστοῦ, τοῦ θεοῦ ἡμῶν, τῇ ἐκκλησίᾳ τῇ ἀξιομακαρίστῳ, τῇ οὔσῃ ἐν Ἐφέσῳ [τῆς Ἀσίας], πλεῖστα ἐν Ἰησοῦ Χριστῷ καὶ ἐν ἀμώμῳ χαρᾷ χαίρειν.

1 ₁Ἀποδεξάμενος [ὑμῶν] ἐν θεῷ τὸ πολυαγάπητον ὄνομα,[1] κέκτησθε φύσει [ἐν γνώμῃ ὀρθῇ καὶ] δικαίᾳ κατὰ πίστιν καὶ ἀγάπην ἐν Χριστῷ Ἰησοῦ τῷ σωτῆρι ἡμῶν· μιμηταὶ ὄντες θεοῦ, ἀναζωπυρήσαντες ἐν αἵματι θεοῦ, τὸ συγγενικὸν ἔργον τελείως ἀπηρτίσατε· ₂ἀκούσαντες γὰρ δεδεμένον ἀπὸ Συρίας ὑπὲρ τοῦ κοινοῦ ὀνόματος καὶ ἐλπίδος, ἐλπίζοντα τῇ προσευχῇ ὑμῶν ἐπιτυχεῖν ἐν Ῥώμῃ θηριομαχῆσαι, ἵνα διὰ τοῦ ἐπιτυχεῖν δυνηθῶ μαθητὴς εἶναι, ἱστορῆσαι[2] ἐσπουδάσατε· ₃ἐπεὶ οὖν τὴν πολυπληθίαν ὑμῶν ἐν ὀνόματι θεοῦ ἀπείληφα ἐν Ὀνησίμῳ, τῷ ἐν ἀγάπῃ ἀδιηγήτῳ, ὑμῶν δὲ [ἐν σαρκὶ] ἐπισκόπῳ, ὃν εὔχομαι κατὰ Ἰησοῦν Χριστὸν ὑμᾶς ἀγαπᾶν καὶ πάντας ὑμᾶς αὐτῷ ἐν ὁμοιότητι εἶναι. εὐλογητὸς γὰρ ὁ χαρισάμενος ὑμῖν ἀξίοις οὖσιν τοιοῦτον ἐπίσκοπον κεκτῆσθαι.

2 ₁Περὶ δὲ τοῦ συνδούλου μου Βούρρου, τοῦ κατὰ θεὸν διακόνου ὑμῶν [καὶ] ἐν πᾶσιν εὐλογημένου, εὔχομαι παραμεῖναι αὐτὸν εἰς τιμὴν ὑμῶν καὶ τοῦ ἐπισκόπου· καὶ Κρόκος δέ, ὁ θεοῦ ἄξιος καὶ ὑμῶν, ὃν ἐξεμπλάριον τῆς ἀφ' ὑμῶν ἀγάπης ἀπέλαβον, κατὰ πάντα με ἀνέπαυσεν· ὡς καὶ αὐτὸν ὁ πατὴρ Ἰησοῦ Χριστοῦ ἀναψύξαι ἅμα. Ὀνησίμῳ καὶ Βούρρῳ καὶ Εὔπλῳ καὶ Φρόντωνι, δι' ὧν πάντας ὑμᾶς κατὰ ἀγάπην εἶδον. ₂ὀναίμην ὑμῶν διὰ παντός, ἐάνπερ ἄξιος ὦ. πρέπον οὖν ἐστιν κατὰ πάντα τρόπον δοξάζειν Ἰησοῦν Χριστὸν τὸν

---

[1]So Lightfoot. Cf. more recent texts which omit ὑμῶν and read πολυαγάπητόν σου ὄνομα at the end of the sentence.
[2]So Lightfoot. Cf. the majority of versions which supply ἰδεῖν to complete a defective text.

IGNATIUS TO THE EPHESIANS:

Ignatius, who is also God-carrier, to the church blessed in greatness by the fullness of God the Father, which was foreordained before the ages to possess at all times a glory which is enduring and unchanging, which is united and elected in true suffering, by the will of the Father and of Jesus Christ, our God, the church which is worthy of good fortune, which is in Ephesus of Asia, warmest greetings in a blameless joy.

1   ₁I have received your much-desired name in God, which you have obtained through your just nature, in accordance with the faith and love in Christ Jesus, our Savior. You are imitators of God; rekindling in the blood of God the task we share, you have brought it to perfection. ₂For when you heard that I was coming, in chains, from Syria, on account of our common name and that I hoped, through your intercession, to have the chance to fight wild beasts in Rome, so that I might be able thereby to be a disciple, you were keen to see me. ₃Since, therefore, I have, in Onesimus, who is in a love beyond telling your bishop in the flesh, received your fullness in the name of God, I pray, in Jesus Christ, that you love him and that you should all be of his likeness. For blessed is the one who has given you the grace, worthy as you are, to obtain such a bishop.

2   ₁Now concerning my fellow-slave Burrhus, your deacon in God, blessed in everything: I pray that he should remain for your honor and that of the bishop. And Crocus also, who is worthy of God and of you, whom I received as an embodiment of your love. He has revived me in every way, and so may the Father of Jesus Christ refresh him, as well as Onesimus and Burrhus and Euplus and Fronto, through whom I saw all of you, in accordance with love. ₂May I delight in you at all times, should I be worthy. Thus it is proper for you to give glory to Jesus Christ in every way, as he glorified you, so that you may be

δοξάσαντα ὑμᾶς· ἵνα ἐν μιᾷ ὑποταγῇ κατηρτισμένοι, ὑποτασσόμενοι τῷ ἐπισκόπῳ καὶ τῷ πρεσβυτέρῳ, κατὰ πάντα ἦτε ἡγιασμένοι.

3 ₁Οὐ διατάσσομαι ὑμῖν ὡς ὤν τι. εἰ γὰρ καὶ δέδεμαι ἐν τῷ ὀνόματι, οὔπω ἀπήρτισμαι ἐν Ἰησοῦ Χριστῷ. νῦν [γὰρ] ἀρχὴν ἔχω τοῦ μαθητεύεσθαι καὶ προσλαλῶ ὑμῖν ὡς συνδιδασκαλίταις μου. ἐμὲ γὰρ ἔδει ὑφ᾽ ὑμῶν ὑπαλειφθῆναι πίστει, νουθεσίᾳ, ὑπομονῇ, μακροθυμίᾳ. ₂ἀλλ᾽ ἐπεὶ ἡ ἀγάπη οὐκ ἐᾷ με σιωπᾶν περὶ ὑμῶν, διὰ τοῦτο προέλαβον παρακαλεῖν ὑμᾶς, ὅπως συντρέχητε τῇ γνώμῃ τοῦ θεοῦ. καὶ γὰρ Ἰησοῦς Χριστός, τὸ ἀδιάκριτον ἡμῶν ζῆν, τοῦ πατρὸς ἡ γνώμη, ὡς καὶ οἱ ἐπίσκοποι, οἱ κατὰ τὰ πέρατα ὁρισθέντες ἐν Ἰησοῦ Χριστοῦ γνώμῃ εἰσίν.

4 ₁Ὅθεν πρέπει ὑμῖν συντρέχειν τῇ τοῦ ἐπισκόπου γνώμῃ· ὅπερ καὶ ποιεῖτε. τὸ γὰρ ἀξιονόμαστον ὑμῶν πρεσβυτέριον τοῦ θεοῦ ἄξιον, οὕτως συνήρμοσται τῷ ἐπισκόπῳ, ὡς χορδαὶ κιθάρᾳ. διὰ τοῦτο ἐν τῇ ὁμονοίᾳ ὑμῶν καὶ συμφώνῳ ἀγάπῃ Ἰησοῦς Χριστὸς ᾄδεται. ₂καὶ οἱ κατ᾽ ἄνδρα δὲ χορὸς γίνεσθε, ἵνα σύμφωνοι ὄντες ἐν ὁμονοίᾳ, χρῶμα θεοῦ λαβόντες, ἐν ἑνότητι, ᾄδητε ἐν φωνῇ μιᾷ διὰ Ἰησοῦ Χριστοῦ τῷ πατρί, ἵνα ὑμῶν καὶ ἀκούσῃ καὶ ἐπιγινώσκῃ, δι᾽ ὧν εὖ πράσσετε· μέλη ὄντας τοῦ υἱοῦ αὐτοῦ. χρήσιμον οὖν ἐστιν ὑμᾶς ἐν ἀμώμῳ ἑνότητι εἶναι, ἵνα καὶ θεοῦ πάντοτε μετέχητε.

5 ₁Εἰ γὰρ ἐγὼ ἐν μικρῷ χρόνῳ τοιαύτην συνήθειαν ἔσχον πρὸς τὸν ἐπίσκοπον ὑμῶν, οὐκ ἀνθρωπίνην οὖσαν ἀλλὰ πνευματικήν, πόσῳ μᾶλλον ὑμᾶς μακαρίζω τοὺς ἐγκεκραμένους αὐτῷ, ὡς ἡ ἐκκλησία Ἰησοῦ Χριστῷ καὶ ὡς Ἰησοῦς Χριστὸς τῷ πατρί, ἵνα πάντα ἐν ἑνότητι σύμφωνα ᾖ. ₂μηδεὶς πλανάσθω· ἐὰν μή τις ᾖ ἐντὸς τοῦ θυσιαστηρίου, ὑστερεῖται τοῦ ἄρτου [τοῦ θεοῦ]. εἰ γὰρ ἑνὸς καὶ δευτέρου προσευχὴ τοσαύτην ἰσχὺν ἔχει, πόσῳ μᾶλλον ἥ τε τοῦ ἐπισκόπου καὶ πάσης τῆς ἐκκλησίας. ₃ὁ οὖν μὴ ἐρχόμενος ἐπὶ τὸ αὐτό, οὗτος ἤδη ὑπερηφανεῖ καὶ ἑαυτὸν διέκρινεν· γέγραπται

complete in a single subjection, being subject to the bishop and to the presbytery, so being hallowed in every way.

3 ₁I do not direct you as though I were a somebody. For even though I am in chains on behalf of the name, I have not yet been perfected in Jesus Christ. Only now am I at the beginning of my instruction, and I address you as my fellow-pupils. I am in need of your anointing me with faith, with instruction, with patience, with longsuffering. ₂But since love does not permit me to be silent concerning you, I have determined to exhort you, that you should run together in union with the mind of God. For Jesus Christ, our inseparable life, is the mind of the Father, as the bishops, who are established to the ends of the earth, are in the mind of Christ.

4 ₁It is thus fitting that you should run together in accordance with the mind of your bishop, as indeed you do. For your justly renowned presbytery, worthy of God, is so attuned to the bishop as the strings are to the harp. Therefore Jesus Christ is sung in your concord and harmonious love. ₂And each of you should join the chorus, so that in a harmonious concord, and taking up God's note in unity, you may sing to the Father with a single voice through Jesus Christ, so that he may both hear you, and acknowledge you, through what you do well, as limbs of his own Son. It is profitable, therefore, that you should enjoy blameless unity, so that you may participate in God always.

5 ₁For since, in such a short space of time, I obtained such an intimate acquaintance with your bishop, which was not human but spiritual, how much more do I reckon you fortunate to be enmeshed with him, as the church is with Jesus Christ and as Jesus Christ is with the Father, so that everything may be harmonious in unity. ₂Let nobody be deceived. Anyone who is not within the sanctuary lacks the bread of God. For if the intercession of one or two has such power, how much more is that of the bishop and the entire church? ₃Therefore anyone who does not join the congregation is

γάρ· ὑπερηφάνοις ὁ θεὸς ἀντιτάσσεται. σπουδάσωμεν οὖν μὴ ἀντιτάσσεσθαι τῷ ἐπισκόπῳ, ἵνα ὦμεν θεῷ ὑποτασσόμενοι.

6 ₁Καὶ ὅσον βλέπει τις σιγῶντα ἐπίσκοπον, πλειόνως αὐτὸν φοβείσθω. πάντα γὰρ ὃν πέμπει ὁ οἰκοδεσπότης εἰς ἰδίαν οἰκονομίαν, οὕτως δεῖ ἡμᾶς αὐτὸν δέχεσθαι, ὡς αὐτὸν τὸν πέμψαντα. τὸν οὖν ἐπίσκοπον δῆλονότι ὡς αὐτὸν τὸν κύριον δεῖ προσβλέπειν. ₂αὐτὸς μὲν οὖν Ὀνήσιμος ὑπερεπαινεῖ ὑμῶν τὴν ἐν θεῷ εὐταξίαν, ὅτι πάντες κατὰ ἀλήθειαν ζῆτε καὶ ὅτι ἐν ὑμῖν οὐδεμία αἵρεσις κατοικεῖ· ἀλλ᾽ οὐδὲ ἀκούετέ τινος πλέον ἢ περὶ Ἰησοῦ Χριστοῦ λαλοῦντος ἐν ἀληθείᾳ.

7 ₁Εἰώθασιν γάρ τινες δόλῳ πονηρῷ τὸ ὄνομα περιφέρειν, ἄλλα τινὰ πράσσοντες ἀνάξια θεοῦ· οὓς δεῖ ὑμᾶς ὡς θηρία ἐκκλίνειν· εἰσὶν γὰρ κύνες λυσσῶντες, λαθροδῆκται, οὓς δεῖ ὑμᾶς φυλάσσεσθαι ὄντας δυσθεραπεύτους. ₂εἷς ἰατρός ἐστιν, σαρκικός τε καὶ πνευματικός, γεννητὸς καὶ ἀγέννητος, ἐν ἀνθρώπῳ[3] γενόμενος θεός, ἐν θανάτῳ ζωὴ ἀληθινή, καὶ ἐκ Μαρίας καὶ ἐκ θεοῦ, πρῶτον παθητὸς καὶ τότε ἀπαθής, Ἰησοῦς Χριστὸς ὁ κύριος ἡμῶν.

8 ₁Μὴ οὖν τις ὑμᾶς ἐξαπατάτω, ὥσπερ οὐδὲ ἐξαπατᾶσθε, ὅλοι ὄντες θεοῦ. ὅταν γὰρ μηδεμία ἐπιθυμία[4] ἐνήρεισται ἐν ὑμῖν ἡ δυναμένη ὑμᾶς βασανίσαι, ἄρα κατὰ θεὸν ζῆτε. περίψημα ὑμῶν καὶ ἁγνίζομαι ὑπὲρ ὑμῶν Ἐφεσίων, ἐκκλησίας τῆς διαβοήτου τοῖς αἰῶσιν. ₂οἱ σαρκικοὶ τὰ πνευματικὰ πράσσειν οὐ δύνανται οὐδὲ οἱ πνευματικοὶ τὰ σαρκικά, ὥσπερ οὐδὲ ἡ πίστις τὰ τῆς ἀπιστίας οὐδὲ ἡ ἀπιστία τὰ τῆς πίστεως. Ἃ δὲ καὶ κατὰ σάρκα πράσσετε, ταῦτα πνευματικά ἐστιν· ἐν Ἰησοῦ γὰρ Χριστῷ πάντα πράσσετε.

9 ₁Ἔγνων δὲ παροδεύσαντάς τινας ἐκεῖθεν, ἔχοντας κακὴν διδαχήν· οὓς οὐκ εἰάσατε σπεῖραι εἰς ὑμᾶς, βύσαντες τὰ ὦτα εἰς τὸ μὴ παραδέξασθαι τὰ σπειρόμενα ὑπ᾽ αὐτῶν· ὡς ὄντες λίθοι ναοῦ πατρός,

---

[3]So Lightfoot. I have read σαρκὶ.
[4]So Lightfoot, as in the long recension. I have read ἔρις.

already supercilious and has passed judgement upon himself. For it is written: "God opposes the supercilious."[1] Therefore we should be anxious not to oppose the bishop, so that we may be subject to God.

6 ₁And insofar as anyone sees that the bishop is silent, they should hold him in awe all the more. For we should receive anyone whom the master sends to look after his household as though he were the sender. That we should look upon the bishop as the Lord himself is thus clear. ₂Onesimus himself highly praises your good order in God, because you all live in accordance with the truth and because there is no factionalism dwelling among you. Rather you will not even listen to anyone apart from somebody who speaks in truth of Jesus Christ.

7 ₁For some are accustomed to bearing the name in wicked deceit, whilst acting in a manner unworthy of God. You should shun them like wild animals, for they are raving dogs who bite in secret. You should be on your guard against them as they are hard to tame. ₂There is one physician, fleshly and spiritual, begotten and unbegotten, God in the flesh, true life in death, both from Mary and from God, first suffering and then impassible, Jesus Christ, our Lord.

8 ₁Let nobody fool you, as indeed you are not fooled, as you are all God's, for when no troubling strife is established among you then indeed you are living in accordance with God. I am your expiation, and am being consecrated as such on your behalf, Ephesians, church celebrated into eternity. ₂The fleshly cannot perform anything spiritual, nor can spiritual people perform anything fleshly, just as neither can faith do anything faithless, nor faithlessness do anything faithful. Whatever you do that is in accordance with the flesh is entirely spiritual, for you do everything in Jesus Christ.

9 ₁I know that some have passed in by you from there who hold a wicked teaching. You did not allow them to sow among you, but stopped your ears, so that you would not receive anything sowed

[1]Prov 3.34.

προητοιμασμένοι[5] εἰς οἰκοδομὴν θεοῦ πατρός, ἀναφερόμενοι εἰς τὰ ὕψη διὰ τῆς μηχανῆς Ἰησοῦ Χριστοῦ, ὅς ἐστιν σταυρός, σχοινίῳ χρώμενοι τῷ πνεύματι τῷ ἁγίῳ· ἡ δὲ πίστις ὑμῶν ἀναγωγεὺς ὑμῶν, ἡ δὲ ἀγάπη ὁδὸς ἡ ἀναφέρουσα εἰς θεόν. ₂ἐστὲ οὖν καὶ σύνοδοι πάντες, θεοφόροι καὶ ναοφόροι, χριστοφόροι, ἁγιοφόροι, κατὰ πάντα κεκοσμημένοι ἐν ταῖς ἐντολαῖς Ἰησοῦ Χριστοῦ· οἷς καὶ ἀγαλλιώμενος ἠξιώθην, δι' ὧν γράφω, προσομιλῆσαι ὑμῖν, καὶ συγχαρῆναι ὅτι κατ' ἀνθρώπων[6] βίον οὐδὲν ἀγαπᾶτε, εἰ μὴ μόνον τὸν θεόν.

10 ₁Καὶ ὑπὲρ τῶν ἄλλων δὲ ἀνθρώπων ἀδιαλείπτως προσεύχεσθε· ἔστιν γὰρ [ἐν] αὐτοῖς ἐλπὶς μετανοίας, ἵνα θεοῦ τύχωσιν. ἐπιτρέψατε οὖν αὐτοῖς κἂν ἐκ τῶν ἔργων ὑμῖν μαθητευθῆναι. ₂πρὸς τὰς ὀργὰς αὐτῶν ὑμεῖς πραεῖς, πρὸς τὰς μεγαλορημοσύνας αὐτῶν ὑμεῖς ταπεινόφρονες, πρὸς τὰς βλασφημίας αὐτῶν ὑμεῖς τὰς προσευχάς, πρὸς τὴν πλάνην αὐτῶν ὑμεῖς ἑδραῖοι τῇ πίστει, πρὸς τὸ ἄγριον αὐτῶν ὑμεῖς ἥμεροι· μὴ σπουδάζοντες ἀντιμιμήσασθαι αὐτούς. ₃ἀδελφοὶ αὐτῶν εὑρεθῶμεν τῇ ἐπιεικείᾳ· μιμηταὶ δὲ τοῦ κυρίου σπουδάζωμεν εἶναι· τίς πλέον ἀδικηθῇ, τίς ἀποστερηθῇ, τίς ἀθετηθῇ;[7] ἵνα μὴ τοῦ διαβόλου βοτάνη τις εὑρεθῇ ἐν ὑμῖν, ἀλλ' ἐν πάσῃ ἁγνείᾳ καὶ σωφροσύνῃ μένητε ἐν Ἰησοῦ Χριστῷ σαρκικῶς καὶ πνευματικῶς.

11 ₁Ἔσχατοι καιροί. λοιπὸν αἰσχυνθῶμεν, φοβηθῶμεν τὴν μακροθυμίαν τοῦ θεοῦ, ἵνα μὴ ἡμῖν εἰς κρίμα γένηται. ἡ γὰρ τὴν μέλλουσαν ὀργὴν φοβηθῶμεν, ἢ τὴν ἐνεστῶσαν χάριν ἀγαπήσωμεν, ἓν τῶν δύο· μόνον ἐν Χριστῷ Ἰησοῦ εὑρεθῆναι εἰς τὸ ἀληθινὸν ζῆν. ₂χωρὶς τούτου μηδὲν ὑμῖν πρεπέτω, ἐν ᾧ τὰ δεσμὰ περιφέρω, τοὺς πνευματικοὺς μαργαρίτας· ἐν οἷς γένοιτό μοι ἀναστῆναι τῇ προσευχῇ ὑμῶν, ἧς γένοιτό μοι ἀεὶ μέτοχον εἶναι, ἵνα ἐν κλήρῳ

---

[5]A conjectural emendation from Lightfoot, instead of the πατρός ἡτοιμασμένοι of the mss.

[6]A conjecture of Lightfoot, rather than the rather meaningless ἄλλον of the mss.

[7]Here I have deviated from Lightfoot's punctuation.

by them, as you are stones for the temple of the Father, prepared in advance for the building of God the Father, carried up to the heights through the crane of Jesus Christ, which is his cross, using the Holy Spirit as a rope. Your faith is your hoist, your love the way which carries you up to God. ₂For you are all travelling companions, God-carriers and temple-carriers, Christ-carriers, carriers of holy things, entirely decorated with the commandments of Jesus Christ. I exult because I have been found worthy of conversing with you through what I write, and I rejoice with you because you love nothing in human life except God alone.

10 ₁And intercede for others without ceasing, for there is hope for their repentance, that they may attain to God. Therefore permit them to be instructed, by your deeds at least. ₂You are to be meek in response to their anger, humble in response to their pride, interceding in response to their blasphemies, firm in the faith in response to their error, gentle in response to their wildness, with no desire to follow their example. ₃May they come to be our brothers through our reasonableness. Let us be anxious to be imitators of the Lord. Who was wronged more than he, who was more defrauded, who was more despised? Thus shall no plant of the devil be found in you, but you may abide in Jesus Christ in all holiness and self-control, both fleshly and spiritually.

11 ₁These are the last times. For the rest, let us be shamed, and fearful of God's long-suffering, lest it become a judgement made against us. For we should either be fearful of the wrath that is to come or else love the gracious gift which is now present to us—one of the two, as long as we obtain true life in Jesus Christ. ₂Apart from him there is nothing of value for you. In him I am carrying around these chains, spiritual pearls, in which it may be granted that I should rise again, through your intercession. May I always have a share in it, so that I may be found sharing the lot of the Ephesian Christians,

Ἐφεσίων εὑρεθῶ τῶν Χριστιανῶν, οἳ καὶ τοῖς ἀποστόλοις πάντοτε συνήνεσαν ἐν δυνάμει Ἰησοῦ Χριστοῦ.

12 ₁Οἶδα τίς εἰμι καὶ τίσιν γράφω. ἐγὼ κατάκριτος, ὑμεῖς ἐλεημένοι· ἐγὼ ὑπὸ κίνδυνον, ὑμεῖς ἐστηριγμένοι. ₂πάροδός ἐστε τῶν εἰς θεὸν ἀναιρουμένων, Παύλου συμμύσται, τοῦ ἡγιασμένου, τοῦ μεμαρτυρημένου, ἀξιομακαρίστου, οὗ γένοιτό μοι ὑπὸ τὰ ἴχνη εὑρεθῆναι, ὅταν θεοῦ ἐπιτύχω· ὃς ἐν πάσῃ ἐπιστολῇ μνημονεύει ὑμῶν ἐν Χριστῷ Ἰησοῦ.

13 ₁Σπουδάζετε οὖν πυκνότερον συνέρχεσθαι εἰς εὐχαριστίαν θεοῦ καὶ εἰς δόξαν· ὅταν γὰρ πυκνῶς ἐπὶ τὸ αὐτὸ γίνεσθε, καθαιροῦνται αἱ δυνάμεις τοῦ σατανᾶ, καὶ λύεται ὁ ὄλεθρος αὐτοῦ ἐν τῇ ὁμονοίᾳ ὑμῶν τῆς πίστεως. ₂οὐδέν ἐστιν ἄμεινον εἰρήνης, ἐν ᾗ πᾶς πόλεμος καταργεῖται ἐπουρανίων καὶ ἐπιγείων.

14 ₁Ὧν οὐδὲν λανθάνει ὑμᾶς, ἐὰν τελείως εἰς Ἰησοῦν Χριστὸν ἔχητε τὴν πίστιν καὶ τὴν ἀγάπην· ἥτις ἐστὶν ἀρχὴ ζωῆς καὶ τέλος· ἀρχὴ μὲν πίστις, τέλος δὲ ἀγάπη. τὰ δὲ δύο ἐν ἑνότητι γενόμενα θεός ἐστιν, τὰ δὲ ἄλλα πάντα εἰς καλοκαγαθίαν ἀκόλουθά ἐστιν. ₂οὐδεὶς πίστιν ἐπαγγελλόμενος ἁμαρτάνει οὐδὲ ἀγάπην κεκτημένος μισεῖ. φανερὸν τὸ δένδρον ἀπὸ τοῦ καρποῦ αὐτοῦ· οὕτως οἱ ἐπαγγελλόμενοι Χριστοῦ εἶναι δι᾽ ὧν πράσσουσιν ὀφθήσονται. οὐ γὰρ νῦν ἐπαγγελίας τὸ ἔργον, ἀλλ᾽ ἐν δυνάμει πίστεως ἐάν τις εὑρεθῇ εἰς τέλος.

15 ₁Ἄμεινόν ἐστιν σιωπᾶν καὶ εἶναι, ἢ λαλοῦντα μὴ εἶναι· καλὸν τὸ διδάσκειν, ἐὰν ὁ λέγων ποιῇ. εἷς οὖν διδάσκαλος, ὃς εἶπεν καὶ ἐγένετο· καὶ σιγῶν δὲ πεποίηκεν, ἄξια τοῦ πατρός ἐστιν.
₂ὁ λόγον Ἰησοῦ κεκτημένος ἀληθῶς δύναται καὶ τῆς ἡσυχίας αὐτοῦ ἀκούειν, ἵνα τέλειος ᾖ· ἵνα δι᾽ ὧν λαλεῖ πράσσῃ καὶ δι᾽ ὧν σιγᾷ γινώσκηται.

who have always been in agreement with the apostles in the power of Jesus Christ.

12 ₁I know who I am, and those to whom I write. I am under judgement; you are those who have received mercy. I am in danger, and you are safe. ₂You are a passageway for those being carried away on Christ's account. You are fellow-initiates with Paul, who was sanctified, martyred, most worthily blessed. May I be found in his footsteps, as of those of the rest of the saints, when I attain to God. He, in every letter, makes mention of you in Christ Jesus.

13 ₁Seek, therefore, to come together more closely to give thanks to God and to glorify him. For when you are each together closely the powers of Satan are cast down and his destructive power is brought low by your agreement in the faith. ₂There is nothing better than peace in which every war, heavenly and earthly, is undone.

14 ₁Nothing of this will be overlooked by you if you have perfect faith in Jesus Christ and love, as these are the cause and end of life. Faith is the cause, love the end. When the two are brought together, that is God, and everything else which is noble and good follows on. ₂Nobody who professes faith sins, nor does anyone who has obtained love hate. The tree is recognized by its fruit, so those who profess Christ are apparent through what they do. The task is not the present profession, but is that of being found at the conclusion in the power of faith.

15 ₁To be silent and to be authentic is better than speaking whilst being inauthentic. Teaching is good if the one who teaches is acting. Thus there is one teacher who spoke and so it happened. And what he did, even in silence, is worthy of the Father.

₂Whoever truly possesses the word of Jesus can also hear his quietness, so that he may be perfect, so that he may act through what he says and have knowledge through his silence.

₃οὐδὲν λανθάνει τὸν κύριον, ἀλλὰ καὶ τὰ κρυπτὰ ἡμῶν ἐγγὺς αὐτῷ ἐστιν. πάντα οὖν ποιῶμεν, ὡς αὐτοῦ ἐν ἡμῖν κατοικοῦντος, ἵνα ὦμεν αὐτοῦ ναοὶ καὶ αὐτὸς ἐν ἡμῖν θεὸς ἡμῶν,⁸ ὅπερ καὶ ἔστιν καὶ φανήσεται πρὸ προσώπου ἡμῶν, ἐξ ὧν δικαίως ἀγαπῶμεν αὐτόν.

16 ₁μὴ πλανᾶσθε, ἀδελφοί μου· οἱ οἰκοφθόροι βασιλείαν θεοῦ οὐ κληρονομήσουσιν. ₂εἰ οὖν οἱ κατὰ σάρκα ταῦτα πράσσοντες ἀπέθανον, πόσῳ μᾶλλον ἐὰν πίστιν θεοῦ ἐν κακοδιδασκαλίᾳ φθείρῃ, ὑπὲρ ἧς Ἰησοῦς Χριστὸς ἐσταυρώθη. ὁ τοιοῦτος ῥυπαρὸς γενόμενος εἰς τὸ πῦρ τὸ ἄσβεστον χωρήσει ὁμοίως καὶ ὁ ἀκούων αὐτοῦ.

17 ₁Διὰ τοῦτο μύρον ἔλαβεν ἐπὶ τῆς κεφαλῆς [αὐτοῦ] ὁ κύριος, ἵνα πνέῃ τῇ ἐκκλησίᾳ ἀφθαρσίαν. μὴ ἀλείφεσθε δυσωδίαν τῆς διδασκαλίας τοῦ ἄρχοντος τοῦ αἰῶνος τούτου, μὴ αἰχμαλωτίσῃ ὑμᾶς ἐκ τοῦ προκειμένου ζῆν. ₂διὰ τί δὲ οὐ πάντες φρόνιμοι γινόμεθα λαβόντες θεοῦ γνῶσιν, ὅ ἐστιν Ἰησοῦς Χριστός; τί μωρῶς ἀπολλύμεθα, ἀγνοοῦντες τὸ χάρισμα ὃ πέπομφεν ἀληθῶς ὁ κύριος;

18 ₁Περίψημα τὸ ἐμὸν πνεῦμα τοῦ σταυροῦ, ὅ ἐστιν σκάνδαλον τοῖς ἀπιστοῦσιν, ἡμῖν δὲ σωτηρία καὶ ζωὴ αἰώνιος. ποῦ σοφός; ποῦ συζητητής; ποῦ καύχησις τῶν λεγομένων συνετῶν; ₂ὁ γὰρ θεὸς ἡμῶν Ἰησοῦς ὁ Χριστὸς ἐκυοφορήθη ὑπὸ Μαρίας κατ᾽ οἰκονομίαν θεοῦ⁹ ἐκ σπέρματος μὲν Δαυείδ, πνεύματος δὲ ἁγίου· ὃς ἐγεννήθη καὶ ἐβαπτίσθη ἵνα τῷ πάθει τὸ ὕδωρ καθαρίσῃ.

19 ₁Καὶ ἔλαθεν τὸν ἄρχοντα τοῦ αἰῶνος τούτου ἡ παρθενία Μαρίας καὶ ὁ τοκετὸς αὐτῆς ὁμοίως καὶ ὁ θάνατος τοῦ κυρίου· τρία μυστήρια κραυγῆς, ἅτινα ἐν ἡσυχίᾳ θεοῦ ἐπράχθη. ₂πῶς οὖν

⁸ἡμῶν, found in some mss but not all, is omitted by Lightfoot.
⁹θεοῦ is omitted by Lightfoot, though widely attested.

₃Nothing is hidden from the Lord, but even what we have hidden is close to him. Therefore everything we do should be done as though he were dwelling in us, so that we may be his temples and he may be our God in us. This is indeed so, and will be apparent to us by the love which we justly bear towards him.

16 ₁Do not be deceived, my brothers. Those who corrupt their households shall not inherit the kingdom of God. ₂If those who do this in accordance with the flesh should suffer death, how much more so, if somebody should corrupt the faith of God, for which Jesus Christ was crucified, with evil teaching. Anyone such, vile as he is, shall go to the unquenchable fire, as shall anyone who listens to him.

17 ₁The Lord received ointment on his head for this reason, that he should breathe incorruption upon the church. Do not be anointed with the foul smell of the teaching of the ruler of this age, lest he lead you away as a prisoner from the life set before you. ₂Why indeed are all not sensible, as we receive understanding of God, who is Jesus Christ? Why do we perish in folly, in ignorance of the gracious gift which the Lord has truly sent?

18 ₁My spirit is an expiation on the cross, which is an offense to those who do not believe, but to us is salvation and eternal life. Where is the wise one? Where is the debater?[2] Where is the boasting of those who are termed understanding? ₂For our God, Jesus the Christ, was conceived by Mary, in accordance with God's plan, of the seed of David and the Holy Spirit. He was born and was baptized, so that he might purify the water through his submission.

19 ₁The virginity of Mary and her giving birth, and likewise the death of the Lord, elude the ruler of this world. Three mysteries of crying out were performed in the quietness of God. ₂How, then,

[2]1 Cor 1.20.s

ἐφανερώθη τοῖς αἰῶσιν; ἀστὴρ ἐν οὐρανῷ ἔλαμψεν ὑπὲρ πάντας τοὺς ἀστέρας καὶ τὸ φῶς αὐτοῦ ἀνεκλάλητον ἦν, καὶ ξενισμὸν παρεῖχεν ἡ καινότης αὐτοῦ· τὰ δὲ λοιπὰ πάντα ἄστρα ἅμα ἡλίῳ καὶ σελήνῃ χορὸς ἐγένετο τῷ ἀστέρι, αὐτὸς δὲ ἦν ὑπερβάλλων τὸ φῶς αὐτοῦ ὑπὲρ πάντα· ταραχή τε ἦν πόθεν ἡ καινότης ἡ ἀνόμοιος αὐτοῖς. ₃ὅθεν ἐλύετο πᾶσα μαγεία καὶ πᾶς δεσμός, ἠφανίζετο κακίας ἄγνοια, καθῃρεῖτο παλαιὰ βασιλεία διεφθείρετο [θεοῦ] ἀνθρωπίνως φανερουμένου εἰς καινότητα ἀϊδίου ζωῆς· ἀρχὴν δὲ ἐλάμβανεν τὸ παρὰ θεῷ ἀπηρτισμένον. ἔνθεν τὰ πάντα συνεκινεῖτο διὰ τὸ μελετᾶσθαι θανάτου κατάλυσιν.

20 ₁Ἐάν με καταξιώσῃ Ἰησοῦς Χριστὸς ἐν τῇ προσευχῇ ὑμῶν, καὶ θέλημα ᾖ, ἐν τῷ δευτέρῳ βιβλιδίῳ, ὃ μέλλω γράφειν ὑμῖν, προσδηλώσω ὑμῖν ἧς ἠρξάμην οἰκονομίας εἰς τὸν καινὸν ἄνθρωπον Ἰησοῦν Χριστόν, ἐν τῇ αὐτοῦ πίστει καὶ ἐν τῇ αὐτοῦ ἀγάπῃ, ἐν πάθει αὐτοῦ καὶ ἀναστάσει, ₂μάλιστα ἐὰν ὁ κύριός μοι ἀποκαλύψῃ ὅτι οἱ κατ᾽ ἄνδρα κοινῇ πάντες ἐν χάριτι ἐξ ὀνόματος συνέρχεσθε ἐν μιᾷ πίστει καὶ ἐν Ἰησοῦ Χριστῷ, τῷ κατὰ σάρκα ἐκ γένους Δαυείδ, τῷ υἱῷ ἀνθρώπου καὶ υἱῷ θεοῦ, εἰς τὸ ὑπακούειν ὑμᾶς τῷ ἐπισκόπῳ καὶ τῷ πρεσβυτερίῳ ἀπερισπάστῳ διανοίᾳ· ἕνα ἄρτον κλῶντες, ὅς ἐστιν φάρμακον ἀθανασίας, ἀντίδοτος τοῦ μὴ ἀποθανεῖν ἀλλὰ ζῆν ἐν Ἰησοῦ Χριστῷ διὰ παντός.

21 ₁Ἀντίψυχον ὑμῶν ἐγώ, καὶ ὧν ἐπέμψατε εἰς θεοῦ τιμὴν εἰς Σμύρναν· ὅθεν καὶ γράφω ὑμῖν, εὐχαριστῶν τῷ κυρίῳ, ἀγαπῶν Πολύκαρπον ὡς καὶ ὑμᾶς. μνημονεύετέ μου, ὡς καὶ ὑμῶν Ἰησοῦς Χριστός.

₂προσεύχεσθε ὑπὲρ τῆς ἐκκλησίας τῆς ἐν Συρίᾳ, ὅθεν δεδεμένος εἰς Ῥώμην ἀπάγομαι, ἔσχατος ὢν τῶν ἐκεῖ πιστῶν, ὥσπερ ἠξιώθην εἰς τιμὴν θεοῦ εὑρεθῆναι. ἔρρωσθε ἐν θεῷ πατρὶ καὶ ἐν Ἰησοῦ Χριστῷ, τῇ κοινῇ ἐλπίδι ἡμῶν.

did he appear to the ages? A star shone in heaven brighter than all the stars, and its light was indescribable and its newness brought amazement. All the other stars, with the sun and the moon, formed a chorus to the star, whose light surpassed all other. There was agitation regarding its origin, as it was new, and unlike any other.

₃So was all sorcery undone, and every bond of evil brought to nothing. Ignorance was destroyed and the ancient realm brought down as God appeared in a human manner for the renewal of eternal life. What had been prepared by God received its beginning, as from then on everything was in turmoil as the destruction of death came about.

20   ₁If Jesus Christ finds me worthy through your intercession, and should he so will, I shall clarify for you, in the second booklet which I would like to write to you, what I have already begun, regarding the divine plan proposed on the basis of the new man Jesus Christ, on his fidelity and his love, on his passion and resurrection. ₂Especially shall I do so if the Lord reveals to me that each and all of you are gathering in a common grace, one by one, in a single faith and in Jesus Christ. He is of the race of David in the flesh, he is Son of Man and Son of God, so that you may obey the bishop and the presbytery in an undisturbed conscience, breaking a single bread, which is the medicine of immortality, an antidote which prevents death, yet enables us to live at all times in Jesus Christ.

21   ₁I am a ransom for you, and for those whom you sent to Smyrna for the honor of God. I am writing to you from there, giving thanks to the Lord and loving Polycarp as I love you. Remember me, as Jesus Christ remembers you.

₂Intercede for the church which is in Syria, whence I am taken to Rome in chains, though I am the least of those who are believers there, as I have been found worthy of honoring God. Fare well in God the Father and in Jesus Christ, our common hope.

Magnesians

Having received a visit from Damas, bishop of the Magnesians, Ignatius responds by praying that there may be unity of flesh and spirit among the Magnesians. This Ignatian language is a prayer that the eucharistic celebration of the Magnesians might be both authentically spiritual, showing forth the unity of the church, and authentic in supporting the needy. The fundamental warning here is against those who Judaize. In particular he warns against keeping the Sabbath. The particular point of this is that this is a time in which the main eucharistic celebration is moving from the eve of Sabbath to the Sunday morning; this means that the exercise of patronage in the Eucharist is no longer a matter of providing a meal, but that gifts for the poor have to be given outside the eucharistic context. Thus the role of the bishop, who was the main agent of the church's charity, becomes all the more critical. However, the bishop of the Magnesians is young, and therefore not himself a presbyter (the term means "an older man," and as such mirrors the usage of associations, who had elders as patrons). As such he is the agent of the presbyters. It is in this light that we must understand what Ignatius says about the movement of the liturgy to a Sunday, for to retain a celebration on Saturday evening means that the patrons might exercise their power, including their power over the bishop, more readily.

ΜΑΓΝΗΣΙΕΥΣΙΝ ΙΓΝΑΤΙΟΣ

Ἰγνάτιος, ὁ καὶ Θεοφόρος, τῇ εὐλογημένῃ ἐν χάριτι θεοῦ πατρὸς ἐν Χριστῷ Ἰησοῦ τῷ σωτῆρι [ἡμῶν], ἐν ᾧ ἀσπάζομαι τὴν ἐκκλησίαν τὴν οὖσαν ἐν Μαγνησίᾳ τῇ πρὸς Μαιάνδρῳ, καὶ εὔχομαι ἐν θεῷ πατρὶ καὶ ἐν Ἰησοῦ Χριστῷ πλεῖστα χαίρειν.

1   ₁Γνοὺς ὑμῶν τὸ πολυεύτακτον τῆς κατὰ θεὸν ἀγάπης, ἀγαλλιώμενος προειλόμην ἐν πίστει Ἰησοῦ Χριστοῦ προσλαλῆσαι ὑμῖν. ₂καταξιωθεὶς γὰρ ὀνόματος θεοπρεπεστάτου, ἐν οἷς περιφέρω δεσμοῖς ᾄδω τὰς ἐκκλησίας, ἐν αἷς ἕνωσιν εὔχομαι σαρκὸς καὶ πνεύματος Ἰησοῦ Χριστοῦ τοῦ διὰ παντὸς ἡμῶν ζῆν, πίστεώς τε καὶ ἀγάπης, ἧς οὐδὲν προκέκριται, τὸ δὲ κυριώτερον, Ἰησοῦ καὶ πατρός· ἐν ᾧ ὑπομένοντες τὴν πᾶσαν ἐπήρειαν τοῦ ἄρχοντος τοῦ αἰῶνος τούτου καὶ διαφυγόντες θεοῦ τευξόμεθα.

2   Ἐπεὶ οὖν ἠξιώθην ἰδεῖν ὑμᾶς διὰ Δαμᾶ τοῦ ἀξιοθέου ὑμῶν ἐπισκόπου καὶ πρεσβυτέρων ἀξίων Βάσσου καὶ Ἀπολλωνίου καὶ τοῦ συνδούλου μου διακόνου Ζωτίωνος, οὗ ἐγὼ ὀναίμην, ὅτι ὑποτάσσεται τῷ ἐπισκόπῳ ὡς χάριτι θεοῦ καὶ τῷ πρεσβυτερίῳ ὡς νόμῳ Ἰησοῦ Χριστοῦ.

3   ₁Καὶ ὑμῖν δὲ πρέπει μὴ συγχρᾶσθαι τῇ ἡλικίᾳ τοῦ ἐπισκόπου, ἀλλὰ κατὰ δύναμιν θεοῦ πατρὸς πᾶσαν ἐντροπὴν αὐτῷ ἀπονέμειν, καθὼς ἔγνων καὶ τοὺς ἁγίους πρεσβυτέρους οὐ προσειληφότας τὴν φαινομένην νεωτερικὴν τάξιν, ἀλλ᾿ ὡς φρονίμους ἐν θεῷ συγχωροῦντας αὐτῷ· οὐκ αὐτῷ δέ, ἀλλὰ τῷ πατρὶ Ἰησοῦ Χριστοῦ, τῷ πάντων ἐπισκόπῳ. ₂εἰς τιμὴν οὖν ἐκείνου τοῦ θελήσαντος ἡμᾶς πρέπον ἐστὶν ἐπακούειν κατὰ μηδεμίαν ὑπόκρισιν· ἐπεὶ οὐχ ὅτι τὸν ἐπίσκοπον τοῦτον τὸν βλεπόμενον πλανᾷ τις, ἀλλὰ τὸν ἀόρατον παραλογίζεται· τὸ δὲ τοιοῦτον, οὐ πρὸς σάρκα ὁ λόγος ἀλλὰ πρὸς θεὸν τὸν τὰ κρύφια εἰδότα.

IGNATIUS TO THE MAGNESIANS:

Ignatius, who is also God-carrier, to the one blessed in the grace of God the Father, in Christ Jesus our Savior, in whom I greet the church which is in Magnesia, on the Meander, for which I pray utmost rejoicing in God the Father and the Lord Jesus Christ.

1 ₁Being aware of the well-ordered nature of your godly love, rejoicingly I determined to address you in the faith of Jesus Christ. ₂For being made worthy of a most God-befitting name, in the chains which I carry around I sing the churches, in which I pray that there may be the unity of flesh and spirit from Jesus Christ, our life lasting always, of faith and love, to which nothing is to yield precedence, above all of Jesus and the Father. Abiding in him we may attain to God, escaping all the abuse of the ruler of this age.

2 Since, therefore, I have been deemed worthy to behold you through Damas, your God-worthy bishop, and your worthy presbyters Bassus and Apollonius, and my fellow-slave the deacon Zotion, in whom may I delight, because he is subject to the bishop as to the grace of God, and to the presbytery as to the law of Jesus Christ.

3 ₁It is proper that you should not exploit the age of the bishop, but in accordance with the power of God you should yield every respect to him, as I am aware that your holy presbyters have not taken advantage of his evident youthful rank, but have deferred to him as understanding in God, yet not to him but to the Father of Jesus Christ who is overseer[1] of all. ₂For the honor of the one whose desire is for us it is proper that we should listen carefully, entirely without hypocrisy, since one does not deceive the visible bishop, but gives a false account to the one who is invisible. In such a case the account is not to be given in a fleshly manner, but towards God who sees whatever is hidden.

[1]The word generally rendered "bishop" literally means "overseer."

4 Πρέπον οὖν ἐστὶν μὴ μόνον καλεῖσθαι Χριστιανούς ἀλλὰ καὶ εἶναι· ὥσπερ καί τινες ἐπίσκοπον μὲν καλοῦσιν, χωρὶς δὲ αὐτοῦ πάντα πράσσουσιν. οἱ τοιοῦτοι [δὲ] οὐκ εὐσυνείδητοί μοι εἶναι φαίνονται διὰ τὸ μὴ βεβαίως κατ᾽ ἐντολὴν συναθροίζεσθαι.

5 ₁Ἐπεὶ οὖν τέλος τὰ πράγματα ἔχει, καὶ πρόκειται τὰ δύο ὁμοῦ, ὅ τε θάνατος καὶ ἡ ζωή, καὶ ἕκαστος εἰς τὸν ἴδιον τόπον μέλλει χωρεῖν· ₂ὥσπερ γάρ ἐστιν νομίσματα δύο, ὃ μὲν θεοῦ, ὃ δὲ κόσμου, καὶ ἕκαστον αὐτῶν ἴδιον χαρακτῆρα ἐπικείμενον ἔχει, οἱ ἄπιστοι τοῦ κόσμου τούτου, οἱ δὲ πιστοὶ ἐν ἀγάπῃ χαρακτῆρα θεοῦ πατρὸς διὰ Ἰησοῦ Χριστοῦ, δι᾽ οὗ ἐὰν μὴ αὐθαιρέτως ἔχωμεν τὸ ἀποθανεῖν εἰς τὸ αὐτοῦ πάθος, τὸ ζῆν αὐτοῦ οὐκ ἔστιν ἐν ἡμῖν.

6 ₁Ἐπεὶ οὖν ἐν τοῖς προγεγραμμένοις προσώποις τὸ πᾶν πλῆθος ἐθεώρησα ἐν πίστει καὶ ἠγάπησα, παραινῶ, ἐν ὁμονοίᾳ θεοῦ σπουδάζετε πάντα πράσσειν, προκαθημένου τοῦ ἐπισκόπου εἰς τύπον¹ θεοῦ καὶ τῶν πρεσβυτέρων εἰς τύπον συνεδρίου τῶν ἀποστόλων, καὶ τῶν διακόνων τῶν ἐμοὶ γλυκυτάτων, πεπιστευμένων διακονίαν Ἰησοῦ Χριστοῦ, ὃς πρὸ αἰώνων παρὰ πατρὶ ἦν καὶ ἐν τέλει ἐφάνη. ₂πάντες οὖν ὁμοήθειαν θεοῦ λαβόντες ἐντρέπεσθε ἀλλήλους, καὶ μηδεὶς κατὰ σάρκα βλεπέτω τὸν πλησίον, ἀλλ᾽ ἐν Ἰησοῦ Χριστῷ ἀλλήλους διὰ παντὸς ἀγαπᾶτε. μηδὲν ἔστω ἐν ὑμῖν ὃ δυνήσεται ὑμᾶς μερίσαι, ἀλλ᾽ ἑνώθητε τῷ ἐπισκόπῳ καὶ τοῖς προκαθημένοις εἰς τύπον καὶ διδαχὴν ἀφθαρσίας.

7 ₁Ὥσπερ οὖν ὁ κύριος ἄνευ τοῦ πατρὸς οὐδὲν ἐποίησεν [ἡνωμένος ὤν], οὔτε δι᾽ ἑαυτοῦ οὔτε διὰ τῶν ἀποστόλων, οὕτως μηδὲ ὑμεῖς ἄνευ τοῦ ἐπισκόπου καὶ τῶν πρεσβυτέρων μηδὲν πράσσετε· μηδὲ πειράσητε εὔλογόν τι φαίνεσθαι ἰδίᾳ ὑμῖν· ἀλλ᾽ ἐπὶ τὸ αὐτό· μία προσευχή, μία δέησις, εἷς νοῦς, μία ἐλπὶς, ἐν ἀγάπῃ, ἐν τῇ χαρᾷ τῇ

¹So Lightfoot, cf. the mss which read τόπον.

4 So it is proper not only to be called Christians but to be such as well, just as there are some who call a person bishop yet do everything without him. Such persons do not seem to me to have a good conscience as they do not hold firm gatherings in accordance with the commandment.

5 Thus, since there is an end to things and the two, death and life, are simultaneously laid before us, and each is to go to his or her own place, ₂for just as there are two coins, one of God, one of the world, and each of them bears its own imprint, the faithless of this world, the faithful in love the imprint of God the Father through Jesus Christ, whose life, if we do not choose willingly to die for truth in likeness of his passion, is not in us.

6 Therefore, since I have in faith discerned the entire congregation, and loved it, in the persons of whom I have already written, I urge you to be anxious to do everything in the concord of God, as the bishop is seated first, as representing[2] God and the presbyters as representing the council of the apostles and the deacons, especially dear to me, entrusted with the ministry of Jesus Christ, who was with the Father before the ages and who will appear at the end. ₂Adopting a manner like that of God, all of you should respect one another, and nobody should look upon a neighbor in a fleshly manner, but at all times should love one another in Jesus Christ. There should be nothing among you which is capable of dividing you, but be united with the bishop and with those in the first seats, representing the teaching of incorruptibility.

7 Therefore, just as, without regard to the Father (being united with him), the Lord did nothing, either of himself or through the apostles, so you are to undertake nothing without regard to the bishop and the presbyters. Do not attempt to consider a private purpose reasonable, but for a common purpose there should be one

[2]Or "in the place of," if *topos* is read here.

ἀμώμῳ, ὅς ἐστιν Ἰησοῦς Χριστός, οὗ ἄμεινον οὐθέν ἐστιν. ₂πάντες ὡς εἰς ἕνα ναὸν συντρέχετε †θεοῦ†, ὡς ἐπὶ ἓν θυσιαστήριον, ἐπὶ ἕνα Ἰησοῦν Χριστόν τὸν ἀφ᾽ ἑνὸς πατρὸς προελθόντα καὶ εἰς ἕνα ὄντα καὶ χωρήσαντα.

8 ₁Μὴ πλανᾶσθε ταῖς ἑτεροδοξίαις μηδὲ μυθεύμασιν τοῖς παλαιοῖς ἀνωφελέσιν οὖσιν· εἰ γὰρ μέχρι νῦν κατὰ ἰουδαϊσμὸν² ζῶμεν, ὁμολογοῦμεν χάριν μὴ εἰληφέναι. ₂οἱ γὰρ θειότατοι προφῆται κατὰ Χριστὸν Ἰησοῦν ἔζησαν. διὰ τοῦτο καὶ ἐδιώχθησαν, ἐμπνεόμενοι ὑπὸ τῆς χάριτος [αὐτοῦ] εἰς τὸ πληροφορηθῆναι τοὺς ἀπειθοῦντας, ὅτι εἷς θεός ἐστιν ὁ φανερώσας ἑαυτὸν διὰ Ἰησοῦ Χριστοῦ τοῦ υἱοῦ αὐτοῦ, ὅς ἐστιν αὐτοῦ λόγος ἀπὸ σιγῆς προελθών, ὃς κατὰ πάντα εὐηρέστησεν τῷ πέμψαντι αὐτόν.

9 ₁Εἰ οὖν οἱ ἐν παλαιοῖς πράγμασιν ἀναστραφέντες εἰς καινότητα ἐλπίδος ἦλθον, μηκέτι σαββατίζοντες ἀλλὰ κατὰ κυριακὴν ζῶντες, ἐν ᾗ καὶ ἡ ζωὴ ἡμῶν ἀνέτειλεν δι᾽ αὐτοῦ καὶ τοῦ θανάτου αὐτοῦ, ὅ τινες ἀρνοῦνται· δι᾽ οὗ μυστηρίου ἐλάβομεν, τὸ πιστεύειν καὶ διὰ τοῦτο ὑπομένομεν, ἵνα εὑρεθῶμεν μαθηταὶ Ἰησοῦ Χριστοῦ τοῦ μόνου διδασκάλου ἡμῶν· ₂πῶς ἡμεῖς δυνησόμεθα ζῆσαι χωρὶς αὐτοῦ; οὗ καὶ οἱ προφῆται μαθηταὶ ὄντες τῷ πνεύματι ὡς διδάσκαλον αὐτὸν προσεδόκων. καὶ διὰ τοῦτο, ὃν δικαίως ἀνέμενον, παρὼν ἤγειρεν αὐτοὺς ἐκ νεκρῶν.

10 ₁Μὴ οὖν ἀναισθητῶμεν τῆς χρηστότητος αὐτοῦ. ἐὰν γὰρ ἡμᾶς μιμήσηται καθὰ πράσσομεν, οὐκ ἔτι ἐσμέν. διὰ τοῦτο, μαθηταὶ αὐτοῦ γενόμενοι, μάθωμεν κατὰ Χριστιανισμὸν ζῆν. ὃς γὰρ ἄλλῳ ὀνόματι καλεῖται πλέον τούτου, οὐκ ἔστιν τοῦ θεοῦ.

---

²So Lightfoot. There is some doubt about the text here; νόμον ἰουδαϊσμόν is also a plausible reading.

prayer, one petition, one mind, one hope in love, in blameless joy, which is Jesus Christ, to whom nothing is superior. ₂As to a single temple of God you should all run together, as upon one altar, upon one Jesus Christ, who came forth from one Father and is one with him, to whom he returned.

8 Do not be deceived by strange opinions, nor by ancient legends, which are useless. For if, even now, we live in accordance with Judaism, we admit that we have not received grace. ₂For the most godly prophets lived in accordance with Christ Jesus. On this account they were persecuted, being inspired by grace fully to convict the unpersuaded that there is one God, who made himself manifest through Jesus Christ his Son, who is his Word coming forth from silence, who is well pleasing in everything to the one who sent him.

9 Therefore, if those who conducted themselves in accordance with the ancient ways came to a newness of hope, no longer keeping the Sabbath but living in accordance with the Lord's day,[3] on which our life appeared through him and through his death, which some deny, we receive our faith through this mystery, and remain constant in it, so that we may be found to be disciples of Jesus Christ our only teacher, ₂how could we live without regard to him? It is of him that the prophets were disciples in the Spirit, expecting him as a teacher. For this reason the one whom they righteously expected raised them from the dead on his appearance.

10 ₁Therefore we should not fail to perceive his kindness. For if he were to act in imitation of our actions, we would not still exist. For this reason, being his disciples, let us learn to live in accordance with Christianity, for whoever is known by a name other than this is not God's.

[3]There is no noun in the original. Although the adjective alone comes to mean "the Lord's day," it may not have done so at the time of Ignatius. Nonetheless the context emboldens us to supply the word "day," though one ms supplies the word "life," which is entirely plausible.

₂ὑπέρθεσθε οὖν τὴν κακὴν ζύμην, τὴν παλαιωθεῖσαν καὶ ἐνοξίσασαν, καὶ μεταβάλεσθε εἰς νέαν ζύμην, ὅς ἐστιν Ἰησοῦς Χριστός. ἀλίσθητε ἐν αὐτῷ, ἵνα μὴ διαφθαρῇ τις ἐν ὑμῖν, ἐπεὶ ἀπὸ τῆς ὀσμῆς ἐλεγχθήσεσθε. ₃ἄτοπόν ἐστιν Ἰησοῦν Χριστὸν λαλεῖν καὶ ἰουδαΐζειν. ὁ γὰρ Χριστιανισμὸς οὐκ εἰς Ἰουδαϊσμὸν ἐπίστευσεν, ἀλλ᾽ Ἰουδαϊσμὸς εἰς Χριστιανισμόν, εἰς ὃν³ πᾶσα γλῶσσα πιστεύσασα εἰς θεὸν συνήχθη.

11 Ταῦτα δέ, ἀγαπητοί μου, οὐκ ἐπεὶ ἔγνων τινὰς ἐξ ὑμῶν οὕτως ἔχοντας, ἀλλ᾽ ὡς μικρότερος ὑμῶν θέλω προφυλάσσεσθαι ὑμᾶς μὴ ἐμπεσεῖν εἰς τὰ ἄγκιστρα τῆς κενοδοξίας, ἀλλὰ πεπληροφορῆσθαι ἐν τῇ γεννήσει καὶ τῷ πάθει καὶ τῇ ἀναστάσει τῇ γενομένῃ ἐν καιρῷ τῆς ἡγεμονίας Ποντίου Πιλάτου· πραχθέντα ἀληθῶς καὶ βεβαίως ὑπὸ Ἰησοῦ Χριστοῦ, τῆς ἐλπίδος ἡμῶν, ἧς ἐκτραπῆναι μηδενὶ ὑμῶν γένοιτο.

12 Ὀναίμην ὑμῶν κατὰ πάντα, ἐάνπερ ἄξιος ὦ. εἰ γὰρ καὶ δέδεμαι, πρὸς ἕνα τῶν λελυμένων ὑμῶν οὐκ εἰμί. οἶδα ὅτι οὐ φυσιοῦσθε· Ἰησοῦν γὰρ Χριστὸν ἔχετε ἐν ἑαυτοῖς. καὶ μᾶλλον, ὅταν ἐπαινῶ ὑμᾶς, οἶδα ὅτι ἐντρέπεσθε· ὡς γέγραπται, ὅτι ὁ δίκαιος ἑαυτοῦ κατήγορος.

13 ₁Σπουδάζετε οὖν βεβαιωθῆναι ἐν τοῖς δόγμασιν τοῦ κυρίου καὶ τῶν ἀποστόλων, ἵνα πάντα ὅσα ποιεῖτε κατευοδωθῆτε σαρκὶ καὶ πνεύματι, πίστει καὶ ἀγάπῃ, ἐν υἱῷ καὶ πατρὶ καὶ ἐν πνεύματι, ἐν ἀρχῇ καὶ ἐν τέλει, μετὰ τοῦ ἀξιοπρεπεστάτου ἐπισκόπου ὑμῶν καὶ ἀξιοπλόκου πνευματικοῦ στεφάνου τοῦ πρεσβυτερίου ὑμῶν καὶ τῶν κατὰ θεὸν διακόνων. ₂ὑποτάγητε τῷ ἐπισκόπῳ καὶ ἀλλήλοις, ὡς Ἰησοῦς Χριστὸς τῷ πατρὶ [κατὰ σάρκα] καὶ οἱ ἀπόστολοι τῷ Χριστῷ καὶ τῷ πατρὶ καὶ τῷ πνεύματι, ἵνα ἕνωσις ᾖ σαρκική τε καὶ πνευματική.

³Cf. Lightfoot ᾧ. There is some confusion in the ms tradition, though the overall meaning is clear enough.

₂Therefore put aside the evil yeast, which is aged and soured, and be changed into new yeast, which is Jesus Christ. Be salted in him, so that nothing in you can get corrupted, since you will be convicted by your smell.

₃It is outlandish to speak of Jesus Christ and to Judaize. For Christianity did not put its faith in Judaism but Judaism in Christianity, in which every tongue which believes has been gathered together into God.[4]

11   My beloved, these are (written) not because I know that any of you is acting thus, but I wish to put you on your guard, as one who is less than you, so that you should not be hooked by the barbs of vain doctrine, but that you should have the fullest conviction regarding the birth and the suffering and the resurrection that occurred in the period of the governor Pontius Pilate. Truly and assuredly were these undertaken by our hope, Jesus Christ, from which may none of you turn aside.

12   May I delight in you in every way, should I prove worthy. For although I am enchained, I am nothing compared to any of you who are freed. That you are not haughty, I know, for you have Jesus Christ among you. When I praise you, moreover, I know that you feel compunction: as it is written, "The just person is his own accuser."[5]

13   Therefore be keen to stand strong in the opinions of the Lord and the apostles, so that you may prosper in all that you undertake, in flesh and spirit, in faith and love, in the Son and the Father and in the Spirit, in the beginning and the end, together with your most worthy bishop and your presbytery, well woven into a spiritual crown, and your godly deacons. ₂Be subject to the bishop and to each other, as Jesus Christ was to the Father and the apostles to Christ and to the Father and to the Spirit, so that there may be fleshly and spiritual unity.

[4]Or "in which every tongue which believes in God has been gathered."
[5]Prov 18.17.

14 Εἰδὼς ὅτι θεοῦ γέμετε, συντόμως παρεκάλεσα[4] ὑμᾶς. μνημονεύετέ μου ἐν τοῖς προσευχαῖς ὑμῶν, ἵνα θεοῦ ἐπιτύχω, καὶ τῆς ἐν Συρίᾳ ἐκκλησίας, ὅθεν οὐκ ἄξιός εἰμι καλεῖσθαι. ἐπιδέομαι γὰρ τῆς ἡνωμένης ὑμῶν ἐν θεῷ προσευχῆς καὶ ἀγάπης εἰς τὸ ἀξιωθῆναι τὴν ἐν Συρίᾳ ἐκκλησίαν διὰ τῆς ἐκκλησίας ὑμῶν δροσισθῆναι.

15 Ἀσπάζονται ὑμᾶς Ἐφέσιοι ἀπὸ Σμύρνης, ὅθεν καὶ γράφω ὑμῖν, παρόντες εἰς δόξαν θεοῦ, ὥσπερ καὶ ὑμεῖς, οἳ κατὰ πάντα με ἀνέπαυσαν, ἅμα Πολυκάρπῳ ἐπισκόπῳ Σμυρναίων. καὶ αἱ λοιπαὶ δὲ ἐκκλησίαι ἐν τιμῇ Ἰησοῦ Χριστοῦ ἀσπάζονται ὑμᾶς. ἔρρωσθε ἐν ὁμονοίᾳ θεοῦ, κεκτημένοι ἀδιάκριτον πνεῦμα, ὅς ἐστιν Ἰησοῦς Χριστός.

[4]So Lighfoot, though παρεκέλευσα is also a possible reading.

14   Knowing that you are filled with God I have exhorted you concisely. Remember me in your prayers so that I may attain to God, and the church in Syria, from which I am not worthy to derive my name. For I am in need of your unified prayer and love in God, so that the church in Syria may prove worthy to be bedewed through your church.

15   The Ephesians greet you from Smyrna, from where I am writing to you. They are here for the glory of God, as are you. In every way they have refreshed me, as has Polycarp, the bishop of the Smyrnaeans. The rest of the churches also greet you in the honor of Jesus Christ. Fare well, in the concord of God, to you who have obtained an undivided spirit, who is Jesus Christ.

Trallians

Having received the bishop of the Trallians, a city described by Strabo as a flourishing city, peopled by persons of wealth,[1] Ignatius responds by encouraging the church to unity under its bishop and presbytery. There is a generalized warning given against Docetism, which is seen as more a threat than a present danger. Behind the general statement of submission to the bishop and presbyters, there is perhaps a hint that such submission has not taken place. In view of the statement in 12.2 that ". . . it is proper that every one of you, and especially the presbyters, should refresh the bishop for the honor of the Father and Jesus Christ and the apostles . . ." it is possible that the reason for this is that the presbyters had not acted adequately as patrons (the term "refresh" meaning "to supply material goods"). Thus when Ignatius urges that the Trallians should use only Christian food we may suggest that Trallian Christians were participating in civic sacrifice and other cults, a possibility which would be particularly alluring if there is an impoverished Christian community in a prosperous city. In this light we may explain Ignatius' assertion that deacons are not ministers of food and drink, whereas their role in the Eucharist is precisely this. Christian diakonoi *(deacons) are being contrasted with the* diakonoi *of the civic cults (ritual waiters who assisted with the distribution of meat at civil sacrifices).*

[1] Strabo *Geography* 14.1.42

ΤΡΑΛΛΙΑΝΟΙΣ ΙΓΝΑΤΙΟΣ

Ἰγνάτιος, ὁ καὶ Θεοφόρος, ἠγαπημένῃ θεῷ, πατρὶ Ἰησοῦ Χριστοῦ, ἐκκλησίᾳ ἁγίᾳ τῇ οὔσῃ ἐν Τράλλεσιν τῆς Ἀσίας, ἐκλεκτῇ καὶ ἀξιοθέῳ, εἰρηνευούσῃ ἐν σαρκὶ καὶ πνεύματι τῷ πάθει Ἰησοῦ Χριστοῦ τῆς ἐλπίδος ἡμῶν ἐν τῇ εἰς αὐτὸν ἀναστάσει· ἣν καὶ ἀσπάζομαι ἐν τῷ πληρώματι ἐν ἀποστολικῷ χαρακτῆρι, καὶ εὔχομαι πλεῖστα χαίρειν.

1 ₁Ἄμωμον διάνοιαν καὶ ἀδιάκριτον ἐν ὑπομονῇ ἔγνων ὑμᾶς ἔχοντας, οὐ κατὰ χρῆσιν ἀλλὰ κατὰ φύσιν· καθὼς ἐδήλωσέν μοι Πολύβιος, ὁ ἐπίσκοπος ὑμῶν, ὃς παρεγένετο θελήματι θεοῦ καὶ Ἰησοῦ Χριστοῦ ἐν Σμύρνῃ, καὶ οὕτως μοι συνεχάρη δεδεμένῳ ἐν Χριστῷ Ἰησοῦ, ὥστε με τὸ πᾶν πλῆθος ὑμῶν ἐν αὐτῷ θεωρεῖσθαι. ₂ἀποδεξάμενος οὖν τὴν κατὰ θεὸν εὔνοιαν δι᾽ αὐτοῦ, ἐδόξασα, εὑρὼν ὑμᾶς, ὡς ἔγνων, μιμητὰς ὄντας θεοῦ.

2 ₁Ὅταν γὰρ τῷ ἐπισκόπῳ ὑποτάσσησθε ὡς Ἰησοῦ Χριστῷ, φαίνεσθέ μοι οὐ κατὰ ἄνθρωπον ζῶντες, ἀλλὰ κατὰ Ἰησοῦν Χριστὸν, τὸν δι᾽ ἡμᾶς ἀποθανόντα ἵνα πιστεύσαντες εἰς τὸν θάνατον αὐτοῦ τὸ ἀποθανεῖν ἐκφύγητε. ₂ἀναγκαῖον οὖν ἐστίν, ὥσπερ ποιεῖτε, ἄνευ τοῦ ἐπισκόπου μηδὲν πράσσειν ὑμᾶς· ἀλλ᾽ ὑποτάσσεσθαι καὶ τῷ πρεσβυτερίῳ, ὡς [τοῖς] ἀποστόλοις Ἰησοῦ Χριστοῦ, τῆς ἐλπίδος ἡμῶν, ἐν ᾧ διάγοντες [ἐν αὐτῷ]¹ εὑρεθησόμεθα. ₃δεῖ δὲ καὶ τοὺς διακόνους ὄντας μυστηρίων Ἰησοῦ Χριστοῦ κατὰ πάντα τρόπον πᾶσιν ἀρέσκειν· οὐ γὰρ βρωμάτων καὶ ποτῶν εἰσιν διάκονοι, ἀλλ᾽ ἐκκλησίας θεοῦ ὑπηρέται· δέον οὖν αὐτοὺς φυλάσσεσθαι τὰ ἐγκλήματα ὡς πῦρ.

3 ₁Ὁμοίως πάντες ἐντρεπέσθωσαν τοὺς διακόνους ὡς Ἰησοῦν Χριστόν, ὡς καὶ τὸν ἐπίσκοπον ὄντα τύπον τοῦ πατρός, τοὺς δὲ πρεσβυτέρους ὡς συνέδριον θεοῦ καὶ [ὡς]² σύνδεσμον ἀποστόλων· χωρὶς τούτων ἐκκλησία οὐ καλεῖται. ₂περὶ ὧν πέπεισμαι ὑμᾶς

---

¹Words inserted by Lightfoot, as by the long recension. It is possible that the text stood without these words, but it is very awkward without them.

²There is some confusion in the text here. I have omitted ὡς in the translation.

IGNATIUS TO THE TRALLIANS:

Ignatius, who is also God-carrier, to the holy church which is at Tralles, in Asia, beloved of God, the Father of Jesus Christ, chosen and God-worthy, brought to peace in flesh and spirit through the suffering of Jesus Christ, our hope for resurrection into his self, which (church) also I greet in its completeness, in the apostolic manner, and wish abundance of happiness.

1   ₁I came to know that you possess a blameless and unwavering mind in patience, that is not by habit but by nature, just as Polybius, your bishop, has shown me in coming to Smyrna by the will of God and Jesus Christ. So he rejoiced with me, who am bound in Christ Jesus, so that in him I discerned your whole congregation. ₂I gloried in receiving through him your godly goodwill, discovering that, as I had known, you were imitators of God.

2   ₁For when you are subject to the bishop as to Jesus Christ you seem to me not to be living in a human way but in accordance with Jesus Christ who died for us so that, believing in his death, you may escape death. ₂Thus it is required that you should undertake nothing apart from the bishop, as is already the case, but also that you be subject to the presbytery as to the apostles of Jesus Christ our hope, in whom we will be found through living in him. ₃And it is necessary that the deacons of the mysteries of Jesus Christ should be pleasing to all in every way. For they are not deacons of food and drink, but ministers of the church of God, who should guard themselves against accusations as against fire.

3   ₁Likewise everyone should respect the deacons like Jesus Christ, and also the bishop, who is a representation of the Father, and the presbyters as a sanhedrin of God and company of the apostles. Apart from these nothing can be called a church. ₂I am sure that you agree in this, for I have received the proof of your love and I have it with

οὕτως ἔχειν·τὸ γὰρ ἐξεμπλάριον τῆς ἀγάπης ὑμῶν ἔλαβον καὶ ἔχω
μεθ' ἑαυτοῦ ἐν τῷ ἐπισκόπῳ ὑμῶν, οὗ αὐτὸ τὸ κατάστημα μεγάλη
μαθητεία, ἡ δὲ πραότης αὐτοῦ δύναμις· ὃν λογίζομαι καὶ τοὺς
ἀθέους ἐντρέπεσθαι. 3ἀγαπῶν ὑμᾶς οὕτως³ φείδομαι, συντονώτερον
δυνάμενος γράφειν ὑπὲρ τούτου·[ἀλλ' οὐχ ἱκανὸν ἑαυτὸν]⁴ εἰς
τοῦτο ᾠήθην, ἵνα ὢν κατάκριτος ὡς ἀπόστολος ὑμῖν διατάσσωμαι.

4 1Πολλὰ φρονῶ ἐν θεῷ· ἀλλ' ἐμαυτὸν μετρῶ, ἵνα μὴ ἐν καυχήσει
ἀπόλωμαι· νῦν γάρ με δεῖ πλέον φοβεῖσθαι καὶ μὴ προσέχειν τοῖς
φυσιοῦσίν με· οἱ γὰρ λέγοντές μοι μαστιγοῦσίν με. 2ἀγαπῶ μὲν γὰρ
τὸ παθεῖν, ἀλλ' οὐκ οἶδα εἰ ἄξιός εἰμι· τὸ γὰρ ζῆλος πολλοῖς μὲν
οὐ φαίνεται, ἐμὲ δὲ [πλέον]⁵ πολεμεῖ. χρῄζω οὖν πραότητος, ἐν ᾗ
καταλύεται ὁ ἄρχων τοῦ αἰῶνος τούτου.

5 1Μὴ οὐ δύναμαι ὑμῖν τὰ ἐπουράνια γράψαι; ἀλλὰ φοβοῦμαι μὴ
νηπίοις οὖσιν ὑμῖν βλάβην παραθῶ. καὶ συγγνωμονεῖτέ μοι, μήποτε
οὐ δυνηθέντες χωρῆσαι στραγγαλωθῆτε. 2καὶ γὰρ ἐγώ, οὐ καθότι
δέδεμαι καὶ δύναμαι νοεῖν τὰ ἐπουράνια καὶ τὰς τοποθεσίας τὰς
ἀγγελικὰς καὶ τὰς συστάσεις τὰς ἀρχοντικάς, ὁρατά τε καὶ ἀόρατα,
παρὰ τοῦτο ἤδη καὶ μαθητής εἰμι· πολλὰ γὰρ ἡμῖν λείπει, ἵνα θεοῦ
μὴ λειπώμεθα.

6 1Παρακαλῶ οὖν ὑμᾶς, οὐκ ἐγώ ἀλλ' ἡ ἀγάπη Ἰησοῦ Χριστοῦ,
μόνῃ τῇ χριστιανῇ τροφῇ χρῆσθε, ἀλλοτρίας δὲ βοτάνης ἀπέχεσθε,
ἥτις ἐστὶν αἵρεσις· 2οἳ καὶ ἰῷ⁶ παρεμπλέκουσιν Ἰησοῦν Χριστὸν,
καταξιοπιστευόμενοι, ὥσπερ θανάσιμον φάρμακον διδόντες μετὰ
οἰνομέλιτος, ὅπερ ὁ ἀγνοῶν ἡδέως λαμβάνει ἐν ἡδονῇ κακῇ τὸ
ἀποθανεῖν.

---

³This word is inserted by Lightfoot, in an attempt to reconcile the variations in
the textual tradition. It is not rendered in the translation opposite.

⁴Lightfoot inserts these words, in the belief that some words are omitted here. It
is quite possible that there is some disruption in the text, but such a bold conjecture
is not justified. I have, however, read and translated οὐκ, found in some mss here.

⁵Lightfoot brackets this word, suspecting interpolation.

⁶Such is Lightfoot's conjecture. The text is very confused at this point. I have
translated, however, οἳ ἑαυτοῖς.

me still in your bishop, whose very appearance is highly instructive, whose meekness itself is powerful. I reckon that even the godless respect him. ₃Though I could write to you more sharply on this matter, I refrain out of love for you. It did not seem proper that, as a condemned man, I should direct you like an apostle.

4 ₁I understand much in God, but I limit myself so that I should not be destroyed by boasting. At present I have to be all the more fearful, and pay no attention to those who would puff me up. For those who speak to me are scourging me. ₂For indeed I am a lover of suffering, but I do not know whether I am worthy. For envy is not obvious to many, whilst it wars against me all the more. Therefore I am in need of humility, by which the ruler of this age is undone.

5 Am I not able to write to you about heavenly things? Yet I am afraid to do so lest, being infants, I should harm you. Yet allow me this, as otherwise you might choke, being unable to swallow. ₂For even I, whilst in bondage and able to understand heavenly matters, the disposition of the angels and the hierarchies of the rulers, visible and invisible, am not yet a disciple. For much is still lacking to us, but we are not lacking in God.

6 ₁I entreat you, therefore, yet not I, but the love of Jesus Christ, to use only Christian nourishment, to abstain from a foreign plant, that is factionalism. ₂For such people appear trustworthy through mingling Jesus Christ with themselves, so that they are like those who dispense a deadly drug mixed with honeyed wine, so that the ignorant should die, after gladly taking it with a guilty enjoyment.

7 ₁Φυλάττεσθε οὖν τοὺς τοιούτους. τοῦτο δὲ ἔσται ὑμῖν μὴ φυσιουμένοις καὶ οὖσιν ἀχωρίστοις [θεοῦ] Ἰησοῦ Χριστοῦ καὶ τοῦ ἐπισκόπου καὶ τῶν διαταγμάτων τῶν ἀποστόλων. ₂ὁ ἐντὸς θυσιαστηρίου ὢν καθαρός ἐστιν, ὁ δὲ ἐκτὸς θυσιαστηρίου ὢν οὐ καθαρός ἐστιν· τοῦτ᾿ ἔστιν, ὁ χωρὶς ἐπισκόπου καὶ πρεσβυτερίου καὶ διακόνων πράσσων τι, οὗτος οὐ καθαρός ἐστιν τῇ συνειδήσει.

8 ₁Οὐκ ἐπεὶ ἔγνων τοιοῦτόν τι ἐν ὑμῖν, ἀλλὰ προφυλάσσω ὑμᾶς ὄντας μου ἀγαπητούς, προορῶν τὰς ἐνέδρας τοῦ διαβόλου. ὑμεῖς οὖν τὴν πραϋπάθειαν ἀναλαβόντες ἀνακτίσασθε ἑαυτοὺς ἐν πίστει, ὅ ἐστιν σὰρξ τοῦ κυρίου, καὶ ἐν ἀγάπῃ, ὅ ἐστιν αἷμα Ἰησοῦ Χριστοῦ. ₂μηδεὶς ὑμῶν κατὰ τοῦ πλησίον ἐχέτω· μὴ ἀφορμὰς δίδοτε τοῖς ἔθνεσιν, ἵνα μὴ δι᾿ ὀλίγους ἄφρονας τὸ ἔνθεον πλῆθος βλασφημῆται· οὐαὶ γάρ, δι᾿ οὗ ἐπὶ ματαιότητι τὸ ὄνομά μου ἐπί τινων βλασφημεῖται.

9 Κωφώθητε οὖν, ὅταν ὑμῖν χωρὶς Ἰησοῦ Χριστοῦ λαλῇ τις, τοῦ ἐκ γένους Δαυείδ, τοῦ ἐκ Μαρίας, ὃς ἀληθῶς ἐγεννήθη, ἔφαγέν τε καὶ ἔπιεν, ἀληθῶς ἐδιώχθη ἐπὶ Ποντίου Πιλάτου, ἀληθῶς ἐσταυρώθη καὶ ἀπέθανεν, βλεπόντων [τῶν] ἐπουρανίων καὶ ἐπιγείων καὶ ὑποχθονίων· ₂ὃς καὶ ἀληθῶς ἠγέρθη ἀπὸ νεκρῶν, ἐγείραντος αὐτὸν τοῦ πατρὸς αὐτοῦ, κατὰ τὸ ὁμοίωμα ὃς καὶ ἡμᾶς τοὺς πιστεύοντας αὐτῷ οὕτως ἐγερεῖ ὁ πατὴρ αὐτοῦ ἐν Χριστῷ Ἰησοῦ, οὗ χωρὶς τὸ ἀληθινὸν ζῆν οὐκ ἔχομεν.

10 Εἰ δέ, ὥσπερ τινὸς ἄθεοι ὄντες, τουτέστιν ἄπιστοι, λέγουσιν, τὸ δοκεῖν πεπονθέναι αὐτόν, αὐτοὶ ὄντες τὸ δοκεῖν, ἐγὼ τί δέδεμαι; τί δὲ καὶ εὔχομαι θηριομαχῆσαι; δωρεὰν οὖν ἀποθνήσκω. Ἄρα οὖν καταψεύδομαι τοῦ κυρίου.

7 ₁Therefore be on your guard against such people. This will be possible for you if you are not puffed up and are unseparated from God, Jesus Christ, and the bishop and the injunctions of the apostles. ₂Whoever is within the sanctuary is pure. Whoever is outside the sanctuary is not pure. That is to say, whoever undertakes anything apart from the bishop and the presbytery and the deacons is not pure in conscience.

8 ₁I am not aware of anything of this nature among you, but I am protecting you in advance, my beloved, foreseeing the devil's ambushes. Therefore you should adopt gentleness, and remake yourselves in faith, which is the flesh of the Lord, and in love, which is the blood of Jesus Christ. ₂Let none of you hold anything against your neighbor. Do not give any entry-point to heathens, lest the whole congregation in God be blasphemed through a few silly people. For woe to the one through whom my name is blasphemed, on account of stupidity.[2]

9 ₁Be deaf, therefore, when anyone speaks to you apart from Jesus Christ, who is of the race of David, who is from Mary, who was truly born, who ate and drank, who truly was persecuted under Pontius Pilate, who truly was crucified and died, as those in the heavens, and on the earth, and under the earth looked on. ₂He was truly raised from the dead, raised by his Father, as his Father will similarly raise us who believe in him, in Christ Jesus, apart from whom we do not have true life.

10 Thus if some people, atheists, that is unbelievers, say that he suffered in appearance only, it is they who are the appearance. Why am I bound? Why do I beg to fight the wild beasts? Am I therefore dying in vain? Am I, even more, lying about the Lord?

---

[2] Cf. Is 53.5, cited verbatim at this point in ps-Ignatius.

11 ₁Φεύγετε οὖν τὰς κακὰς παραφυάδας τὰς γεννώσας καρπὸν θανατοφόρον, οὗ ἐὰν γεύσηταί τις, παρ' αὐτὰ ἀποθνήσκει. οὗτοι γὰρ οὔκ εἰσιν φυτεία πατρός· ₂εἰ γὰρ ἦσαν, ἐφαίνοντο ἂν κλάδοι τοῦ σταυροῦ, καὶ ἦν ἂν ὁ καρπὸς αὐτῶν ἄφθαρτος· δι' οὗ ἐν τῷ πάθει αὐτοῦ προσκαλεῖται ὑμᾶς, ὄντας μέλη αὐτοῦ. οὐ δύναται οὖν κεφαλὴ χωρὶς γεννηθῆναι ἄνευ μελῶν, τοῦ θεοῦ ἕνωσιν ἐπαγγελλομένου, ὅς ἐστιν αὐτός.

12 ₁Ἀσπάζομαι ὑμᾶς ἀπὸ Σμύρνης, ἅμα ταῖς συμπαρούσαις μοι ἐκκλησίαις τοῦ θεοῦ, οἳ κατὰ πάντα με ἀνέπαυσαν σαρκί τε καὶ πνεύματι. ₂παρακαλεῖ ὑμᾶς τὰ δεσμά μου, ἃ ἕνεκεν Ἰησοῦ Χριστοῦ περιφέρω, αἰτούμενος θεοῦ ἐπιτυχεῖν· διαμένετε ἐν τῇ ὁμονοίᾳ ὑμῶν καὶ τῇ μετ' ἀλλήλων προσευχῇ. πρέπει γὰρ ὑμῖν τοῖς καθ' ἕνα, ἐξαιρέτως καὶ τοῖς πρεσβυτέροις, ἀναψύχειν τὸν ἐπίσκοπον εἰς τιμὴν πατρὸς [καὶ εἰς τιμην]⁷ Ἰησοῦ Χριστοῦ καὶ τῶν ἀποστόλων. ₃εὔχομαι ὑμᾶς ἐν ἀγάπη ἀκοῦσαί μου, ἵνα μὴ εἰς μαρτύριον ὦ [ἐν] ὑμῖν γράψας. καὶ περὶ ἐμοῦ δὲ προσεύχεσθε, τῆς ἀφ' ὑμῶν ἀγάπης χρήζοντος ἐν τῷ ἐλέει τοῦ θεοῦ, εἰς τὸ καταξιωθῆναί με τοῦ κλήρου οὗ περίκειμαι ἐπιτυχεῖν, ἵνα μὴ ἀδόκιμος εὑρεθῶ.

13 ₁Ἀπάζεται ὑμᾶς ἡ ἀγάπη Σμυρναίων καὶ Ἐφεσίων. μνημονεύετε ἐν ταῖς προσευχαῖς ὑμῶν τῆς ἐν Συρίᾳ ἐκκλησίας· ὅθεν [καὶ] οὐκ ἄξιός εἰμι λέγεσθαι ὢν ἔσχατος ἐκείνων. ₂ἔρρωσθε ἐν Ἰησοῦ Χριστῷ, ὑποτασσόμενοι τῷ ἐπισκόπῳ ὡς τῇ ἐντολῇ, ὁμοίως καὶ τῷ πρεσβυτερίῳ· καὶ οἱ κατ' ἄνδρα ἀλλήλους ἀγαπᾶτε ἐν ἀμερίστῳ καρδίᾳ. ₃ἁγνίζεται ὑμῶν τὸ ἐμὸν πνεῦμα οὐ μόνον νῦν, ἀλλὰ καὶ ὅταν θεοῦ ἐπιτύχω. ἔτι γὰρ ὑπὸ κίνδυνόν εἰμι· ἀλλὰ πιστὸς ὁ πατὴρ ἐν Ἰησοῦ Χριστῷ πληρῶσαί μου τὴν αἴτησιν καὶ ὑμῶν· ἐν ᾧ εὑρεθείημεν⁸ ἄμωμοι.

---

⁷These words are inserted by Lightfoot, with an eye to the long recension. It is possible that something of this sort should be included, but the text without the conjectural insertion is rendered opposite nonetheless.

⁸So Lighfoot. However, I have read, and translated, εὑρεθείητε.

11 ₁Therefore flee the wicked offshoots which produce death-dealing fruit; anyone who tastes of it dies instantly. For these are not of the Father's planting, ₂for if they were they would appear as stems of the cross and their fruit would be imperishable. Through it,³ in his passion, he invites you to be parts of his body, as a head cannot be born without body-parts, as God promises unity, which he is.

12 ₁I greet you from Smyrna, along with the churches of God which are present with me, who in all manner of ways have refreshed me, both in body and in spirit. ₂My chains, which I wear on account of Jesus Christ, are exhorting you, as I ask that I may attain to God. Remain in your concord and in prayer with one another. For it is proper that every one of you, and especially the presbyters, should refresh the bishop for the honor of the Father of Jesus Christ and the apostles. ₃I pray that you hear me in love, and that my writing should not stand as a witness against you. And pray for me, in need of your love through the mercy of God, that I be found worthy of the lot which is to fall to me, lest I be found undeserving.

13 ₁The love of the Smyrnaeans and Ephesians salutes you. Remember in your prayers the church in Syria, after whom I am not worthy to be called, being the least of them. ₂Fare well in Jesus Christ, remaining subject to the bishop as to the commandment, also likewise to the presbytery. And every one of you, love one another with an undivided heart. ₃My spirit is consecrated for you, not only now, but also when I attain to God. For I am still in danger. But the Father is faithful in Jesus Christ, fulfilling both my request and yours, that you may be found blameless in him.

³Namely the cross.

Romans

Unlike the other letters, directed to churches which Ignatius had visited on his journey through Asia, Romans is addressed to a church with which he had no personal acquaintance. Its purpose is primarily to introduce himself. In both respects, therefore, it is like Paul's letter to the Christian communties of the same city.

Unlike Paul, however, Ignatius writes in full expectation and knowledge of his coming death, and he is principally concerned in this letter to ensure that his martyrdom take place and not be frustrated by any well-meaning attempt to save him. His martyrdom is to enact the Eucharist in the arena, to be an offering like that of Christ.

ΡΩΜΑΙΟΙΣ ΙΓΝΑΤΙΟΣ

Ἰγνάτιος, ὁ καὶ Θεοφόρος, τῇ ἐλεημένῃ ἐν μεγαλειότητι πατρὸς ὑψίστου καὶ Ἰησοῦ Χριστοῦ τοῦ μόνου υἱοῦ αὐτοῦ, ἐκκλησίᾳ ἠγαπημένῃ καὶ πεφωτισμένῃ ἐν θελήματι τοῦ θελήσαντος τὰ πάντα ἃ ἔστιν, κατὰ πίστιν καὶ ἀγάπην Ἰησοῦ Χριστοῦ τοῦ θεοῦ ἡμῶν, ἥτις καὶ προκάθηται ἐν τόπῳ χωρίου Ῥωμαίων, ἀξιόθεος, ἀξιοπρεπής, ἀξιομακάριστος, ἀξιέπαινος, ἀξιοεπίτευκτος, ἀξιόαγνος καὶ προκαθημένη τῆς ἀγάπης, χριστόνομος, πατρώνυμος, ἣν καὶ ἀσπάζομαι ἐν ὀνόματι Ἰησοῦ Χριστοῦ υἱοῦ πατρός· κατὰ σάρκα καὶ πνεῦμα ἡνωμένοις πάσῃ ἐντολῇ αὐτοῦ, πεπληρωμένοις χάριτος θεοῦ ἀδιακρίτως καὶ ἀποδιϋλισμένοις ἀπὸ παντὸς ἀλλοτρίου χρώματος, πλεῖστα ἐν Ἰησοῦ Χριστῷ, τῷ θεῷ ἡμῶν, ἀμώμως χαίρειν.

1 ₁Ἐπεὶ εὐξάμενος θεῷ ἐπέτυχον ἰδεῖν ὑμῶν τὰ ἀξιόθεα πρόσωπα, ὡς καὶ πλέον ἠτούμην λαβεῖν· δεδεμένος γὰρ ἐν Χριστῷ Ἰησοῦ ἐλπίζω ὑμᾶς ἀσπάσασθαι, ἐάνπερ θέλημα ᾖ τοῦ ἀξιωθῆναί με εἰς τέλος εἶναι· ₂ἡ μὲν γὰρ ἀρχὴ εὐοικονόμητός ἐστιν, ἐάνπερ χάριτος ἐπιτύχω εἰς τὸ τὸν κλῆρόν μου ἀνεμποδίστως ἀπολαβεῖν. φοβοῦμαι γὰρ τὴν ὑμῶν ἀγάπην, μὴ αὐτή με ἀδικήσῃ· ὑμῖν γὰρ εὐχερές ἐστιν, ὃ θέλετε ποιῆσαι· ἐμοὶ δὲ δύσκολόν ἐστιν τοῦ θεοῦ ἐπιτυχεῖν, ἐάνπερ ὑμεῖς μὴ φείσησθέ μου.

2 ₁Οὐ γὰρ θέλω ὑμᾶς ἀνθρωπαρεσκῆσαι, ἀλλὰ θεῷ ἀρέσαι, ὥσπερ καὶ ἀρέσκετε. οὔτε γὰρ ἐγώ ποτε ἕξω καιρὸν τοιοῦτον θεοῦ ἐπιτυχεῖν· οὔτε ὑμεῖς, ἐὰν σιωπήσητε, κρείττονι ἔργῳ ἔχετε ἐπιγραφῆναι. ἐὰν γὰρ σιωπήσητε ἀπ᾽ ἐμοῦ, ἐγὼ λόγος θεοῦ· ἐὰν δὲ ἐρασθῆτε τῆς σαρκός μου, πάλιν ἔσομαι φωνή.

Ignatius to the Romans:

Ignatius, who is also God-carrier, to the church which has obtained mercy, through the majesty of the most high God the Father, and of Jesus Christ, his only Son, a church hallowed and beloved[1] by the will of God, who willed all that is, in accordance with the faith and love of Jesus Christ, our God, which presides in the place of the region of the Romans, and which is worthy of God, worthy of honor, worthy of blessedness, worthy of praise, worthy of success, worthy of sanctification, presiding out of love, keeping the law of Christ, named after the Father, whom I also greet in the name of Jesus Christ the Son of the Father; to those who are united both in flesh and spirit to every one of his commandments, who are filled unwaveringly with every grace of God and are purified from every strange taint: many greetings, blamelessly, in God the Father and our Lord Jesus Christ.

1 ₁Since I have been able to perceive your God-worthy faces through prayer to God, I have asked to receive more yet. For chained in Christ Jesus I hope to greet you, should this be the will of the one who has made me worthy to continue to the end. ₂For the beginning is well-arranged, yet to attain grace I have to obtain my lot unhindered. For I fear your love, lest it do me harm. For it is easy for you to do what you wish but it is hard for me to attain to God, if you spare me not.

2 ₁For I do not wish that you should be people-pleasers but that you please God, as you already do. For I shall have no further opportunity such as this to attain to God, nor shall you, if you keep silent, be enrolled in a better task. For if you keep silent about me, I shall be a word of God, but if you are deeply concerned about my flesh I shall once again simply be a voice.

---

[1] *Ēgapēmenē*. Possibly "sanctified" (*ēgiasmenē*), as in the long recension.

₂πλέον [δὲ] μοι μὴ παράσχησθε τοῦ σπονδισθῆναι θεῷ, ὡς ἔτι θυσιαστήριον ἕτοιμόν ἐστιν, ἵνα ἐν ἀγάπῃ χορὸς γενόμενοι ᾄσητε τῷ πατρὶ ἐν Χριστῷ Ἰησοῦ, ὅτι τὸν ἐπίσκοπον Συρίας κατηξίωσεν ὁ θεὸς εὑρεθῆναι εἰς δύσιν ἀπὸ ἀνατολῆς μεταπεμψάμενος. καλὸν τὸ δῦναι ἀπὸ κόσμου πρὸς θεόν, ἵνα εἰς αὐτὸν ἀνατείλω.

3   ₁Οὐδέποτε ἐβασκάνατε οὐδενί· ἄλλους ἐδιδάξατε. ἐγὼ δὲ θέλω, ἵνα κἀκεῖνα βέβαια ᾖ, ἃ μαθητεύοντες ἐντέλλεσθε.

₂μόνον μοι δύναμιν αἰτεῖσθε ἔσωθέν τε καὶ ἔξωθεν, ἵνα μὴ μόνον λέγω, ἀλλὰ καὶ θέλω· ἵνα μὴ μόνον λέγωμαι Χριστιανός ἀλλὰ καὶ εὑρεθῶ. ἐὰν γὰρ εὑρεθῶ, καὶ λέγεσθαι δύναμαι, καὶ τότε πιστὸς εἶναι, ὅταν κόσμῳ μὴ φαίνωμαι.

₃οὐδὲν φαινόμενον καλόν.¹ ὁ γὰρ θεὸς ἡμῶν Ἰησοῦς Χριστὸς, ἐν πατρὶ ὤν, μᾶλλον φαίνεται. οὐ πεισμονῆς τὸ ἔργον ἀλλὰ μεγέθους ἐστὶν ὁ Χριστιανισμός, ὅταν μισῆται ὑπὸ κόσμου.

4   ₁Ἐγὼ γράφω πάσαις ταῖς ἐκκλησίαις καὶ ἐντέλλομαι πᾶσιν ὅτι [ἐγὼ] ἑκὼν ὑπὲρ θεοῦ ἀποθνήσκω, ἐάνπερ ὑμεῖς μὴ κωλύσητε. παρακαλῶ ὑμᾶς, μὴ εὔνοια ἄκαιρος γένησθέ μοι. ἄφετέ με θηρίων εἶναι,² δι᾽ ὧν [ἔν]εστιν θεοῦ ἐπιτυχεῖν. σῖτός εἰμι θεοῦ, καὶ δι᾽ ὀδόντων θηρίων ἀλήθομαι, ἵνα καθαρὸς ἄρτος εὑρεθῶ [τοῦ Χριστοῦ].

₂μᾶλλον κολακεύσατε τὰ θηρία, ἵνα μοι τάφος γένωνται, καὶ μηθὲν καταλίπωσι τῶν τοῦ σώματός μου, ἵνα μὴ κοιμηθεὶς βαρύς τινι γένωμαι. τότε ἔσομαι μαθητὴς ἀληθῶς Ἰησοῦ Χριστοῦ, ὅτε οὐδὲ τὸ σῶμά μου ὁ κόσμος ὄψεται. λιτανεύσατε τὸν Κύριον ὑπὲρ ἐμοῦ, ἵνα διὰ τῶν ὀργάνων τούτων θεοῦ θυσία εὑρεθῶ.

---

¹So Lightfoot. See, however, the note to the translation opposite.
²So Lightfoot. However, many mss and versions add a word here, and I have rendered βοράν here.

₂Do not allow me anything other than being poured out for God, whilst there is an altar still prepared, so that forming a chorus in love you may sing out to the Father in Jesus Christ, because God has made the bishop from Syria worthy of being found at the setting of the sun, after being sent from where it rises. It is good for me to sink to God from the world, so that I may rise up to him.

3 ₁You have never envied anyone; you have taught others. I now wish that what you have enjoined should be secure, as you teach them.

₂For myself, ask simply that I should have the power both inwardly and outwardly, that I do not simply say so but that I actually desire, not only to be called a Christian but to be found to be one. For if I be found to be so, I shall be able both to speak and then to be faithful, when I am no longer apparent to the world.

₃Nothing visible is eternal; for our God Jesus Christ, is all the more apparent, since he is in the Father.[2] The matter is not a work of persuasion, but Christianity is majesty when it is hated by the world.

4 ₁I am writing to all the churches and I am instructing everyone that I am willingly dying for God, unless you prevent me. I beseech you, do not become an unseasonable kindness for me. Leave me to be bread for the beasts, through which I may be able to attain to God. I am God's wheat and through the beasts' teeth I shall be found to be pure bread for Christ.

₂Rather encourage the beasts, so that they may be my tomb and nothing be left over of my body, so that I become no burden to anyone when I am dead. Then I shall truly be a disciple of Jesus Christ, when the world does not see even my body. Beseech the Lord on my behalf, so that I may be found a sacrifice for God through these instruments.

[2]This is something of an eclectic reading. Broadly there are two readings: one states "Nothing visible is good; for our God Jesus Christ, is all the more apparent, since he is in the Father." The other reads "Nothing visible is eternal. 'For whatever is seen is temporary, whatever is not seen is eternal.' For our God Jesus Christ, is all the more apparent, since he is in the Father." Thus here I have taken the adjective "eternal" from one group, but omitted the quotation, leaving it in the long recension.

₃οὐχ ὡς Πέτρος καὶ Παῦλος διατάσσομαι ὑμῖν· ἐκεῖνοι ἀπόστολοι, ἐγὼ κατάκριτος· ἐκεῖνοι ἐλεύθεροι, ἐγὼ δὲ μέχρι νῦν δοῦλος. ἀλλ' ἐὰν πάθω, ἀπελεύθερος Ἰησοῦ Χριστοῦ, καὶ ἀναστήσομαι ἐν αὐτῷ ἐλεύθερος. νῦν μανθάνω δεδεμένος μηδὲν ἐπιθυμεῖν.

5 ₁Ἀπὸ Συρίας μέχρι Ῥώμης θηριομαχῶ, διὰ γῆς καὶ θαλάσσης, νυκτὸς καὶ ἡμέρας, δεδεμένος δέκα λεοπάρδοις, ὅ ἐστιν στρατιωτικὸν τάγμα, οἳ καὶ εὐεργετούμενοι χείρους γίνονται. ἐν δὲ τοῖς ἀδικήμασιν αὐτῶν μᾶλλον μαθητεύομαι·ἀλλ' οὐ παρὰ τοῦτο δεδικαίωμαι. ₂ὀναίμην τῶν θηρίων τῶν ἐμοὶ ἡτοιμασμένων, καὶ εὔχομαι σύντομά μοι εὑρεθῆναι· ἃ καὶ κολακεύσω συντόμως με καταφαγεῖν, οὐχ ὥσπερ τινῶν δειλαινόμενα οὐχ ἥψαντο· κἂν αὐτὰ δὲ ἄκοντα μὴ θελήσῃ, ἐγὼ προσβιάσομαι.

₃συγγνώμην μοι ἔχετε· τί μοι συμφέρει ἐγὼ γινώσκω· νῦν ἄρχομαι μαθητὴς εἶναι· μηθέν με ζηλώσαι τῶν ὁρατῶν καὶ ἀοράτων, ἵνα Ἰησοῦ Χριστοῦ ἐπιτύχω. πῦρ καὶ σταυρὸς θηρίων τε συστάσεις, [ἀνατομαί, διαιρέσεις,] σκορπισμοὶ ὀστέων, συγκοπὴ μελῶν, ἀλεσμοὶ ὅλου τοῦ σώματος, κακαὶ κολάσεις τοῦ διαβόλου ἐπ' ἐμὲ ἐρχέσθωσαν· μόνον ἵνα Ἰησοῦ Χριστοῦ ἐπιτύχω.

6 ₁Οὐδέν μοι ὠφελήσει τὰ τερπνὰ τοῦ κόσμου, οὐδὲν αἱ βασιλεῖαι τοῦ αἰῶνος τούτου· καλόν μοι ἀποθανεῖν εἰς Χριστὸν Ἰησοῦν, ἢ βασιλεύειν τῶν περάτων τῆς γῆς. ἐκεῖνον ζητῶ, τὸν ὑπὲρ ἡμῶν ἀποθανόντα· ἐκεῖνον θέλω, τὸν [δι' ἡμᾶς] ἀναστάντα. ὁ δὲ τοκετός μοι ἐπίκειται.

₂σύγγνωτέ μοι, ἀδελφοί· μὴ ἐμποδίσητέ μοι ζῆσαι, μὴ θελήσητέ με ἀποθανεῖν. τὸν τοῦ θεοῦ θέλοντα εἶναι κόσμῳ μὴ χαρίσησθε· μηδὲ ὕλῃ κολακεύσητε. ἄφετέ με καθαρὸν φῶς λαβεῖν· ἐκεῖ παραγενόμενος ἄνθρωπος ἔσομαι.

₃ἐπιτρέψατέ μοι μιμητὴν εἶναι τοῦ πάθους τοῦ θεοῦ μου. εἴ τις αὐτὸν ἐν ἑαυτῷ ἔχει, νοησάτω ὃ θέλω καὶ συμπαθείτω μοι εἰδὼς τὰ συνέχοντά με.

₃I am not directing you like Peter and Paul. They were apostles, I am a condemned criminal. They were free, I am still a slave. But if I should suffer I shall become a freedman of Jesus Christ, and I shall rise up free in him. And now I am learning, whilst chained, to be desirous of nothing.

5 ₁I am fighting wild beasts from Syria to Rome, through earth and sea, day and night. I am guarded by ten leopards, which is a military unit, who become worse by being well-treated. In their injustices I am becoming more of a disciple, "but I am not made just on this account."[3] ₂May I delight in the beasts prepared for me, and I pray they may be found ready for me. I shall encourage them to devour me speedily, unlike those of whom they take fright and will not touch. So even if they do not wish to do so, I shall force them.

₃Grant me this: I know what is right for me. Now I am beginning to be a disciple. May nothing, visible or invisible, show jealousy towards me, only let me attain to Jesus Christ. Fire and cross, packs of wild beasts, cuttings, rendings, the scattering of bones, the chopping up of limbs, the grinding of the whole body, the evil torments of the devil can come upon me, only let me attain to Jesus Christ.

6 ₁Neither the ends of the world nor the kingdoms of this age profit me anything. It is better for me to die in Jesus Christ than to reign over the ends of the earth. Him I seek, the one who died on our behalf. Him I desire, him who rose up for us. The birth-pangs are laid upon me.

₂Grant me this, brothers: do not hinder me from living, do not wish that I should die. Do not give the world the one who wishes to be God's, nor charm him with the material. Allow me to receive the pure light. When I have arrived there I will truly be human.

₃Allow me to be an imitator of the passion of my God. Anyone who has understanding within would know what I desire and would sympathize with me, knowing what restrains me.

[3]1 Cor 4.4.

7 ₁Ὁ ἄρχων τοῦ αἰῶνος τούτου διαρπάσαι με βούλεται καὶ τὴν
εἰς θεόν μου γνώμην διαφθεῖραι. μηδεὶς οὖν τῶν παρόντων ὑμῶν
βοηθείτω αὐτῷ· μᾶλλον ἐμοῦ γίνεσθε, τουτέστιν τοῦ θεοῦ. μὴ
λαλεῖτε Ἰησοῦν Χριστόν κόσμον δὲ ἐπιθυμεῖτε.

₂βασκανία ἐν ὑμῖν μὴ κατοικείτω· μηδ᾽ ἂν ἐγὼ παρὼν παρακαλῶ
ὑμᾶς, πείσθητέ μοι, τούτοις δὲ μᾶλλον πείσθητε, οἷς γράφω ὑμῖν. ζῶν
[γὰρ] γράφω ὑμῖν, ἐρῶν τοῦ ἀποθανεῖν· ὁ ἐμὸς ἔρως ἐσταύρωται, καὶ
οὐκ ἔστιν ἐν ἐμοὶ πῦρ φιλόϋλον, ὕδωρ δὲ ζῶν †καὶ λαλοῦν† ἐν ἐμοί,
ἔσωθέν μοι λέγον· Δεῦρο πρὸς τὸν πατέρα.

₃οὐχ ἥδομαι τροφῇ φθορᾶς οὐδὲ ἡδοναῖς τοῦ βίου τούτου·
ἄρτον θεοῦ θέλω, ὅ ἐστιν σὰρξ τοῦ Χριστοῦ[3] τοῦ ἐκ σπέρματος
Δαυείδ, καὶ πόμα θέλω τὸ αἷμα αὐτοῦ, ὅ ἐστιν ἀγάπη ἄφθαρτος.

8 ₁Οὐκ ἔτι θέλω κατὰ ἀνθρώπους ζῆν· τοῦτο δὲ ἔσται, ἐὰν ὑμεῖς
θελήσητε. θελήσατε, ἵνα καὶ ὑμεῖς θεληθῆτε.

₂δι᾽ ὀλίγων γραμμάτων αἰτοῦμαι ὑμᾶς· πιστεύσατέ μοι. Ἰησοῦς
δὲ Χριστὸς ὑμῖν ταῦτα φανερώσει, ὅτι ἀληθῶς λέγω· τὸ ἀψευδὲς
στόμα, ἐν ᾧ ὁ πατὴρ ἐλάλησεν [ἀληθῶς].

₃αἰτήσασθε περὶ ἐμοῦ, ἵνα ἐπιτύχω [ἐν πνευματι ἁγίῳ]. οὐ κατὰ
σάρκα ὑμῖν ἔγραψα, ἀλλὰ κατὰ γνώμην θεοῦ. ἐὰν πάθω, ἠθελήσατε·
ἐὰν ἀποδοκιμασθῶ, ἐμισήσατε.

9 ₁Μνημονεύετε ἐν τῇ προσευχῇ ὑμῶν τῆς ἐν Συρίᾳ ἐκκλησίας,
ἥτις ἀντὶ ἐμοῦ ποιμένι τῷ θεῷ χρῆται· μόνος αὐτὴν Ἰησοῦς Χριστὸς
ἐπισκοπήσει καὶ ἡ ὑμῶν ἀγάπη.

₂ἐγὼ δὲ αἰσχύνομαι ἐξ αὐτῶν λέγεσθαι· οὐδὲ γὰρ ἄξιός εἰμι,
ὢν ἔσχατος αὐτῶν καὶ ἔκτρωμα· ἀλλ᾽ ἠλέημαί τις εἶναι, ἐὰν θεοῦ
ἐπιτύχω.

₃ἀσπάζεται ὑμᾶς τὸ ἐμὸν πνεῦμα καὶ ἡ ἀγάπη τῶν ἐκκλησιῶν
τῶν δεξαμένων με εἰς ὄνομα Ἰησοῦ Χριστοῦ, οὐχ ὡς παροδεύοντα·

[3]So Lightfoot. However, I have read, and rendered, Ἰησοῦ Χριστοῦ, in common
with the majority witness.

7 ₁The ruler of this age wishes to snatch me and desires to corrupt my understanding of God. Let none of those with you help him! Rather be on my side, that is to say, on God's. Do not speak of Jesus Christ whilst longing for the world.

₂Envy should find no place among you. Even if, when I arrive, I beseech you otherwise, be persuaded by me, rather be persuaded by this which I am writing to you. For while I live I am writing to you, anxious to die. My desire is crucified, and there is no love of the material burning in me. Rather there is living water speaking in me, saying to me, within, "Come to the Father."

₃I have no pleasure in corruptible food nor in the pleasures of this life; I desire the bread of God which is the flesh of Jesus Christ, of the seed of David, and I desire his blood for my drink, which is incorruptible love.

8 ₁No longer do I wish to live in a human manner. This will come about if you wish it. So wish it, so that you may also be wanted.

₂I ask you in a few letters: believe me! Jesus Christ shall make plain to you that I speak the truth. He is the mouth incapable of falsehood, in whom the Father truly spoke.

₃Pray for me, that I may win through. I do not write to you in the flesh, but in accordance with God's mind. If I suffer, you have wished it so. If I am rejected, you have despised me.

9 ₁In your intercession remember the church in Syria, which employs God as its shepherd, instead of me. Jesus Christ alone will watch over it, as well as your love.

₂I am ashamed to be called one of them, for I am not worthy, being the least of them and untimely born. But through mercy I gain authenticity, should I attain to God.

₃My spirit greets you, as does the love of the churches which have received me in the name of Jesus Christ, and not as a wayfarer.

καὶ γὰρ αἱ μὴ προσήκουσαί μοι τῇ ὁδῷ τῇ κατὰ σάρκα κατὰ πόλιν
με προῆγον.

10   ₁Γράφω δὲ ὑμῖν ταῦτα ἀπὸ Σμύρνης δι᾿ Ἐφεσίων τῶν
ἀξιομακαρίστων. ἔστιν δὲ καὶ ἅμα ἐμοὶ σὺν ἄλλοις πολλοῖς καὶ
Κρόκος, τὸ ποθητόν [μοι] ὄνομα. ₂περὶ τῶν προελθόντων με ἀπὸ
Συρίας εἰς Ῥώμην εἰς δόξαν [τοῦ] θεοῦ πιστεύω ὑμᾶς ἐπεγνωκέναι.
οἷς καὶ δηλώσατε ἐγγύς με ὄντα- πάντες γάρ εἰσιν ἄξιοι [τοῦ] θεοῦ
καὶ ὑμῶν· οὓς πρέπον ὑμῖν ἐστὶν κατὰ πάντα ἀναπαῦσαι. ₃ἔγραψα δὲ
ὑμῖν ταῦτα τῇ πρὸ ἐννέα καλανδῶν Σεπτεμβρίων. ἔρρωσθε εἰς τέλος
ἐν ὑπομονῇ Ἰησοῦ Χριστοῦ.

For those who did not lie on my route in the flesh preceded me city by city.

10   ₁I am writing this to you from Smyrna, through the Ephesians who are worthily blessed. Along with many others, Crocus is with me, whose name is longed for. ₂I trust that you are aware of those who have gone ahead of me from Syria to Rome for the glory of God. Inform them that I am nearby, for they are all worthy of God, as of yourselves. It is right that you should refresh them in every way. ₃I am writing this to you on the ninth before the kalends of September.[4] Fare well to the last in the endurance of Jesus Christ.

[4]24 August.

Philadelphians

It is apparent from this letter that Ignatius had spent some time in Philadelphia on his journey, and had met members of the church. His concern here is with teachers of Judaism within the Christian context, those who put particular emphasis on the "archives," on written teaching. Against this Ignatius prophecies, stating that the church should be united around the bishop. Ignatius is opposed to the scholasticization of Christianity, in part, I suggest, because the offering of patronage to teachers detracted from the patronage which might be offered to the poor.

It has been suggested, on the basis of this letter, that Ignatius is opposing those who, in turn, opposed episcopal structures in Christian circles, who favored leadership by prophets.[1] I have criticized such a view extensively elsewhere, suggesting that there was never such a thing as prophetic leadership and that the whole picture is based on a misunderstanding of Weber, who used the term "charismatic" to describe leadership as well as religious phenomena such as prophecy, but that the term was used in different ways in different contexts, and so Weber does not lend support to the idea that leadership might have been in the hands of religiously charismatic functionaries.[2] Ignatius' concern here, as elsewhere, is that the church should be united in offering a single Eucharist, and that the single bishop, as agent of God and broker of God's gifts, should be a sign of that unity.

---

[1] In particular note Christine Trevett, "Prophecy and Anti-episcopal Activity: A Third Error Combatted by Ignatius?" *JEH* 34 (1983): 1–18

[2] In particular in my "Prophecy and Patronage: The Relationship between Charismatic Functionaries and Household Officers in early Christianity" in C.M. Tuckett and A. Gregory (eds), *Trajectories through the New Testament and the Apostolic Fathers* (Oxford: OUP, 2005), 165–189.

ΦΙΛΑΔΕΛΦΕΥΣΙΝ ΙΓΝΑΤΙΟΣ

Ἰγνάτιος, ὁ καὶ Θεοφόρος, ἐκκλησίᾳ θεοῦ πατρὸς καὶ κυρίου Ἰησοῦ Χριστοῦ τῇ οὔσῃ ἐν Φιλαδελφίᾳ τῆς Ἀσίας, ἐλεημένῃ καὶ ἡδρασμένῃ ἐν ὁμονοίᾳ θεοῦ καὶ ἀγαλλιωμένῃ ἐν τῷ πάθει τοῦ κυρίου ἡμῶν ἀδιακρίτως καὶ ἐν τῇ ἀναστάσει αὐτοῦ, πεπληροφορημένῃ ἐν παντὶ ἐλέει· ἣν ἀσπάζομαι ἐν αἵματι Ἰησοῦ Χριστοῦ, ἥτις ἐστὶν χαρὰ αἰώνιος καὶ παράμονος· μάλιστα ἐὰν ἐν ἑνὶ ὦσιν σὺν τῷ ἐπισκόπῳ καὶ τοῖς σὺν αὐτῷ πρεσβυτέροις καὶ διακόνοις ἀποδεδειγμένοις ἐν γνώμῃ Ἰησοῦ Χριστοῦ, οὓς κατὰ τὸ ἴδιον θέλημα ἐστήριξεν ἐν βεβαιωσύνῃ τῷ ἁγίῳ αὐτοῦ πνεύματι.

1 ₁Ὃν ἐπίσκοπον ἔγνων οὐκ ἀφ' ἑαυτοῦ οὐδὲ δι' ἀνθρώπων κεκτῆσθαι τὴν διακονίαν τὴν εἰς τὸ κοινὸν ἀνήκουσαν, οὐδὲ κατὰ κενοδοξίαν, ἀλλ' ἐν ἀγάπῃ θεοῦ πατρὸς καὶ κυρίου Ἰησοῦ Χριστοῦ· οὗ καταπέπληγμαι τὴν ἐπιείκειαν, ὃς σιγῶν πλείονα δύναται τῶν λαλούντων·[1] ₂συνευρύθμισται γὰρ ταῖς ἐντολαῖς, ὡς χορδαῖς κιθάρα. διὸ μακαρίζει μου ἡ ψυχὴ τὴν εἰς θεὸν αὐτοῦ γνώμην, ἐπιγνοὺς ἐνάρετον καὶ τέλειον οὖσαν, τὸ ἀκίνητον αὐτοῦ καὶ τὸ ἀόργητον [αὐτοῦ] ἐν πάσῃ ἐπιεικείᾳ θεοῦ ζῶντος.

2 ₁Τέκνα οὖν [φωτὸς] ἀληθείας, φεύγετε τὸν μερισμὸν καὶ τὰς κακοδιδασκαλίας· ὅπου δὲ ὁ ποιμήν ἐστιν, ἐκεῖ ὡς πρόβατα ἀκολουθεῖτε· ₂πολλοὶ γὰρ λύκοι ἀξιόπιστοι ἡδονῇ κακῇ αἰχμαλωτίζουσιν τοὺς θεοδρόμους· ἀλλ' ἐν τῇ ἑνότητι ὑμῶν οὐχ ἕξουσιν τόπον.

3 ₁Ἀπέχεσθε τῶν κακῶν βοτανῶν, ἅστινας οὐ γεωργεῖ Ἰησοῦς Χριστός, διὰ τὸ μὴ εἶναι αὐτοὺς φυτείαν πατρός. οὐχ ὅτι παρ' ὑμῖν μερισμὸν εὗρον, ἀλλ' ἀποδιϋλισμόν. ₂ὅσοι γὰρ θεοῦ εἰσιν καὶ Ἰησοῦ

---

[1] Most published texts read μάταια λαλούντων, but the object is unnecessary.

IGNATIUS TO THE PHILADELPHIANS:

Ignatius, who is also God-carrier, to the church of God the Father and the Lord Jesus Christ which is in Philadelphia of Asia, which has received mercy and is established in the agreement of God and which rejoices in the passion of our Lord without distinction, as in his resurrection, which is fully satisfied in all mercy, which I greet in the blood of Jesus Christ, which is an eternal and lasting joy, especially if they are at one with the bishop and those with him, the presbyters and deacons who are appointed in the knowledge of Jesus Christ, who, in accordance with his own desire, set them firmly in place by his Holy Spirit.

1 ₁I am aware that the bishop did not receive the ministry to the community which is his from himself, nor through any human agency, nor on account of vainglory, but in the love of God the Father and the Lord Jesus Christ. I have been astonished by his fairness, as being silent he can achieve more than those who speak.[3] ₂For he is attuned to the commandments like a harp to its strings. So my soul blesses his understanding of God, knowing it to be virtuous and perfect, together with his calm and composed nature, in all fairness, deriving from the living God.

2 Therefore, children of the light of truth, avoid division and evil teachings. Where the shepherd is, there you, the sheep, should follow. ₂For many apparently trustworthy wolves imprison, by means of wicked pleasure, those who go the way of God, but in your unity shall they have no place.

3 Stay away from wicked plants, those which Jesus Christ does not cultivate, since they are not a planting of the Father. Not that I have found division among you, but purity.[4] ₂Those who are of God, and

[3]Some mss add "vanity." I have followed Lightfoot in omitting this word.
[4]Literally, "a filter." The idea seems to be that impurities have been filtered out.

Χριστοῦ, οὗτοι μετὰ τοῦ ἐπισκόπου εἰσίν· καὶ ὅσοι ἂν μετανοήσαντες
ἔλθωσιν ἐπὶ τὴν ἑνότητα τῆς ἐκκλησίας, καὶ οὗτοι θεοῦ ἔσονται, ἵνα
ὦσιν κατὰ Ἰησοῦν Χριστὸν ζῶντες. ₃μὴ πλανᾶσθε, ἀδελφοί μου·
εἴ τις σχίζοντι ἀκολουθεῖ, βασιλείαν θεοῦ οὐ κληρονομεῖ· εἴ τις ἐν
ἀλλοτρίᾳ γνώμῃ περιπατεῖ, οὗτος τῷ πάθει οὐ συγκατατίθεται.

4 σπουδάσατε οὖν μιᾷ εὐχαριστίᾳ χρῆσθαι· μία γὰρ σὰρξ τοῦ
κυρίου ἡμῶν Ἰησοῦ Χριστοῦ, καὶ ἓν ποτήριον εἰς ἕνωσιν τοῦ αἵματος
αὐτοῦ· ἓν θυσιαστήριον, ὡς εἷς ἐπίσκοπος, ἅμα τῷ πρεσβυτερίῳ
καὶ διακόνοις τοῖς συνδούλοις μου· ἵνα ὃ ἐὰν πράσσητε κατὰ θεὸν
πράσσητε.

5 ₁Ἀδελφοί μου λίαν ἐκκέχυμαι ἀγαπῶν ὑμᾶς, καὶ ὑπεραγαλλό-
μενος ἀσφαλίζομαι ὑμᾶς· οὐκ ἐγὼ δέ, ἀλλ᾿ Ἰησοῦς Χριστός, ἐν
ᾧ δεδεμένος φοβοῦμαι μᾶλλον, ὡς ἔτι ὢν ἀναπάρτιστος. ἀλλ᾿ ἡ
προσευχὴ ὑμῶν [εἰς θεόν] με ἀπαρτίσει, ἵνα ἐν ᾧ κλήρῳ ἠλεήθην
ἐπιτύχω, προσφυγὼν τῷ εὐαγγελίῳ ὡς σαρκὶ Ἰησοῦ καὶ τοῖς
ἀποστόλοις ὡς πρεσβυτερίῳ ἐκκλησίας. ₂καὶ τοὺς προφήτας δὲ
ἀγαπῶμεν, διὰ τὸ καὶ αὐτοὺς εἰς τὸ εὐαγγέλιον κατηγγελκέναι
καὶ εἰς αὐτὸν ἐλπίζειν καὶ αὐτὸν ἀναμένειν· ἐν ᾧ καὶ πιστεύσαντες
ἐσώθησαν ἐν ἑνότητι Ἰησοῦ Χριστοῦ, ὄντες ἀξιαγάπητοι καὶ
ἀξιοθαύμαστοι ἅγιοι, ὑπὸ Ἰησοῦ Χριστοῦ μεμαρτυρημένοι καὶ
συνηριθμημένοι ἐν τῷ εὐαγγελίῳ τῆς κοινῆς ἐλπίδος.

6 ₁Ἐὰν δέ τις Ἰουδαϊσμὸν ἑρμηνεύῃ ὑμῖν, μὴ ἀκούετε αὐτοῦ.
ἄμεινον γάρ ἐστιν παρὰ ἀνδρὸς περιτομὴν ἔχοντος Χριστιανισμὸν
ἀκούειν ἢ παρὰ ἀκροβύστου Ἰουδαϊσμόν. ἐὰν δὲ ἀμφότεροι περὶ
Ἰησοῦ Χριστοῦ μὴ λαλῶσιν, οὗτοι ἐμοὶ στῆλαί εἰσιν καὶ τάφοι
νεκρῶν, ἐφ᾿ οἷς γέγραπται μόνον ὀνόματα ἀνθρώπων. ₂φεύγετε
οὖν τὰς κακοτεχνίας καὶ ἐνέδρας τοῦ ἄρχοντος τοῦ αἰῶνος τούτου,
μήποτε θλιβέντες τῇ γνώμῃ αὐτοῦ ἐξασθενήσετε ἐν τῇ ἀγάπῃ· ἀλλὰ
πάντες ἐπὶ τὸ αὐτὸ γίνεσθε ἐν ἀμερίστῳ καρδίᾳ. ₃εὐχαριστῶ δὲ τῷ
θεῷ μου, ὅτι εὐσυνείδητός εἰμι ἐν ὑμῖν, καὶ οὐκ ἔχει τις καυχήσασθαι

Jesus Christ, are with the bishop. Those who are repentant and who come into the unity of the church will also be God's, so that they may live in accordance with Jesus Christ. ₃Do not be deceived, my brothers, anyone who follows the one who separates shall not inherit the kingdom of God. Anyone who acts in accordance with an alien opinion is not conformed to the passion.

4 Therefore be eager to celebrate one Eucharist. For there is one flesh of our Lord Jesus Christ and one cup of unity in his blood, one altar, just as there is one bishop together with the presbytery and the deacons, my fellow-slaves. In this way, whatever you do, you will do in accordance with God.

5 ₁My brothers, in loving you I am overflowing greatly, and rejoicing exceedingly I safeguard you. Rather, not I, but Jesus Christ. Although I am bound in him my fear is greater, being still incomplete. But your prayer to God will complete me, so that I may attain to the lot which I have received in mercy, as I flee to the gospel as to the flesh of Jesus and the apostles as to the presbytery of the church. ₂And we should also love the prophets, since their proclamation was of the gospel; they hoped for it and awaited it, and by believing in it they were saved, as they were in the unity of Jesus Christ, saints deserving of love and deserving of admiration, receiving the testimony of Jesus Christ in the gospel of the hope we hold in common.

6 ₁Do not listen to anyone who should interpret Judaism to you. For it is better to hear about Christianity from a circumcised man than Judaism from one uncircumcised. Yet if either fails to speak of Jesus Christ, they seem to me to be headstones and tombs for the dead, on which simply human names are written. ₂Therefore flee the evil arts and the snares of the ruler of this age, so that you are not weakened in your love through the oppression of his will. But all of you should stand in agreement and with an undivided heart. ₃I thank my God that I am of a clear conscience in regard to you, and that nobody has

οὔτε λάθρα οὔτε φανερῶς, ὅτι ἐβάρησά τινα ἐν μικρῷ ἢ ἐν μεγάλῳ. καὶ πᾶσι δὲ, ἐν οἷς ἐλάλησα, εὔχομαι ἵνα μὴ εἰς μαρτύριον αὐτὸ κτήσωνται.

7 ₁Εἰ γὰρ καὶ κατὰ σάρκα μέ τινες ἠθέλησαν πλανῆσαι, ἀλλὰ τὸ πνεῦμα οὐ πλανᾶται, ἀπὸ θεοῦ ὄν· οἶδεν γάρ πόθεν ἔρχεται καὶ ποῦ ὑπάγει, καὶ τὰ κρυπτὰ ἐλέγχει. ἐκραύγασα μεταξὺ ὤν, ἐλάλουν μεγάλῃ φωνῇ, θεοῦ φωνῇ· Τῷ ἐπισκόπῳ προσέχετε καὶ τῷ πρεσβυτερίῳ καὶ διακόνοις. ₂οἱ δὲ ὑποπτεύσαντές με, ὡς προειδότα τὸν μερισμόν τινων, λέγειν ταῦτα. μάρτυς δέ μοι, ἐν ᾧ δέδεμαι, ὅτι ἀπὸ σαρκὸς ἀνθρωπίνης οὐκ ἔγνων·τὸ δὲ πνεῦμα ἐκήρυσσεν, λέγον τάδε· Χωρὶς τοῦ ἐπισκόπου μηδὲν ποιεῖτε· τὴν σάρκα ὑμῶν ὡς ναὸν θεοῦ τηρεῖτε· τὴν ἕνωσιν ἀγαπᾶτε· τοὺς μερισμοὺς φεύγετε· μιμηταὶ γίνεσθε Ἰησοῦ Χριστοῦ, ὡς καὶ αὐτὸς τοῦ πατρὸς αὐτοῦ.

8 ₁Ἐγὼ μὲν οὖν τὸ ἴδιον ἐποίουν, ὡς ἄνθρωπος εἰς ἕνωσιν κατηρτισμένος. Οὗ δὲ μερισμός ἐστιν καὶ ὀργή, θεὸς οὐ κατοικεῖ. πᾶσιν οὖν μετανοοῦσιν ἀφίει ὁ κύριος, ἐὰν μετανοήσωσιν εἰς ἑνότητα θεοῦ καὶ συνέδριον τοῦ ἐπισκόπου. πιστεύω τῇ χάριτι Ἰησοῦ Χριστοῦ, ὃς λύσει ἀφ᾿ ὑμῶν πάντα δεσμόν· ₂παρακαλῶ δὲ ὑμᾶς, μηδὲν κατ᾿ ἐρίθειαν πράσσειν, ἀλλὰ κατὰ χριστομαθίαν. ἐπεὶ ἤκουσά τινων λεγόντων ὅτι, Ἐὰν μὴ ἐν τοῖς ἀρχείοις εὕρω, ἐν τῷ εὐαγγελίῳ οὐ πιστεύω· καὶ λέγοντός μου αὐτοῖς ὅτι Γέγραπται, ἀπεκρίθησάν μοι ὅτι Πρόκειται. ἐμοὶ δὲ ἀρχεῖά ἐστιν Ἰησοῦς Χριστός, τὰ ἄθικτα ἀρχεῖα ὁ σταυρὸς αὐτοῦ καὶ ὁ θάνατος καὶ ἡ ἀνάστασις αὐτοῦ καὶ ἡ πίστις ἡ δι᾿ αὐτοῦ· ἐν οἷς θέλω ἐν τῇ προσευχῇ ὑμῶν δικαιωθῆναι.

9 ₁Καλοὶ καὶ οἱ ἱερεῖς· κρεῖσσον δὲ ὁ ἀρχιερεὺς ὁ πεπιστευμένος τὰ ἅγια τῶν ἁγίων, ὃς μόνος πεπίστευται τὰ κρυπτὰ τοῦ θεοῦ· αὐτὸς

cause to boast, whether privately or publicly, that I weighed anyone down in any matter, small or great, and I pray that all with whom I conversed, should not find it a witness against themselves.

7 ₁For even if some people desired to deceive me in the flesh, the spirit which is of God is not deceived, for it knows whence it came and where it is going, and it exposes what is hidden.[5] Amongst you I cried out, I spoke with a great voice, the voice of God: "Give mind to the bishop and to the presbytery and to the deacons." ₂There were some who suspected me of having foreknowledge of the division among you when I said this, but the one in whom I am bound bears witness to me that I knew this not from any human source, but the Spirit was proclaiming in speaking thus. "Do nothing apart from the bishop, keep your flesh as a temple of God, love unity, shun divisions, be imitators of Jesus Christ, as he is of his Father."

8 ₁I, therefore, was acting of my own accord as a person fixed on unity. For God does not dwell where there is division and anger. The Lord forgives all who repent if they repent in the unity of God and the council of the bishop. I have faith in the grace of Jesus Christ, who will release you from all your chains. ₂I exhort you to do nothing in a discordant manner, but in accordance with the teaching of Christ. Since I heard some saying "If I do not find it in the ancient writings,[6] I do not believe it in the gospel." And when I said to them, "It is written," they replied to me, "That is the question." For me the archives are Jesus Christ, the sacred archives, his cross and death and his resurrection and the faith which comes from him, by which I desire, by your prayer, to be made righteous.

9 ₁The priests are indeed good, but better is the high priest who is entrusted with the holy of holies, who alone is entrusted with

[5]Cf. Jn 3.8; 1 Cor 2.10.

[6]Reading *archaiois*. It is possible that the word should be *archeiois*, as employed below and in the long recension.

ὧν θύρα τοῦ πατρός, δι᾽ ἧς εἰσέρχονται Ἀβραὰμ καὶ Ἰσαὰκ καὶ Ἰακὼβ καὶ οἱ προφῆται καὶ οἱ ἀπόστολοι καὶ ἡ ἐκκλησία. πάντα ταῦτα εἰς ἑνότητα θεοῦ.

₂ἐξαίρετον δέ τι ἔχει τὸ εὐαγγέλιον, τὴν παρουσίαν τοῦ σωτῆρος, κυρίου ἡμῶν Ἰησοῦ Χριστοῦ, τὸ πάθος αὐτοῦ, τὴν ἀνάστασιν. οἱ γὰρ ἀγαπητοὶ προφῆται κατήγγειλαν εἰς αὐτόν· τὸ δὲ εὐαγγέλιον ἀπάρτισμά ἐστιν ἀφθαρσίας. πάντα ὁμοῦ καλά ἐστιν, ἐὰν ἐν ἀγάπῃ πιστεύητε.

10 ₁Ἐπειδὴ κατὰ τὴν προσευχὴν ὑμῶν, καὶ κατὰ τὰ σπλάγχνα ἃ ἔχετε ἐν Χριστῷ Ἰησοῦ, ἀπηγγέλη μοι εἰρηνεύειν τὴν ἐκκλησίαν τὴν ἐν Ἀντιοχείᾳ τῆς Συρίας, πρέπον ἐστὶν ὑμῖν, ὡς ἐκκλησίᾳ θεοῦ, χειροτονῆσαι διάκονον εἰς τὸ πρεσβεῦσαι ἐκεῖ θεοῦ πρεσβείαν, εἰς τὸ συγχαρῆναι αὐτοῖς ἐπὶ τὸ αὐτὸ γενομένοις καὶ δοξάσαι τὸ ὄνομα· ₂μακάριος ἐν Ἰησοῦ Χριστῷ, ὃς καταξιωθήσεται τῆς τοιαύτης διακονίας· καὶ ὑμεῖς δοξασθήσεσθε. θέλουσιν δὲ ὑμῖν οὐκ ἔστιν ἀδύνατον ὑπὲρ ὀνόματος θεοῦ· ὡς καὶ αἱ ἔγγιστα ἐκκλησίαι ἔπεμψαν ἐπισκόπους, αἱ δὲ πρεσβυτέρους καὶ διακόνους.

11 ₁Περὶ δὲ Φίλωνος τοῦ διακόνου ἀπὸ Κιλικίας, ἀνδρὸς μεμαρτυρημένου, ὃς καὶ νῦν ἐν λόγῳ θεοῦ ὑπηρετεῖ μοι, ἅμα Ῥαΐῳ Ἀγαθόποδι, ἀνδρὶ ἐκλεκτῷ, ὃς ἀπὸ Συρίας μοι ἀκολουθεῖ ἀποταξάμενος τῷ βίῳ· οἳ καὶ μαρτυροῦσιν ὑμῖν. κἀγὼ τῷ θεῷ εὐχαριστῶ ὑπὲρ ὑμῶν, ὅτι ἐδέξασθε αὐτούς, ὡς καὶ ὑμᾶς ὁ κύριος. οἱ δὲ ἀτιμάσαντες αὐτοὺς λυτρωθείησαν ἐν τῇ χάριτι τοῦ Ἰησοῦ Χριστοῦ.

₂ἀσπάζεται ὑμᾶς ἡ ἀγάπη τῶν ἀδελφῶν τῶν ἐν Τρωάδι· ὅθεν καὶ γράφω ὑμῖν διὰ Βούρρου πεμφθέντος ἅμα ἐμοὶ ἀπὸ Ἐφεσίων καὶ Σμυρναίων εἰς λόγον τιμῆς. τιμήσει αὐτοὺς ὁ κύριος Ἰησοῦς Χριστός, εἰς ὃν ἐλπίζουσιν σαρκί, ψυχῇ, πνεύματι, πίστει, ἀγάπῃ, ὁμονοίᾳ. ἔρρωσθε ἐν Χριστῷ Ἰησοῦ, τῇ κοινῇ ἐλπίδι ἡμῶν.

the secrets of God, who is himself the door of the Father, through which enter Abraham and Isaac and Jacob and the prophets and the apostles and the church. All these are of the unity of God.

₂Yet there is something distinct in the gospel, the presence of the Savior, our Lord Jesus Christ, his passion, the resurrection. The proclamation of the beloved prophets was aimed at him, but the gospel is the completed work of incorruption. All things together are good, as long as you believe lovingly.

10 ₁Since, in accordance with your prayers and in accordance with the compassion which you possess in Christ Jesus, it is reported to me that the church which is in Syrian Antioch is at peace, it would be fitting for you, as the church of God, to elect a deacon to be delegated as God's ambassador there, so that you can rejoice with those who have a common purpose and glorify the name. ₂Whoever is found worthy of such a ministry is happy in Jesus Christ, and you will yourselves be glorified. For you who desire to do this, for the name of God, this is not impossible, as the closer churches have sent bishops, and others presbyters and deacons.

11 ₁Now regarding Philo, the deacon from Cilicia, a man who has received a good testimony, who even now serves me in the Word of God, alongside Rheus Agathopus, a chosen man, who follows me from Syria, bidding life farewell, who also bear witness to you, as indeed I thank God on behalf of you, because you received them as the Lord received you. May those who dishonored them be redeemed in the grace of Jesus Christ.

₂The love of the brothers in Troas greets you. I write to you from there through Burrhus, who has been sent alongside me from the Ephesians and the Smyrneans as a pledge of honor. The Lord Jesus Christ will honor them; they hope in him in flesh, in soul, spirit, faith, love, concord. Fare well in Christ Jesus, who is our common hope.

Smyrneans

It is apparent from Ignatius' comments and itinerary, insofar as it can be reconstructed, that some time was spent in Smyrna on his journey to Rome. Given Hadrian's close relationship with the city, this is consistent with the suggestion in the introduction that Ignatius was part of an imperial journey from Antioch.

Ignatius' particular concern in addressing this church was to warn of the dangers of Docetic teachers; he points out that such teachers, through denying the fleshly nature of Christ, evacuate both agapē and Eucharist of any significance. Not only do they deny any fleshly reality to Christ, so making it impossible for the Eucharist to convey the spirit of Christ, but they also neglect the bodily needs of the poor and distressed through the failure to celebrate the meal at which both spiritual and fleshly food is shared. In this light we understand what Ignatius means by the unity of flesh and spirit. A true Eucharist is that held with the bishop as broker of God's gifts, the means by which the goods of the church may properly be shared.

ΣΜΥΡΝΑΙΟΙΣ ΙΓΝΑΤΙΟΣ

Ἰγνάτιος, ὁ καὶ Θεοφόρος, ἐκκλησίᾳ θεοῦ πατρὸς καὶ τοῦ ἠγαπημένου Ἰησοῦ Χριστοῦ, ἠλεημένῃ ἐν παντὶ χαρίσματι, πεπληρωμένῃ ἐν πίστει καὶ ἀγάπῃ, ἀνυστερήτῳ οὔσῃ παντὸς χαρίσματος, θεοπρεπεστάτῃ καὶ ἁγιοφόρῳ, τῇ οὔσῃ ἐν Σμύρνῃ τῆς Ἀσίας, ἐν ἀμώμῳ πνεύματι καὶ λόγῳ θεοῦ πλεῖστα χαίρειν.

1   ₁Δοξάζω Ἰησοῦν Χριστὸν τὸν θεὸν τὸν οὕτως ὑμᾶς σοφίσαντα· ἐνόησα γὰρ ὑμᾶς κατηρτισμένους ἐν ἀκινήτῳ πίστει, ὥσπερ καθηλωμένους ἐν τῷ σταυρῷ τοῦ κυρίου Ἰησοῦ Χριστοῦ, σαρκί τε καὶ πνεύματι, καὶ ἡδρασμένους ἐν ἀγάπῃ ἐν τῷ αἵματι Χριστοῦ, πεπληροφορημένους εἰς τὸν κύριον ἡμῶν ἀληθῶς ὄντα ἐκ γένους Δαυεὶδ κατὰ σάρκα, υἱὸν θεοῦ κατὰ θέλημα καὶ δύναμιν,[1] γεγεννημένον ἀληθῶς ἐκ παρθένου, βεβαπτισμένον ὑπὸ Ἰωάννου ἵνα πληρωθῇ πᾶσα δικαιοσύνη ὑπ᾽ αὐτοῦ, ₂ἀληθῶς ἐπὶ Ποντίου Πιλάτου καὶ Ἡρώδου τετράρχου καθηλωμένον ὑπὲρ ἡμῶν ἐν σαρκί· ἀφ᾽ οὗ καρποῦ ἡμεῖς ἀπὸ τοῦ θεομακαρίστου αὐτοῦ πάθους· ἵνα ἄρῃ σύσσημον εἰς τοὺς αἰῶνας διὰ τῆς ἀναστάσεως εἰς τοὺς ἁγίους καὶ πιστοὺς αὐτοῦ, εἴτε ἐν Ἰουδαίοις εἴτε ἐν ἔθνεσιν, ἐν ἑνὶ σώματι τῆς ἐκκλησίας αὐτοῦ.

2   Ταῦτα γὰρ πάντα ἔπαθεν δι᾽ ἡμᾶς, ἵνα [σωθῶμεν]· καὶ ἀληθῶς ἔπαθεν, ὡς καὶ ἀληθῶς ἀνέστησεν ἑαυτόν· οὐχ ὥσπερ ἄπιστοί τινες λέγουσιν τὸ δοκεῖν αὐτὸν πεπονθέναι, αὐτοὶ τὸ δοκεῖν ὄντες· καὶ καθὼς φρονοῦσιν, καὶ συμβήσεται αὐτοῖς, οὖσιν ἀσωμάτοις καὶ δαιμονικοῖς.

3   ₁Ἐγὼ γὰρ καὶ μετὰ τὴν ἀνάστασιν ἐν σαρκὶ αὐτὸν οἶδα καὶ πιστεύω ὄντα· ₂καὶ ὅτε πρὸς τοὺς περὶ Πέτρον ἦλθεν, ἔφη αὐτοῖς· Λάβετε, ψηλαφήσατέ με, καὶ ἴδετε ὅτι οὐκ εἰμὶ δαιμόνιον ἀσώματον.

---

[1]So Lightfoot. However, I have read, and translated, θέλημα καὶ δύναμιν θεοῦ. Lighfoot suggests that θέλημα simply means "divine will" and that the inclusion of θεοῦ is the result of scribal ignorance.

IGNATIUS TO THE SMYRNEANS:

Ignatius, who is also God-carrier, to the church of God the Father and the beloved Jesus Christ, which has received mercy in every good gift, which is filled in faith and love, which is second to none in every good gift, which is most worthy of God and carries sanctification, which is in Smyrna of Asia, many greetings in the spotless Spirit and the Word of God.

1 ₁I glorify Jesus Christ, the God who has given you such wisdom. I am aware that you have been equipped in an unmoving faith, just as if you were nailed to the cross of the Lord Jesus Christ in both flesh and spirit, settled in love in the blood of Christ, and fully convinced with regard to our Lord, that he was truly of the race of David in the flesh, the Son of God according to the will and the power of God, truly begotten from the virgin, baptized by John so that all righteousness might be fulfilled by him. ₂He was truly nailed for us in the flesh, under Pontius Pilate and Herod the tetrarch, as we ourselves derive from the fruit of his divinely blessed passion, so that through the resurrection he could lift up the standard for his holy and faithful ones for ever, whether among Jews or among Gentiles, in the single body of his church.

2 For he suffered all this for our sake, so that we might be saved. And he truly suffered, just as he truly raised himself. He did not, as some unbelievers state, suffer in appearance only. It is they who are appearances, and just what they think will happen to them, as they are disembodied and demonlike.

3 ₁For indeed I know that even after the resurrection he was in the flesh, and I believe that it was so. ₂And when he came to those who were with Peter he said to them: "Reach out, touch me and see that

καὶ εὐθὺς αὐτοῦ ἥψαντο, καὶ ἐπίστευσαν κραθέντες τῇ σαρκὶ αὐτοῦ καὶ τῷ αἵματι.[2] διὰ τοῦτο καὶ θανάτου κατεφρόνησαν, ηὑρέθησαν δὲ ὑπὲρ θάνατον. ₃μετὰ δὲ τὴν ἀνάστασιν [καὶ] συνέφαγεν αὐτοῖς καὶ συνέπιεν ὡς σαρκικός, καίπερ πνευματικῶς ἡνωμένος τῷ πατρί.

4 ₁Ταῦτα δὲ παραινῶ ὑμῖν, ἀγαπητοί, εἰδὼς ὅτι καὶ ὑμεῖς οὕτως ἔχετε· προφυλάσσω δὲ ὑμᾶς ἀπὸ τῶν θηρίων τῶν ἀνθρωπομόρφων, οὓς οὐ μόνον δεῖ ὑμᾶς μὴ παραδέχεσθαι, ἀλλ᾽, εἰ δυνατόν, μηδὲ συναντᾶν [αὐτοῖς]· μόνον δὲ προσεύχεσθαι ὑπὲρ αὐτῶν, ἐάν πως μετανοήσωσιν, ὅπερ δύσκολον· τούτου δὲ ἔχει ἐξουσίαν Ἰησοῦς Χριστός, τὸ ἀληθινὸν ἡμῶν ζῆν. ₂εἰ γὰρ τὸ δοκεῖν ταῦτα ἐπράχθη ὑπὸ τοῦ κυρίου ἡμῶν, κἀγὼ τὸ δοκεῖν δέδεμαι. τί δὲ καὶ ἑαυτὸν ἔκδοτον δέδωκα τῷ θανάτῳ, πρὸς πῦρ, πρὸς μάχαιραν, πρὸς θηρία; ἀλλ᾽ ὁ ἐγγὺς μαχαίρας, ἐγγὺς θεοῦ· μεταξὺ θηρίων, μεταξὺ θεοῦ· μόνον ἐν τῷ ὀνόματι Ἰησοῦ Χριστοῦ εἰς τὸ συμπαθεῖν αὐτῷ. πάντα ὑπομένω, αὐτοῦ με ἐνδυναμοῦντος τοῦ τελείου ἀνθρώπου.[3]

5 ₁Ὃν τινες ἀγνοοῦντες ἀρνοῦνται, μᾶλλον δὲ ἠρνήθησαν ὑπ᾽ αὐτοῦ, ὄντες συνήγοροι τοῦ θανάτου μᾶλλον ἢ τῆς ἀληθείας· οὓς οὐκ ἔπεισαν αἱ προφητεῖαι οὐδὲ ὁ νόμος Μωσέως, ἀλλ᾽ οὐδὲ μέχρι νῦν τὸ εὐαγγέλιον, οὐδὲ τὰ ἡμέτερα τῶν κατ᾽ ἄνδρα παθήματα· ₂καὶ γὰρ περὶ ἡμῶν τὸ αὐτὸ φρονοῦσιν. τί γάρ [με] ὠφελεῖ εἰ ἐμὲ ἐπαινεῖ τις, τὸν δὲ κύριόν μου βλασφημεῖ, μὴ ὁμολογῶν αὐτὸν σαρκοφόρον; ὁ δὲ τοῦτο μὴ λέγων τελείως αὐτὸν ἀπήρνηται, ὢν νεκροφόρος. ₃τὰ δὲ ὀνόματα αὐτῶν, ὄντα ἄπιστα, οὐκ ἔδοξέν μοι ἐγγράψαι· ἀλλὰ

---

[2]So Lightfoot, intending that they were intermixed with him entirely, and deriving the noun from the Armenian version. However, I have read, in common with the majority witness, and in line with Ignatius' overall sense, πνεύματι.

[3]So Lightfoot, though many texts add γενομένου after ἀνθρώπου.

I am no bodiless demon."[1] And straightaway they touched him and they believed, as they were intermixed with his flesh and his spirit. It was on this account that they too despised death, for they found themselves beyond death. 3After the resurrection he ate together with them and drank with them as a being of flesh, even though, spiritually, he was united with the Father.

4 1I am encouraging you in these matters, beloved, whilst aware that you are in agreement. I am putting you on your guard in advance against the wild beasts in human guise. Not only should you not receive them, but if possible have nothing to do with them; simply pray for them, that somehow they might repent, which is difficult. Jesus Christ has the authority over this; he is our true life. 2For if these things were undertaken by our Lord in appearance only, then I am chained up only in appearance! Why indeed have I totally given myself up to death, to the fire, to the sword, to wild beasts? But the proximity of a sword is the proximity of God, to be amidst wild beasts is to be amidst God, as long as it is in the name of Jesus Christ. I am bearing all this in order to suffer with him while he, the perfect human being, empowers me.

5 1Some, denying him out of ignorance, are rather denied by him. They are advocates of death rather than of the truth. Neither the prophecies nor the law of Moses has persuaded them, nor, even now, has either the gospel, or our own individual sufferings. 2Indeed, they think the same regarding ourselves. For what does it benefit me if somebody praises me yet insults my Lord, not admitting that he wore flesh? Whoever fails to say this denies him completely as one who wears a corpse. 3There seems no reason to catalogue their names, which are faithless, indeed I would rather

---

[1]According to Jerome, *On Illustrious Men* 2, the citation in Ignatius is from the Gospel according to the Nazarenes. However Eusebius, who was in a position to know the Gospel according to the Nazarenes, does not know the source of this saying (*Ecclesiastical History* 3.36).

μηδὲ γένοιτό μοι αὐτῶν μνημονεύειν, μέχρις οὗ μετανοήσωσιν εἰς
τὸ πάθος, ὅ ἐστιν ἡμῶν ἀνάστασις.

6 ₁Μηδεὶς πλανάσθω. καὶ τὰ ἐπουράνια καὶ ἡ δόξα τῶν ἀγγέλων
καὶ οἱ ἄρχοντες ὁρατοί τε καὶ ἀόρατοι, ἐὰν μὴ πιστεύσωσιν εἰς τὸ
αἷμα Χριστοῦ [τοῦ θεοῦ], κἀκείνοις κρίσις ἐστίν. ὁ χωρῶν χωρείτω·
τόπος μηδένα φυσιούτω· τὸ γὰρ ὅλον ἐστὶν πίστις καὶ ἀγάπη, ὧν
οὐδὲν προκέκριται. ₂καταμάθετε δὲ τοὺς ἑτεροδοξοῦντας εἰς τὴν
χάριν Ἰησοῦ Χριστοῦ τὴν εἰς ἡμᾶς ἐλθοῦσαν, πῶς ἐναντίοι εἰσὶν τῇ
γνώμῃ τοῦ θεοῦ. περὶ ἀγάπης οὐ μέλει αὐτοῖς, οὐ περὶ χήρας, οὐ περὶ
ὀρφανοῦ, οὐ περὶ θλιβομένου, οὐ περὶ δεδεμένου [ἢ λελυμένου], οὐ
περὶ πεινῶντος ἢ διψῶντος·

7 ₁Εὐχαριστίας καὶ προσευχῆς ἀπέχονται διὰ τὸ μὴ ὁμολογεῖν τὴν
εὐχαριστίαν σάρκα εἶναι τοῦ σωτῆρος ἡμῶν Ἰησοῦ Χριστοῦ, τὴν ὑπὲρ
τῶν ἁμαρτιῶν ἡμῶν παθοῦσαν, ἣν τῇ χρηστότητι ὁ πατὴρ ἤγειρεν. οἱ
οὖν ἀντιλέγοντες τῇ δωρεᾷ τοῦ θεοῦ συζητοῦντες ἀποθνήσκουσιν.
συνέφερεν δὲ αὐτοῖς ἀγαπᾶν, ἵνα καὶ ἀναστῶσιν. ₂πρέπον [οὖν] ἐστὶν
ἀπέχεσθαι τῶν τοιούτων, καὶ μήτε κατ᾽ ἰδίαν περὶ αὐτῶν λαλεῖν μήτε
κοινῇ· προσέχειν δὲ τοῖς προφήταις, ἐξαιρέτως δὲ τῷ εὐαγγελίῳ, ἐν
ᾧ τὸ πάθος ἡμῖν δεδήλωται καὶ ἡ ἀνάστασις τετελείωται. τοὺς [δὲ]
μερισμοὺς φεύγετε, ὡς ἀρχὴν κακῶν.

8 ₁Πάντες τῷ ἐπισκόπῳ ἀκολουθεῖτε, ὡς Ἰησοῦς Χριστὸς τῷ
πατρί, καὶ τῷ πρεσβυτερίῳ ὡς τοῖς ἀποστόλοις· τοὺς δὲ διακόνους
ἐντρέπεσθε ὡς θεοῦ ἐντολήν. μηδεὶς χωρὶς τοῦ ἐπισκόπου
τι πρασσέτω τῶν ἀνηκόντων εἰς τὴν ἐκκλησίαν. ἐκείνη βεβαία
εὐχαριστία ἡγείσθω ἡ ὑπὸ ἐπίσκοπον οὖσα, ἢ ᾧ ἂν αὐτὸς ἐπιτρέψῃ.
₂ὅπου ἂν φανῇ ὁ ἐπίσκοπος, ἐκεῖ τὸ πλῆθος ἔστω, ὥσπερ ὅπου ἂν

not bear them in mind until they repent regarding the passion, which is our resurrection.

6 ₁Let nobody be deceived. For the heavenly powers and the glory of the angels, and the visible, as well as the invisible rulers, are all under judgement, if they do not believe in the blood of Christ. Let the one who can receive this receive it. Let position puff up nobody, for faith and love are everything, to which nothing is to be preferred. ₂Take note of those whose opinions regarding the good gift of Jesus Christ which has come to us are false, how opposed they are to the mind of God. Love is of no interest to them, nor the widow, nor the orphan, nor the suffering, nor anyone who is in chains [or who has been released], nor anyone who is hungry or thirsty.[2]

7 ₁They abstain from the Eucharist and prayer, since they do not confess that the Eucharist is the flesh of our Savior Jesus Christ who suffered on account of our sins, and whom the Father raised in his goodness. Those who deny the gifts of God thus die whilst disputing! It would be better for them to engage in acts of love, so that they might also rise up. ₂It is right, therefore, to keep away from such people, and not to speak of them[3] either on one's own or in company, but to give heed to the prophets and especially to the gospel, in which the passion is shown to us and the resurrection brought to completion. Flee divisions as the origin of evils.

8 ₁Follow the bishop, all of you, as Jesus Christ the Father, and the presbytery as the apostles. Respect the deacons as the commandment of God. Without the bishop, nobody should do anything relating to the church. That Eucharist which is under the bishop, or the one to whom he has entrusted it, should be considered sound. ₂The congregation should be wherever the bishop is, just as the catholic

---

[2]This may mean that the love-feast, the *agapē,* is of no interest, as this would be the means by which relief might be offered to the various dispossessed persons mentioned.

[3]Some mss have "speak with them."

ᾗ Χριστὸς Ἰησοῦς, ἐκεῖ ἡ καθολικὴ ἐκκλησία. οὐκ ἐξόν ἐστιν χωρὶς τοῦ ἐπισκόπου οὔτε βαπτίζειν οὔτε ἀγάπην ποιεῖν· ἀλλ᾽ ὃ ἂν ἐκεῖνος δοκιμάσῃ, τοῦτο καὶ τῷ θεῷ εὐάρεστον, ἵνα ἀσφαλὲς ᾖ καὶ βέβαιον πᾶν ὃ πράσσεται.

9 ₁Εὔλογόν ἐστιν λοιπὸν ἀνανῆψαι ἡμᾶς, ὡς [ἔτι] καιρὸν ἔχομεν εἰς θεὸν μετανοεῖν. καλῶς ἔχει θεὸν καὶ ἐπίσκοπον εἰδέναι. ὁ τιμῶν ἐπίσκοπον ὑπὸ θεοῦ τετίμηται· ὁ λάθρα ἐπισκόπου τι πράσσων τῷ διαβόλῳ λατρεύει. ₂πάντα οὖν ὑμῖν ἐν χάριτι περισσευέτω, ἄξιοι γάρ ἐστε. κατὰ πάντα με ἀνεπαύσατε, καὶ ὑμᾶς Ἰησοῦς Χριστός. ἀπόντα με καὶ παρόντα ἠγαπήσατε· ἀμείβοι ὑμῖν θεός, δι᾽ ὃν πάντα ὑπομένοντες αὐτοῦ τεύξεσθε.

10 ₁Φίλωνα καὶ Ῥαῖον Ἀγαθόπουν, οἳ ἐπηκολούθησάν μοι εἰς λόγον θεοῦ, καλῶς ἐποιήσατε ὑποδεξάμενοι ὡς διακόνους [Χριστοῦ] θεοῦ· οἳ καὶ εὐχαριστοῦσιν τῷ κυρίῳ ὑπὲρ ὑμῶν, ὅτι αὐτοὺς ἀνεπαύσατε κατὰ πάντα τρόπον. οὐδὲν ὑμῖν οὐ μὴ ἀπολεῖται. ₂ἀντίψυχον ὑμῶν τὸ πνεῦμά μου καὶ τὰ δεσμά μου, ἃ οὐχ ὑπερηφανήσατε οὐδὲ ἐπῃσχύνθητε· οὐδὲ ὑμᾶς ἐπαισχυνθήσεται ἡ τελεία πίστις,[4] Ἰησοῦς Χριστός.

11 ₁Ἡ προσευχὴ ὑμῶν ἀπῆλθεν ἐπὶ τὴν ἐκκλησίαν τὴν ἐν Ἀντιοχείᾳ τῆς Συρίας· ὅθεν δεδεμένος θεοπρεπεστάτοις δεσμοῖς πάντας ἀσπάζομαι, οὐκ ὢν ἄξιος ἐκεῖθεν εἶναι, ἔσχατος αὐτῶν ὤν· κατὰ θέλημα κατηξιώθην, οὐκ ἐκ συνειδότος, ἀλλ᾽ ἐκ χάριτος θεοῦ, ἣν εὔχομαι τελείαν μοι δοθῆναι, ἵνα ἐν τῇ προσευχῇ ὑμῶν θεοῦ ἐπιτύχω. ₂ἵνα οὖν τέλειον ὑμῶν γένηται τὸ ἔργον καὶ ἐπὶ γῆς καὶ ἐν οὐρανῷ, πρέπει εἰς τιμὴν θεοῦ χειροτονῆσαι τὴν ἐκκλησίαν ὑμῶν θεοπρεσβύτην εἰς τὸ γενόμενον ἕως Συρίας συγχαρῆναι αὐτοῖς ὅτι εἰρηνεύουσιν καὶ ἀπέλαβον τὸ ἴδιον μέγεθος καὶ ἀπεκατεστάθη αὐτοῖς τὸ ἴδιον σωματεῖον. ₃ἐφάνη μοι οὖν ἄξιον πρᾶγμα πέμψαι τινὰ

---

[4]πίστις. So Lightfoot. However, I have read, and translated, ἐλπίς.

church is wherever Christ Jesus may be. Apart from the bishop it is not permissible to baptize or to hold a love-feast, but whatever he approves is pleasing to God, so that everything you do is secure and sound.

9 ₁Moreover, it is sensible that we should recover our sobriety whilst we still have time to turn again to God. It is good to acknowledge God and the bishop. Whoever honors the bishop is honored by God. Whoever undertakes anything behind the bishop's back is worshipping the devil. ₂May all kinds of good gifts abound for you, for you are worthy, you refreshed me in every way and Jesus Christ has refreshed you. In my absence and in my presence have you loved me. Your reward is God, to whom you will attain if, for his sake, you endure everything.

10 ₁You did well to receive Philo and Rheus Agathopous, who have followed me in the Word of God, as deacons of Christ, who is God. They also give thanks to the Lord for you because, in every manner, you refreshed them. Nothing of yours shall be lost. ₂My spirit is your ransom, as are my chains, of which you showed neither haughtiness nor shame. The perfect hope, Jesus Christ, will not be ashamed of you.

11 ₁Your intercession has reached the church of Antioch in Syria, from which I came bound in chains much approved by God, where I greet everyone, not being worthy to be one of them, being the least of them. In accordance with the will of God, not in my own conscience but out of the good gift of God, I pray that I may receive the perfect gift, that I attain to God by your intercession. ₂It is fitting for the honor of God that your church appoint an ambassador for God, to go to Syria and rejoice with them, so that your task will therefore be perfected both on earth and in heaven. Because they are at peace and have taken back their proper greatness, and their proper constitution has been restored to them. ₃Thus it seems to me to be a matter

τῶν ὑμετέρων μετ᾽ ἐπιστολῆς, ἵνα συνδοξάσῃ τὴν κατὰ θεὸν αὐτοῖς γενομένην εὐδίαν, καὶ ὅτι λιμένος ἤδη ἐτύγχανεν τῇ προσευχῇ ὑμῶν. τέλειοι ὄντες τέλεια καὶ φρονεῖτε· θέλουσιν γὰρ ὑμῖν εὐπράσσειν θεὸς ἕτοιμος εἰς τὸ παρασχεῖν.

12   ₁Ἀσπάζεται ὑμᾶς ἡ ἀγάπη τῶν ἀδελφῶν τῶν ἐν Τρωάδι, ὅθεν καὶ γράφω ὑμῖν διὰ Βούρρου, ὃν ἀπεστείλατε μετ᾽ ἐμοῦ ἅμα Ἐφεσίοις τοῖς ἀδελφοῖς ὑμῶν· ὃς κατὰ πάντα με ἀνέπαυσεν. καὶ ὄφελον πάντες αὐτὸν ἐμιμοῦντο, ὄντα ἐξεμπλάριον θεοῦ διακονίας. ἀμείψεται αὐτὸν ἡ χάρις κατὰ πάντα. ₂ἀσπάζομαι τὸν ἀξιόθεον ἐπίσκοπον καὶ θεοπρεπὲς πρεσβυτέριον, [καὶ] τοὺς συνδούλους μου διακόνους καὶ τοὺς κατ᾽ ἄνδρα καὶ κοινῇ πάντας, ἐν ὀνόματι Ἰησοῦ Χριστοῦ, καὶ τῇ σαρκὶ αὐτοῦ καὶ τῷ αἵματι, πάθει τε καὶ ἀναστάσει σαρκικῇ τε καὶ πνευματικῇ, ἑνότητι θεοῦ καὶ ὑμῶν. χάρις ὑμῖν, ἔλεος, εἰρήνη, ὑπομονὴ διὰ παντός.

13   ₁Ἀσπάζομαι τοὺς οἴκους τῶν ἀδελφῶν μου σὺν γυναιξὶ καὶ τέκνοις, καὶ τὰς παρθένους τὰς λεγομένας χήρας. ἔρρωσθέ μοι ἐν δυνάμει πατρός. Ἀσπάζεται ὑμᾶς Φίλων, σὺν ἐμοὶ ὤν. ₂ἀσπάζομαι τὸν οἶκον Γαουΐας, ἣν εὔχομαι ἑδρᾶσθαι πίστει καὶ ἀγάπῃ σαρκικῇ τε καὶ πνευματικῇ. ἀσπάζομαι Ἄλκην, τὸ ποθητόν μοι ὄνομα, καὶ Δάφνον τὸν ἀσύγκριτον καὶ Εὔτεκνον καὶ πάντας κατ᾽ ὄνομα. ἔρρωσθε ἐν χάριτι θεοῦ.

worthy of God that you send one of your own with a letter, so that he may rejoice with them in the tranquility which is theirs in God, and that they have already attained a harbor through your intercession. Being perfect, you should also give consideration to what is perfect. God is prepared to supply you who wish to do good.

12 ₁The love of the brothers who are in Troas greets you. I am writing to you from there through Burrhus, whom you, together with your brothers, the Ephesians, sent alongside me. He has refreshed me in every way. Indeed, would that everyone imitated him as exemplary in the ministry of God. The grace of God will reward him in everything. ₂I greet the God-worthy bishop, the presbytery which God approves, and the deacons, my fellow-slaves, and everyone both individually and collectively in Jesus Christ, both in his flesh and in his blood, in his passion and resurrection both fleshly and spiritual, in the unity which is God's and yours. Grace to you, mercy, peace, endurance, at all times.

13 ₁I greet the households of my brothers together with their wives and children and the virgins who are called widows. Fare well in the power of the Father. Philo, who is with me, greets you. ₂I greet the household of Gavia, which I pray shall remain steadfast in faith and love, both fleshly and spiritual. I greet Alce, a name dear to me, and the incomparable Daphnus, and Eutecnus, and all by name. Fare well in the grace of God.

To Polycarp

Ignatius, in his stay in Smyrna, was under the care of Polycarp as bishop, since the bishop's economic duties extended to the care of the Christian in chains. Ignatius subsequently writes to him to encourage him and to exhort him to a more assiduous performance of his duties, having in mind the particular problems posed in Smyrna through the Docetic beliefs of some. This encouragement to perform the proper duties of a bishop, alongside the direction to appoint ambassadors through convening a council of the Smyrnaean churches in order to demonstrate the unity of the church, provide the content of Ignatius' directions here.

ΠΡΟΣ ΠΟΛΥΚΑΡΠΟΝ ΙΓΝΑΤΙΟΣ

Ἰγνάτιος, ὁ καὶ Θεοφόρος, Πολυκάρπῳ ἐπισκόπῳ ἐκκλησίας Σμυρναίων, μᾶλλον ἐπισκοπημένῳ ὑπὸ θεοῦ πατρὸς καὶ Ἰησοῦ Χριστοῦ,¹ πλεῖστα χαίρειν.

1 ₁ἀποδεχόμενός σου τὴν ἐν θεῷ γνώμην ἡδρασμένην ὡς ἐπὶ πέτραν ἀκίνητον, ὑπερδοξάζω καταξιωθεὶς τοῦ προσώπου σου τοῦ ἀμώμου, οὗ ὀναίμην ἐν θεῷ. ₂παρακαλῶ σε ἐν χάριτι ᾗ ἐνδέδυσαι προσθεῖναι τῷ δρόμῳ σου, καὶ πάντας παρακαλεῖν ἵνα σώζωνται. ἐκδίκει σου τὸν τόπον ἐν πάσῃἐπιμελείᾳ σαρκικῇ τε καὶ πνευματικῇ. τῆς ἑνώσεως φρόντιζε, ἧς οὐδὲν ἄμεινον· πάντας βάσταζε, ὡς καὶ σὲ ὁ κύριος· πάντων ἀνέχου ἐν ἀγάπῃ, ὥσπερ καὶ ποιεῖς· ₃προσευχαῖς σχόλαζε ἀδιαλείπτοις· αἰτοῦ σύνεσιν πλείονα ἧς ἔχεις· γρηγόρει ἀκοίμητον πνεῦμα κεκτημένος· τοῖς κατ' ἄνδρα κατὰ ὁμοήθειαν θεοῦ λάλει· πάντων τὰς νόσους βάσταζε, ὡς τέλειος ἀθλητής· ὅπου πλείων κόπος, πολὺ κέρδος.

2 ₁Καλοὺς μαθητὰς ἐὰν φιλῇς, χάρις σοι οὐκ ἔστιν· μᾶλλον τοὺς λοιμοτέρους ἐν πραότητι ὑπότασσε. οὐ πᾶν τραῦμα τῇ αὐτῇ ἐμπλάστρῳ θεραπεύεται· τοὺς παροξυσμοὺς ἐμβροχαῖς παῦε. ₂φρόνιμος γίνου ὡς ὄφις ἐν ἅπασιν καὶ ἀκέραιος εἰς ἀεὶ ὡς ἡ περιστερά. διὰ τοῦτο σαρκικὸς εἶ καὶ πνευματικός, ἵνα τὰ φαινόμενά σου εἰς πρόσωπον κολακεύῃς· τὰ δὲ ἀόρατα αἴτει ἵνα σοι φανερωθῇ· ἵνα μηδενὸς λείπῃ καὶ παντὸς χαρίσματος περισσεύῃς. ₃ὁ καιρὸς ἀπαιτεῖ σε, ὡς κυβερνῆται ἀνέμους καὶ ὡς χειμαζόμενος λιμένα, εἰς τὸ θεοῦ ἐπιτυχεῖν. νῆφε, ὡς θεοῦ ἀθλητής· τὸ θέμα ἀφθαρσία καὶ ζωὴ αἰώνιος, περὶ ἧς καὶ σὺ πέπεισαι. κατὰ πάντα σου ἀντίψυχον ἐγὼ καὶ τὰ δεσμά μου, ἃ ἠγάπησας.

---

¹So Lightfoot. However, I have read, and translated, κυρίου Ἰησοῦ Χριστοῦ.

IGNATIUS TO POLYCARP:

Ignatius, who is also God-carrier, to Polycarp, bishop of the church of the Smyrnaeans, or rather to him who has God the Father and the Lord Jesus Christ as bishop, abundance of happiness.

1 ₁Welcoming your outlook in God, fixed as upon an immovable rock, I rejoice all the more as I was found worthy to look upon your blameless character, in which, in God, I would delight. ₂I exhort you in the grace with which you are clothed, to progress in your course and to exhort everyone, so that all may be saved. Claim your proper place with every effort, both fleshly and spiritual. Give consideration to unity, for there is nothing better. Bear with all people, just as does the Lord with you. Tolerate everybody in love, as indeed you do already. ₃Be assiduous with constant intercession, asking for an understanding greater than you have. Be alert, in possession of an unsleeping spirit. Address everyone in conformity with the manner of God. Bear the diseases of all as a perfect athlete. Where the labor is more intense, the yield is great.

2 ₁You obtain no merit if you love the good disciples; rather bring the more troublesome to order in compliance. Not every wound is healed by the same plaster; treat irritations with lotions. ₂In every matter be as wise as a serpent, and at all times as pure as a dove. You are fleshly, as well as spiritual, on this account, namely so that you can be gentle with what is apparent to you; yet pray that what is invisible may also be apparent to you, so that you lack nothing and overflow in every good gift. ₃The occasion is calling on you, as helmsmen seek the winds and the storm-tossed the harbor, so that you may attain to God. As God's athlete, be wary. The prize is incorruption and eternal life, of which you are already convinced. In everything I am your ransom, as are my chains, which you have loved.

3 ₁Οἱ δοκοῦντες ἀξιόπιστοι εἶναι καὶ ἑτεροδιδασκαλοῦντες μή σε καταπλησσέτωσαν. στῆθι ἑδραῖος, ὡς ἄκμων τυπτόμενος. μεγάλου ἐστὶν ἀθλητοῦ [τὸ] δέρεσθαι καὶ νικᾶν. μάλιστα δὲ ἕνεκεν θεοῦ πάντα ὑπομένειν ἡμᾶς δεῖ, ἵνα καὶ αὐτὸς ἡμᾶς ὑπομείνῃ. ₂πλέον σπουδαῖος γίνου οὗ εἶ. τοὺς καιροὺς καταμάνθανε· τὸν ὑπὲρ καιρὸν προσδόκα, τὸν ἄχρονον, τὸν ἀόρατον, τὸν δι' ἡμᾶς ὁρατόν, τὸν ἀψηλάφητον, τὸν ἀπαθῆ, τὸν δι' ἡμᾶς παθητόν, τὸν κατὰ πάντα τρόπον δι' ἡμᾶς ὑπομείναντα.

4 ₁Χῆραι μὴ ἀμελείσθωσαν· μετὰ τὸν κύριον σὺ αὐτῶν φροντιστὴς ἔσο. μηδὲν ἄνευ γνώμης σου γινέσθω, μηδὲ σὺ ἄνευ θεοῦ γνώμης τι πρᾶσσε· ὅπερ οὐδὲ πράσσεις. εὐστάθει. ₂πυκνότερον συναγωγαὶ γινέσθωσαν. ἐξ ὀνόματος πάντας ζήτει. ₃δούλους καὶ δούλας μὴ ὑπερηφάνει· ἀλλὰ μηδὲ αὐτοὶ φυσιούσθωσαν, ἀλλ' εἰς δόξαν θεοῦ πλέον δουλευέτωσαν, ἵνα κρείττονος ἐλευθερίας ἀπὸ θεοῦ τύχωσιν· μὴ ἐράτωσαν ἀπὸ τοῦ κοινοῦ ἐλευθεροῦσθαι, ἵνα μὴ δοῦλοι εὑρεθῶσιν ἐπιθυμίας.

5 ₁Τὰς κακοτεχνίας φεῦγε, μᾶλλον δὲ περὶ τούτων ὁμιλίαν ποιοῦ. ταῖς ἀδελφαῖς μου προσλάλει ἀγαπᾶν τὸν κύριον καὶ τοῖς συμβίοις ἀρκεῖσθαι σαρκὶ καὶ πνεύματι. ὁμοίως καὶ τοῖς ἀδελφοῖς μου παράγγελλε ἐν ὀνόματι Ἰησοῦ Χριστοῦ ἀγαπᾶν τὰς συμβίους, ὡς ὁ κύριος τὴν ἐκκλησίαν. ₂εἴ τις δύναται ἐν ἁγνείᾳ μένειν εἰς τιμὴν τῆς σαρκὸς τοῦ κυρίου, ἐν ἀκαυχησίᾳ μενέτω· ἐὰν καυχήσηται, ἀπώλετο· καὶ ἐὰν γνωσθῇ πλὴν τοῦ ἐπισκόπου, ἔφθαρται. πρέπει δὲ τοῖς γαμοῦσι καὶ ταῖς γαμούσαις μετὰ γνώμης τοῦ ἐπισκόπου τὴν ἕνωσιν ποιεῖσθαι, ἵνα ὁ γάμος ᾖ κατὰ κύριον καὶ μὴ κατ' ἐπιθυμίαν. πάντα εἰς τιμὴν θεοῦ γινέσθω.

6 ₁Τῷ ἐπισκόπῳ προσέχετε, ἵνα καὶ ὁ θεὸς ὑμῖν. ἀντίψυχον ἐγὼ τῶν ὑποτασσομένων [τῷ] ἐπισκόπῳ, πρεσβυτέροις, διακόνοις· καὶ μετ' αὐτῶν μοι τὸ μέρος γένοιτο σχεῖν παρὰ θεῷ. συγκοπιᾶτε

3 ₁Do not let those who appear trustworthy and who teach strange doctrines browbeat you. Stand firm as an anvil when it is struck. It is a great athlete who is victorious whilst injured. We should endure everything particularly on behalf of God, so that he too may endure us. ₂Be more eager than you are. Observe the occasions, look out for the one who is beyond the moment, who is timeless, who is invisible, who is visible for us, who is intangible, who is impassible, suffering for us, who endured in every manner on our account.

4 ₁Do not let the widows be neglected. You are to be their care-giver, after the Lord. Let nothing be done without your consent, and do nothing yourself without regard to the mind of God, as indeed you do not. Be steadfast. ₂Let gatherings be closer, seek out everyone by name. ₃Do not look down on male or female slaves, but do not let them become puffed up, but serve all the better for the glory of God, so that they may obtain a better freedom from God. And they should have no desire to be set free out of common funds, so that they may not be slaves of passion.

5 ₁Flee the evil arts, rather discuss them. Instruct my sisters to love the Lord and to be satisfied with their spouses in flesh and spirit. Similarly charge my brothers in the name of Jesus Christ to love their spouses as the Lord the church. ₂Anyone who is able to remain in purity for the honor of the flesh of the Lord should do so without boasting. Whoever boasts is destroyed. And if anyone apart from the bishop becomes aware of it, this is corrupted. It is proper for those men and women who are marrying to form their union with the consent of the bishop, so that their marriage may be in accordance with the Lord and not out of desire. Let everything be done for the honor of God.

6 ₁You all should give heed to the bishop, so that God may do so to you. I am a ransom for those who are subject to the bishop, the pres-byters, deacons. May my lot be with them in God. Labor together

ἀλλήλοις, συναθλεῖτε, συντρέχετε, συμπάσχετε, συγκοιμᾶσθε, συνεγείρεσθε, ὡς θεοῦ οἰκονόμοι καὶ πάρεδροι καὶ ὑπηρέται. ₂ἀρέσκετε ᾧ στρατεύεσθε, ἀφ' οὗ καὶ τὰ ὀψώνια κομίζεσθε. μή τις ὑμῶν δεσέρτωρ εὑρεθῇ. τὸ βάπτισμα ὑμῶν μενέτω ὡς ὅπλα, ἡ πίστις ὡς περικεφαλαία, ἡ ἀγάπη ὡς δόρυ, ἡ ὑπομονὴ ὡς πανοπλία· τὰ δεπόσιτα ὑμῶν τὰ ἔργα ὑμῶν, ἵνα τὰ ἄκκεπτα ὑμῶν ἄξια κομίσησθε. μακροθυμήσατε οὖν μετ' ἀλλήλων ἐν πραΰτητι, ὡς ὁ θεὸς μεθ' ὑμῶν. ὀναίμην ὑμῶν διὰ παντός.

7 ₁Ἐπειδὴ ἡ ἐκκλησία ἡ ἐν Ἀντιοχείᾳ τῆς Συρίας εἰρηνεύει, ὡς ἐδηλώθη μοι, διὰ τῆς προσευχῆς ὑμῶν, κἀγὼ εὐθυμότερος ἐγενόμην ἐν ἀμεριμνίᾳ θεοῦ, ἐάνπερ διὰ τοῦ παθεῖν θεοῦ ἐπιτύχω, εἰς τὸ εὑρεθῆναί με ἐν τῇ αἰτήσει² ὑμῶν μαθητήν. ₂πρέπει, Πολύκαρπε θεομακαριστότατε, συμβούλιον ἀγαγεῖν θεοπρεπέστατον καὶ χειροτονῆσαί τινα ὃν ἀγαπητὸν λίαν ἔχετε καὶ ἄοκνον, ὃς δυνήσεται θεοδρόμος καλεῖσθαι· τοῦτον καταξιῶσαι, ἵνα πορευθεὶς εἰς Συρίαν δοξάσῃ ὑμῶν τὴν ἄοκνον ἀγάπην εἰς δόξαν θεοῦ. ₃Χριστιανὸς ἑαυτοῦ ἐξουσίαν οὐκ ἔχει ἀλλὰ θεῷ σχολάζει. τοῦτο τὸ ἔργον θεοῦ ἐστιν καὶ ὑμῶν, ὅταν αὐτὸ ἀπαρτίσητε. πιστεύω γὰρ τῇ χάριτι, ὅτι ἕτοιμοί ἐστε εἰς εὐποιΐαν θεῷ ἀνήκουσαν. εἰδὼς ὑμῶν τὸ σύντονον τῆς ἀληθείας δι' ὀλίγων ὑμᾶς γραμμάτων παρεκάλεσα.

8 ₁Ἐπεὶ οὖν πάσαις ταῖς ἐκκλησίαις οὐκ ἠδυνήθην γράψαι διὰ τὸ ἐξαίφνης πλεῖν με ἀπὸ Τρωάδος εἰς Νεάπολιν, ὡς τὸ θέλημα προστάσσει, γράψεις ταῖς ἔμπροσθεν ἐκκλησίαις, ὡς θεοῦ γνώμην κεκτημένος, εἰς τὸ καὶ αὐτοὺς τὸ αὐτὸ ποιῆσαι — οἱ μὲν δυνάμενοι πεζοὺς πέμψαι, οἱ δὲ ἐπιστολὰς διὰ τῶν ὑπὸ σοῦ πεμπομένων, ἵνα δοξασθῆτε αἰωνίῳ ἔργῳ — ὡς ἄξιος ὤν. ₂ἀσπάζομαι πάντας ἐξ

---

²So Lightfoot. However, I have read, and translated, ἀναστάσει, whilst uncertain that this reading is correct.

with each other, struggle together, run together, suffer together, lie down together, be raised together as God's stewards, attendants and servants. ₂Be pleasing to the one in whose army you serve, from whom you also receive your wages. None of you should be found deserting, let your baptism remain as weaponry, faith as a helmet, love as a spear, endurance as armor, your works as a downpayment on your wages, so that you may receive the just back-pay.[1] Therefore be patient with one another in gentleness, so that God may be with you. May I delight in you at all times.

7 ₁Since the church which is in Antioch in Syria is at peace, as has been made clear to me, through your intercession, I have become more content in a freedom from care which is of God, even should I attain to God through suffering, so that I may be found to be your disciple in the resurrection.[2] ₂Polycarp, most blessed of God, it is fitting to convene a most God-befitting council and to elect somebody, whom you consider most beloved and resolute, who could be called God's runner. He should be held worthy of going to Syria, to glorify your resolute love in the glory of God. ₃A Christian does not have his own authority, but is devoted to God. This deed is God's and yours, when you accomplish it, for I trust in grace that you are ready for the good deeds which please God. Aware of your zeal for the truth I exhort you in a few lines.

8 ₁Since I have been unable to write to all the churches because of my sudden sailing from Troas to Neapolis, as the will directs, you are to write to the churches which lie on this side as one in possession of God's purpose, and so they may do the same. Some will be able to send foot-messengers, others letters through those sent by you, so that you may be glorified by an eternal work, as you are worthy. ₂I

---

[1]The reference is to the procedure by which monies might be held back from soldiers, and then paid out to them, upon discharge. The works of the Smyrneans will in time receive the full reward which is due.

[2]See the note on the text opposite, and that in the corresponding section of ps-Ignatius.

ὀνόματος καὶ τὴν τοῦ Ἐπιτρόπου σὺν ὅλῳ τῷ οἴκῳ αὐτῆς καὶ τῶν τέκνων· ἀσπάζομαι Ἄτταλον τὸν ἀγαπητόν μου. ἀσπάζομαι τὸν μέλλοντα καταξιοῦσθαι τοῦ εἰς Συρίαν πορεύεθαι. Ἔσται ἡ χάρις μετ' αὐτοῦ διὰ παντός, καὶ τοῦ πέμποντος αὐτὸν Πολυκάρπου.

₃ἐρρῶσθαι ὑμᾶς διὰ παντὸς ἐν θεῷ ἡμῶν Ἰησοῦ Χριστῷ εὔχομαι, ἐν ᾧ διαμείνητε ἐν ἑνότητι θεοῦ καὶ ἐπισκοπῇ. ἀσπάζομαι Ἄλκην τὸ ποθητόν μοι ὄνομα. ἔρρωσθε ἐν κυρίῳ.

greet all by name, and the wife of Epitropus, together with her whole household and children. I greet my beloved Attalus. I greet the one who is to be found worthy of going to Syria. Grace will be with him at all times, as with Polycarp who sends him. ₃I wish you to fare well at all times in our God Jesus Christ, in whom may you remain in the unity of God and in his oversight. I greet Alce, a name dear to me. Fare well in the Lord.

PSEUDO-IGNATIUS

On Pseudo-Ignatius

For many years Ignatius of Antioch was known through what scholars term the "long recension." This was a collection of thirteen letters, twelve of which were supposedly from Ignatius, and one of which was written to him. In the west this collection was further supplemented by a correspondence between Ignatius and the Virgin Mary and with St John.

As critical scholarship began in the west, the authenticity of these letters was much disputed. This dispute was largely bound up with discussion regarding church polity. Because Ignatius is insistent upon the episcopate as a mark of the true church, the tendency was for Protestants to dismiss the collection as a forgery, whereas Anglicans and Roman Catholics would support its authenticity. In 1623 the first breakthrough in determining whether or not the whole collection, or only part, was authentic, was made with the realization by Vedelius that Eusebius, in the fourth century, had cited only seven of these letters; these, he thought, might be authentic, whereas the others were not.[1] He suspected that even the seven texts which he had were interpolated, but had no way of determining the nature or the extent of the interference. However, in 1643 a Latin text of the seven letters was published in England, which differed considerably from that which had previously circulated; in particular, the letters were shorter.[2] This edition was the work of James Ussher who had observed that mediaeval English writers had cited Ignatius in a form very different from that more generally known, and so deduced that

[1]Nicolaus Vedelius, *Ta tou hagiou Ignatiou martyros Episkopou Antiocheias heuriskomena hapanta* (Geneva: Veuve et Héritiers de Pierre de la Rovière, 1623).

[2]*Ignatii, Polycarpi, et Barnabæ, epistolæ at(que) martyria* (Oxford: Henry Hall, 1643).

there had to be a manuscript in England which contained a Latin version of the text in a different form. In the event he found two manuscripts; although they contained letters beyond the seven mentioned by Eusebius, those letters which Eusebius mentioned were found in a distinct, shorter form. This Latin edition of the shorter letters was followed rapidly by a Greek text of six of the seven letters (the letter to the Romans not being included in the Florentine manuscript which was published in this version), again in a shorter form than that previously known.[3] It is this form of the text which is termed the "middle recension" and, insofar as textual criticism allows us, represents the original letters written by Ignatius. It is so called to distinguish it from the long recension, and from the "short recension," an epitome in Syriac of three of the letters.

The publication of this Greek text was not the end of controversy about Ignatius, but the debate moved on nonetheless to concern the authenticity and the date of the seven letters in the version published by Vossius, as well as the date of Ignatius himself, based on the evidence provided by these seven letters. As a result there was little interest in the longer version of the letters, since they were clearly not by Ignatius of Antioch himself.

Nevertheless, the fact that the long recension is not authentic does not mean that it is without interest. The letters may be of no value for the historical figure Ignatius, but insofar as they expand and interpolate the letters of Ignatius himself, as well as providing further letters from a pseudonymous Ignatius, they may give us a clue to the expansion and growth of the Ignatian tradition. In the third century there was a distinct school of Polycarp in Smyrna, responsible not only for the continued circulation of the account of his martyrdom, but also for the production of a biography and for a further collection of Polycarp materials. It does not seem that there was such an intentional Ignatian school in Antioch, but the city was, nonetheless, an intellectual centre for Christians. It would thus

[3] Isaac Vossius, *Epistolae genuinae Ignatii martyris* (Amsterdam: Johannes Blaeu, 1646).

seem possible that an Antiochene Christian school might latch onto the name and identity of Ignatius. Jerome records that the relics of Ignatius are buried in Antioch,[4] which is an indication that there was an awareness of the name and witness of Ignatius in the latter part of the fourth century. These relics were translated within the city, to a church dedicated to Ignatius, in the fifth century. We may thus observe the preservation of the *acta* of Ignatius which concentrate on the relics,[5] and the homily of John Chrysostom on Ignatius,[6] which clearly refers to the presence of the relics in Antioch.

The pseudo-Ignatian epistles are thus to be read as an example of an Antiochene school at work. As such we may have a picture of the church, and her teaching, developing to meet the distinct challenges of the distinct periods of the second and the fourth centuries, these being the periods to which the middle and the long recension respectively are to be attributed.

The Ignatian school and the long recension

As may already have been gathered, the long recension of the letters of Ignatius, alongside letters which were not written by Ignatius, contains versions of the original letters in a form longer than those of the middle recension. The increased length is the result of the interpolation and expansion of the original letters.

As an example of this expansion we may take, as an example, the following passage from *Philadelphians* 3:

Stay away from wicked plants, those which Jesus Christ does not cultivate,	Therefore stay away from the wicked plants, those which Jesus Christ does not cultivate,

[4]*On Illustrious Men* 16.

[5]Found in the appendix below.

[6]To be found in Wendy Mayer with Bronwen Neil, trans., *St John Chrysostom: The Cult of the Saints* Popular Patristics Series no. 31 (Crestwood, NY: St Vladimir's Seminary Press, 2006), 101–117, and reprinted in the appendix below.

since
they are not a planting of the
Father.

Not that I have found
division among you, but purity.

Those who are of God,
and Jesus Christ, are with the
bishop.

Those who are
repentant and who come into
the unity of the church will
also be God's, so that they may
live in accordance with Jesus
Christ.

Do not be deceived, my
brothers, anyone who follows
the one who separates shall not
inherit the kingdom of God.

but the homicidal beast, since
they are not a planting of the
Father but a seed of the evil
one. Not because I have found
division among you do I write,
but to set you on guard in
advance as children of God.

Those who are of Christ
are with the bishop, but those
who incline away from him, and
embrace the communion of the
accursed, will be pruned away
with them, for they are not the
cultivation of Christ but the seed
of the enemy. May you always be
rescued through the prayers of
the shepherd who is set at your
head, who is most faithful and
most gentle. Therefore I exhort
you in the Lord to receive with
all gentleness those who are
repentant and who come into
the unity of the church, that
through your kindness and your
goodness they will escape the
devil's trap, becoming worthy
of Jesus Christ, attaining eternal
salvation in the kingdom of
Christ. Do not be deceived,
brothers. Anyone who follows
the one who separates from
the truth shall not inherit the
kingdom of God. And anyone
who does not distance himself

Anyone who acts in accordance with an alien opinion is not conformed to the passion.

from the preacher of falsehood shall be condemned to Gehenna. One should neither distance oneself from the godly, nor should one consort with the ungodly. Anyone who acts in accordance with an alien opinion is not of Christ, and is not a participant in his passion, but is a fox, a trampler of Christ's vineyard. Have no relations with anyone such, so that you do not perish together, even if he is your father, your son, your brother, or a member of your family. For it says: "Your eye shall not spare him." You should therefore hate those who hate God and waste away on account of his enemies. I do not mean that you should beat them or persecute them, as do the Gentiles who "know not the Lord and God," but should consider them your enemies and keep away from them, whilst warning them and exhorting them to repentance, as it is possible that they might hear, and possible that they submit themselves. For our God is a lover of humanity, and desires that "all people should be saved and should come to knowledge of the truth." So "he causes the

> sun to rise on the wicked and
> the good, and sends rain on the
> just and the unjust." Desiring
> that we should be imitators of
> his kindness the Lord says: "Be
> perfect, just as your heavenly
> Father is perfect."

We may note first of all that the original Ignatius is expanded through the use of Scriptural citations. This is a significant part of the work of the long recension. Ignatius himself wrote before the Scriptures of the new covenant had been recognized as such, and although there is a possibility that he was acquainted with some written gospels, and had read some Pauline letters, they would not have been at hand as he wrote. The long recension ties Ignatius' insight together with Scripture, stringing together the witness of the first and the newer testaments into a harmony.

The second point we may note about this passage is the manner in which Ignatius' words about the reception into the unity of the church are expanded. The issue over the reception of Christians from various of the heresies was a constant preoccupation in the councils of the fourth century; here a clear irenic message is being sent, that those of another party should be received with kindness. This is simply one example of the manner in which the long recension updates the witness and insights of Ignatius to meet the needs of the time.

The updating of Ignatius related fundamentally to the situation of the church at the time, and to the threats posed by the heresies and theological discussions of the period. This is the third point which is significant about the long recension, one which relates to the concerns of the historical Ignatius, even as it is distinct in many ways; namely, the long recension sets out a distinct theology as an attempt to forge reconciliation in a profoundly divided church.

Beyond these expanded letters, the additional letters consist of the correspondence between Mary, a proselyte, and Ignatius; the letter to Hero, Ignatius' fictive successor at Antioch; and letters to the Tarsians, to the Philippians and to the church at Antioch itself. It seems that these forged letters are the work, if not of the same hand, then certainly of the same school, as the interpolated letters. These forged letters are imbued with the language of the original Ignatius to the extent that sometimes they appear to be pastiches of Ignatius. Thus *Philippians* 8 is readily comparable to *Ephesians* 1.1–2:

The virginity of Mary and her giving birth, and likewise the death of the Lord, elude the ruler of this world. Three mysteries of crying out were performed in the quietness of God. How, then, did he appear to the ages? A star shone in heaven brighter than all the stars, and its light was indescribable and its newness brought amazement. All the other stars, with the sun and the moon, formed a chorus to the star, whose light surpassed all other. There was agitation regarding its origin, as it was new, and unlike any other.

For much eludes you: the virginity of Mary, the wonderful birth, the identity of the one who was embodied, the star directing the magi from the east who presented gifts, the archangel's greeting to the virgin, the marvellous conception of the betrothed virgin, the announcement of a child who would proceed in front of the one who was from the virgin as he skipped in the womb at what was foreseen, the angels' hymns for the one who was born, the good news to the shepherds, the fear of Herod at the loss of his kingdom, the command to kill the infants, the removal into Egypt and the return from there to the previous place, the Infant's swaddling bands, the human registration, the feeding with milk, the paternity ascribed to him who had no child, the manger as there was no place, the lack of any human preparation . . .

Similarly we may note the beginning of *Tarsians* 1.

I fight wild beasts from Syria, all the way to Rome. I am not devoured by unreasoning beasts, for as you know they spared Daniel, as God willed, but by those in human form, in which the merciless beast has hidden himself, pricking and wounding me daily.

The first sentence is taken from the beginning of *Romans* 5, whereas what follows, whilst perhaps having an eye on Ignatius' characterization of his guards as "leopards," also employs the language of *Smyrnaeans* 4.2, in which heretics are described as wild animals in human form.

Finally we may note the clear debt of the *Letter to Hero* to Ignatius' *Letter to Polycarp*. Thus:

Claim your proper place with every effort, both fleshly and spiritual. Give consideration to unity, for there is nothing better. Bear with all people, just as does the Lord with you. Tolerate everybody in love, as indeed you do already.	I exhort you to progress in your course and to vindicate your dignity. Be mindful of harmony with all the saints. Support those who are weaker, so that you fulfil the law of Christ.[7]

As well as this stylistic unity across the corpus, obtained through the redeployment of Ignatian material, we may observe a single theological outlook, as will be discussed in more detail below, and a similarly extensive use of proof-texts. Thus the additional letters are either the creations of the interpolator, or of the same school and at the same period.

[7] Gal 6.2.

The date of the long recension

There is a widespread and well-founded consensus placing the long recension in the latter part of the fourth century. The discussion thus centres on when, precisely, within this period the long recension was produced and which of the bewildering variety of theological positions this recension represents.

In describing the basis for the consensus we may first point to a passage in the letter to the Philadelphians, to the import of which we will return:

> The governors should show obedience to Caesar, the soldiers to their commanders, deacons to the presbyters, presbyters to the high priests. And the deacons and the rest of the clergy, as well as all the people, and the soldiers and the governors and Caesar to the bishop. (*Phld.* 4)

We may deduce that this is an Ignatius who is addressing a church set under a Christian emperor.

We may also point to the orders and ministries which the letters presuppose, which are also indicative of a period late in the fourth century. Thus the fictive Ignatius, in *Antiochenes* 12, greets the "sub-deacons, readers, singers, doorkeepers, those who labor, exorcists, confessors . . . the keepers of the holy gates, the deaconesses in Christ . . ." Although relatively little is known of the development of minor orders, the evidence is largely from the fourth century, and this period seems to see a growth in such offices. Thus the Council of Antioch (341) mentions readers, subdeacons and exorcists, apparently as an exhaustive list, as these were the offices to which a rural bishop might appoint. The Council of Laodicea, in around 363, in banning those in orders from entering taverns, mentions subdeacons, readers, singers, exorcists, door-keepers, and ascetics. The institution of deaconesses is of uncertain date, but is first found in the *Didascalia of the Apostles*, at a level of recension probably late in the third century, whereas we can be fairly sure that the institution of laborers is a fourth-century development, since a law of 361 (*Codex* 16.2.15) refers to the order as a recent institution.

Whereas it may be suggested that the external attestation is not decisive, and that since relatively little is known of the development of these minor orders, an earlier date might be feasible, what is decisive is the apparent relationship between the long recension and the *Apostolic Constitutions*.

The issue is complex, but there are many parallel points; the major points are catalogued here, and a number of minor points of concurrence are observed in the annotation:

- The common statement that Solomon was twelve at the beginning of his reign (*Apostolic Constitutions* 2.1, cf. Ignatius *To Mary* 3). This is in the context of a discussion about young bishops, a subject further discussed, following the authentic Ignatius, at *Magnesians* 3. However, it should be observed that this statement derives from the *Didascalia*, and is also found in rabbinic discourse.[8]

- The peculiar passion timing at *Trallians* 9 and *Apostolic Constitutions* 5.14, in which Jesus is condemned at the third hour and crucified at the sixth. In *Apostolic Constitutions* this is an expansion of a statement in the *Didascalia* that Christ was crucified at the sixth hour.

- The parallel between *Magnesians* 4 and *Apostolic Constitutions* 6.2.34. The *Didascalia* had employed the typology of the rebellion of Korah to warn against the divisive effects of heresy. This is taken up by *Apostolic Constitutions* to warn of disobedience to the bishop, and further examples are added. The same use of the typology is found in ps-Ignatius; although this example of rebellion is traditional

[8]Namely in Genesis *Rabbah* 11.

in Christian discourse, being found in *1 Clement*, ps-Ignatius and *Apostolic Constitutions* have in common an error in which Obededom is linked to Absalom in being beheaded on account of opposition to David, whereas it is in fact Sheba who, in the scriptural text, is beheaded on this account.

- The same citations of Isaiah 1.19 and Genesis 9.3 are found to support the same anti-ascetic agenda in *Apostolic Constitutions* 7.20 and *To Hero* 1. These may be collected proof-texts, however, deriving from controversy with Jews.

- The polemic against the keeping of Sabbath by Christians in *Apostolic Constitutions* (e.g. at 2.36) and *Magnesians* 9 (though in the light of Chrysostom's anti-Judaizing polemic, we may suggest that this is a pressing issue in fourth-century Antioch).

- The appearance of Judith and Anna as examples of worthy widows (examples which are not employed in the *Didascalia*) in the common discussion of the behavior of widows (*Apostolic Constitutions* 3.1–7, cf. *Philadelphians* 4).

- The direction of *Antiochenes* 9 that wives should not address their husbands by name, which has has a notable parallel in *Apostolic Constitutions* 6.29, an expansion of the parallel passage in the *Didascalia*, in which it is stated that wives should not address their husbands by name, but should be like Sarah, who simply addressed Abraham as "Lord." However, it should be observed that this is not an exclusive parallel, as the *Gnomes* of the Council of Nicaea, preserved in Coptic, similarly state that a Christian wife should address her husband as "lord."

- The similar appearance, in a catalogue of heresies, in *Trallians* 11, of the "falsely so called Nicolaitians," a term also employed in *Apostolic Constitutions* 6.8 (though Lightfoot notes that Clement of Alexandria had sought to distance Nicolaos from the group which bore his name).[9]

There is no question that the two pseudonymous productions have much in common and must therefore have derived from the same circles at about the same time. There are several possible ways of explaining the relationship: the two have the same author/redactor,[10] ps-Ignatius is dependent on *Apostolic Constitutions*,[11] or else the two draw upon the same pool of (Antiochene) tradition. It does not seem probable that ps-Ignatius was a source for *Apostolic Constitutions* as the parallels are occasional, scattered through the corpus. One argument against identity of authorship lies in the direct contradiction between *Apostolic Constitutions* 7.46, in which the succession of Roman bishops is given as Linus, followed by Clement, whereas in *To Mary* 4 Clement succeeds Anacletus, the order given by Eusebius.[12] If ps-Ignatius is employing *Apostolic Constitutions* as an occasional source the inconsistency may be explained by suggesting that he has chosen at this point to prefer Eusebius, possibly because *Apostolic Constitutions* appears to give a dual episcopate to Antioch. Moreover, evidence for use of *Apostolic Constitutions*

[9] Lightfoot, *Apostolic Fathers* 2.3, 161, with reference to *Miscellanies* 2.20.

[10] Originally maintained by Ussher, more recently supported by, among others, F.E. Brightman, *Liturgies Eastern and Western* 1 (Oxford: Clarendon, 1896), xxvii–xxix; Adolf Harnack, *Die Lehre der zwölf Apostel* (TU 2; Berlin: Akademie, 1886), 241–256, Dieter Hagedorn, *Der Hiobkommentar des Arianers Julian* (Berlin: de Gruyter, 1973), XLI–LII. The most complete treatment, however is that of F.X. Funk, *Die apostolischen Konstitutionen: eine litterar-historische Untersuchung* (Rottenburg: Wilhelm Bader, 1891), 316–355.

[11] Lightfoot, *Apostolic Fathers* 2.1, 262–265.

[12] *Ecclesiastical History* 3.21.6. Zahn explains this by suggesting that ps-Ignatius had employed only the first six books of *Apostolic Constitutions*; this is difficult, as there are parallels between ps-Ignatius and the entire *Apostolic Constitutions*. Funk, *Apostolischen Konstitutionen*, 319–320, thinks this a minor slip, which does not affect the hypothesis of a single redactor for the two documents.

as a source lies in an apparent misunderstanding of the statement of *Apostolic Constitutions* 2.1 that Josiah was eight years old at the beginning of his reign, whereas in *From Mary* 4 he is represented as being of this age when he began his work of extirpating idolatry. Identity of authorship, whilst widely and frequently asserted, is not necessary, as many of the parallels may be explained with reference to a common pool of tradition, for instance the error regarding Obededom may be the result of a common exegetical tradition. Both have the same theology of baptism as baptism into the Lord's death,[13] and there are many creedal passages in common, but all this may result from formation in the same theological tradition.

Whatever the precise relationship between the two, they are certainly rough contemporaries. *Apostolic Constitutions* is dated to the last quarter of the fourth century on the basis of a reference to the feast of Christmas which was a relative newcomer to the eastern festal calendar, and on the basis of the doctrine of the Holy Spirit which it contains, which is barely compatible with the orthodoxy which would emerge after the Council of Constantinople.[14] Such a dating would also make a great deal of sense were it applied to ps-Ignatius. It would, moreover, be hard to date the work any earlier. Amelungk essays a date in the 340s on the basis of similarities between the doctrinal assertions of the false Ignatius and the "makrostichos" creed produced by the council of Antioch in 345,[15] but this is not decisive because, as will be observed below, the theology of the pseudo-Ignatius is a very conservative Antiochene theology of the kind espoused by the council, and so it is entirely possible that the same assertions are being made from some time subsequently. Thus a date between 360 and 380 would seem likely on the basis of the

[13]Thus cf. ps-*Trallians* 2.1 to *Apostolic Constitutions* 3.17.

[14]P.F. Bradshaw, *The Search for the Origins of Christian Worship: Sources and Methods for the Study of early Liturgy* (2nd ed.; London: SPCK, 2002), 84–86.

[15]Arnold Amelungk, *Untersuchungen über Pseudo-Ignatius: ein Beitrag zur Geschichte einer litterarischen Fälschung* (Marburg: G. Otto, 1899), 61–71. A close connection with this creed is also observed by K.J. Woollcombe, "The Doctrinal Connexions of the Pseudo-Ignatian Letters" in F.L. Cross (ed.), *Studia Patristica* 6 (TU 81; Berlin: Akademie, 1962), 269–273, at 271.

relationship between ps-Ignatius and the traditions lying behind the *Apostolic Constitutions* and on the basis of the state of development of minor orders; it will be noted below that this is entirely consistent with the theology espoused by the Ignatian school.

The context and theology of the long recension:

The Christian church in Antioch during the late fourth century was deeply divided. This division grew out of the chaos that ensued on the Council of Nicaea, which had condemned the teaching of an Alexandrian presbyter, Arius, that the Son was a creation, brought about in time, and therefore secondary to the Father. The council had asserted that the Son was *homoousios* with the Father, a term which was itself hard to define and which, in Antioch particularly, was suspect as its use had been condemned in the third century in the condemnation of the beliefs of Paul of Samosata, then bishop of the city, who was deposed. The term means, "of one being," but whereas it might be interpreted to mean that the Father and the Son are equally divine, it might also mean that they were the same being, or the same person.

This is not the place to tell the story of the fourth century controversies regarding Arianism. At different times different emperors supported those who favored Nicaea, or favored Arianism, and bishops were deposed and replaced, only to be re-instated, as imperial favor and opinion swung in different directions, and as factions in the church produced a proliferation of creedal formulae. The result, as far as Antioch was concerned, was that in the 360s there were no fewer than four bishops of Antioch. The difficulties in Antioch had begun with the deposition of the bishop Eustathius in the wake of Nicaea, but reached a new level of complexity at the beginning of the 360s with the election of Meletius, who had been elected bishop with imperial support, but who seems rapidly to have fallen out of favor. It is as hard to characterize Meletius' theology as that of ps-Ignatius,

in particular because the early 360s were a time of intense development; it was in this time that a "neo-Nicene" party formed, in part
perhaps because of the extreme restatement of Arius' views by Aetius
and Eunomius, figures known as "anomoians" because of their claim
that the Son and the Father were utterly unlike (*anomoios*) each
other. Our sources for Meletius' own writings are a sermon preached
not long after his accession,[16] and a letter from a synod of 363, which
assents to the Nicene creed, but appears to give a rather peculiar
interpretation of the vexed term "*homoousios*," as "signifying that
the Son was begotten from the *ousia* of the Father and that he is like
the Father in *ousia*."[17]

Meletius, whilst no advocate of Nicaea prior to 363,[18] at which
point he allies himself with the neo-Nicenes, was likewise distant
from the extreme "Arian" position. On the basis of her study of
his sermon, Spoerl sums up Meletius' theology as "a Homoiousian
one, couched in cautious Homoian terms."[19] That is to say, he was
inclined towards those who held that the Son and the Father had a
fundamental similarity whilst continuing to emphasize the sovereign nature of the Father as the source of Godhead in the Trinity.
As such he was part of the movement that sought reconciliation,
but his language continued to be the conservative language of the
Antiochene tradition. Meletius was expelled from Antioch in 361
and replaced by Euzoius, who had been an associate of Arius himself. Meletius' supporters then separated themselves from the church
and worshipped in distinct assemblies. The following year Julian the
Apostate became emperor, and cancelled the decrees of banishment.
Meletius returned to Antioch, but further complications ensued,

[16]Preserved by Epiphanius *Medicine Chest* 73.29–33.

[17]From the letter of the council preserved by Socrates, *Ecclesiastical History*
3.25.13–15.

[18]He had previously been a supporter of Acacius of Caesarea, interestingly
enough Zahn's candidate as the identity of ps-Ignatius.

[19]Kelley McCarthy Spoerl, "The schism at Antioch since Cavallera," in Michel R.
Barnes and Daniel H. Williams, eds, *Arianism after Arius: Essays on the Development
of the fourth-century Trinitarian Conflicts* (Edinburgh: T&T Clark, 1993), 101–126,
here at 125.

as not all pro-Nicenes in Antioch recognized Meletius. Thus, in an intervention by Italian bishops, a third bishop of Antioch, Paulinus, was ordained. A final complication arose when yet another bishop of Antioch was elected, of the party known as the Apollinarians. This group, whilst maintaining the creed of Nicaea, held the idea that the *logos*, the word of which John speaks, and which is identified with God the Son, replaced the human spirit in the man Jesus.

It is to this situation the school of Ignatius speaks:

> . . . avoid the division of your unity and the evil teachings of the heretics (*Phld.* 3)

> . . . love unity, shun divisions, be imitators of Paul and the other apostles, as they were of Christ . . . God does not dwell where there is difference of opinion and anger and hatred. (*Phld.* 7)

Here the original Ignatius is being cited with relatively little alteration, but we are given the first clue as to the choice of Ignatius as the voice to address the situation: Ignatius is appealing for a united church based on agreed episcopal authority, and this is a voice which speaks deeply to the latter part of the fourth century. We may note that whereas Meletius' homily discussed the relationship between Father and Son, the greater part of it is similarly an appeal for peace within the church.

It is in this light that we may return to the passage adduced above:

> The governors should show obedience to Caesar, the soldiers to their commanders, deacons to the presbyters, presbyters to the high priests. And the deacons and the rest of the clergy, as well as all the people, and the soldiers and the governors and Caesar to the bishop. (*Phld.* 4)

A similar claim is made in *Smyrnaeans* 9, as part of the extended simile between the place of the bishop in the church and that of the emperor in the state. The bishop is responsible solely to God.

The intervention of various emperors had not aided the church; it is thus possible that this passage is written with Euzoius, the imperially supported bishop, in mind, to uphold the claims of one of the Nicene candidates; here one may have in mind the reign of Valens, who explicitly espoused the Arian cause and persecuted Meletians.

On the other hand, we may note that the pseudonymous author has himself been charged with "Arian" sympathies, and may thus be considered a supporter of Euzoius.[20] There are grounds for such an assertion. We may, for instance, note the following alterations of the original Ignatius:

by the will of the Father and of Jesus Christ, our God (Ignatius *Eph.* pref.)	by the will of the Father and of our Lord Jesus Christ, our Savior, (ps-Ignatius *Ephesians* pref.)
rekindling in the blood of God (Ignatius *Eph.* 1)	Rekindling in the blood of Christ (ps-Ignatius *Eph.* 1)
I glorify Jesus Christ, the God who has given you such wisdom (Ignatius *Smyrn.* 1)	I glorify the God and Father of our Lord Jesus Christ who, through him, has given you such wisdom. (ps-Ignatius *Smyrn.* 1)

It is certainly true, moreover, that ps-Ignatius is profoundly opposed to the theology of Marcellus of Ancyra, which would tend to put him in the non-Nicene camp. His concern to protect the mon-

[20]Such is the view of James D. Smith, "On Pseudo-Ignatius' fourth-century Antiochene Assertion of Episcopal Supremacy," in F.M. Young et al., eds, *Studia patristica* 42 (Leuven: Peeters, 2006), 231–236, though Smith is far from the first to see ps-Ignatius as Arian.

archy of God the Father leads him to oppose any form of theology
which would seem, in the interests of sustaining the equality of the
Son, to endanger the Father's monarchy, such as the views of Marcell-
lus or Photinus. Thus we may note such texts as *Magnesians* 6:

> Jesus Christ, who, begotten of the Father before the ages, was
> the Word of God, the only-begotten Son, and at the consum-
> mation of the ages will remain so.

It is not hard to see opposition to Marcellus motivating such an
assertion.

Again, we may compare Meletius' sermon in which, for all the
appeal to peace, there is a clear anti-Marcellan statement of the individual nature of the existence of the Son.

In exploring the possibility that ps-Ignatius might be a supporter
of Euzoius the only material we have is the confession of faith sub-
mitted by Arius and Euzoius:[21]

> We believe in one God, the Father, the ruler of all; and in the
> Lord Jesus Christ, his only Son, the one who was begotten
> from him before all ages, God the Word, through whom all
> things came to be, things in the heavens and things on earth;
> the one who descended and took flesh and suffered and rose
> and ascended into the heavens and is coming again to judge
> living and dead. And in the Holy Spirit, and in the resurrec-
> tion of the flesh and in the life of the age to come and in the
> kingdom of the heavens and in the one catholic church of
> God [extending] from one end of the earth to the other.

This Williams terms a "studiedly uncontroversial composi-
tion,"[22] significant more for what it does not say than for what it actually asserts. Ps-Ignatius goes beyond this in asserting the primacy

---

[21]Socrates *Ecclesiastical History* 1.26.8; Sozomen *Ecclesiastical History* 2.27.
[22]Rowan Williams, *Arius: Heresy and Tradition* (London: DLT, 1987), 256.

of the Father, but also far beyond in asserting the divine nature of the Son.

Moreover, elsewhere ps-Ignatius can sound quite anti-Arian, to the extent that Hanson, pointing to *Philippians* 2 and *Philippians* 5, suggests that these passages must be interpolations.[23] In particular the former passage is difficult because it employs the term *homotimos* (of equal honor), a term employed by Basil of the Holy Spirit and which in usage, if not in meaning, is equivalent to *homoousios*. There is no obvious interpolation here, however, unless one is set on seeing ps-Ignatius as a thoroughgoing Arian, but it may be that the text is corrupt,[24] so too much weight should not be put on this one passage. However, insofar as we may see ps-Ignatius as influenced by Arianism, we may suggest that he is no anomoian either: there are hard words in *Antiochenes* 1 for those who maintain the unity of God by denying Christ's divinity.

Perhaps the clearest example of ps-Ignatius' view of the relationship between the Father and the Son comes in his rewriting of Ephesians 7:

There is one physician, fleshly and spiritual, begotten and unbegotten, God in the flesh, true life in death, both from Mary and from God, first suffering and then impassible, Jesus Christ, our Lord.	Our physician is the one true God, who is unbegotten and unapproachable, the Lord of all, the Father and begetter of the only-begotten one. We also have as a physician the Lord our God, Jesus the Christ, before the ages the only-begotten Son and Word, who afterwards became also man, of Mary the virgin.

---

[23]R.P.C. Hanson, *The Search for the Christian Doctrine of God: The Arian Controversy, 318–381* (Edinburgh: T&T Clark, 1988), 115–116.

[24]See the note in the translation below.

The statement of Ignatius that Christ is "begotten and unbegotten" is clearly unsustainable in a climate in which the nature of the begetting of the Son is the most fundamental debate in the church, and in which the distinction is made between the Father as unbegotten and the Son as the begotten one. However, in "correcting" the original, ps-Ignatius is clear that the begetting takes place before all the ages. A similar understanding is clear from the final words of *Antiochenes*:

> May the one who alone is unbegotten, through the one begotten before the ages, preserve you in spirit and flesh . . . (*Antiochenes* 14)

In understanding this theology we might step back from the 360s, and note, with Amelungk, the degree of common ground between the dogmatic assertions of the forger and the so called *makrostichos* creed produced by the council of Antioch in 345. This creed begins by following the threefold shape of baptismal creeds, with articles on the Father, the Son and the Holy Spirit, and then produces a series of qualifications intended to clarify the Antiochene position. First the creed puts distance between the framers of this confession and the strict Arian position that there was a time when the Son did not exist. We have already observed that the ps-Ignatius does the same. Secondly the creed briefly denies tritheism (as does *Philippians* 2), but the creed does so by asserting the *monarchia* of God the Father, and then qualifies this by stating that this does not involve any denial of the full Godhead of the Son. Having asserted the Son's perfect Godhead the creed then qualifies this in turn by rejecting any version of the Marcellan position that the generation of the Son was a temporary action on the part of the single God, and from there moves on to reject modalism (cf. *Philippians* 7). Finally there is an assertion that there is nothing necessary about the generation of the Son, rather . . .

Believing then in the all-perfect triad, the most holy, that is, in the Father, and the Son, and the Holy Ghost, and calling the Father God, and the Son God, yet we confess in them, not two Gods, but one dignity of Godhead, and one exact harmony of dominion, the Father alone being head over the whole universe wholly, and over the Son Himself, and the Son subordinated to the Father; but, excepting Him, ruling over all things after Him which through Himself have come to be, and granting the grace of the Holy Ghost unsparingly to the saints at the Father's will. For that such is the account of the Divine Monarchy towards Christ, the sacred oracles have delivered to us.

Here we may readily point to *Tarsians* 5 as exhibiting a similar concern to define the relationship of subordination within the Godhead.

There is also common ground between ps-Ignatius and the creed and anathemas of Sirmium (351), as Zahn points out.[25] Thus compare: "For Moses . . . straightaway confessed our Lord in saying, 'The Lord rained fire and brimstone from the Lord upon Sodom and Gomorrah'" (*Antiochenes* 2) to the seventeenth anathema: "Whoever shall explain, 'The Lord rained fire from the Lord' was not the Father and the Son, and says that He rained from Himself, be he anathema. For the Son, being Lord, rained from the Father who is Lord." *Antiochenes* 3, "The prophets, speaking as in the person of God, tell of the Father of all: 'I am God, the first, and I am also the last, and apart from me there is no God . .' similarly may be compared to the eleventh anathema: "Whoever explains, 'I am God, the first, and I am also the last, and apart from me there is no God,' which is said for the denial of idols and of gods that are not, to the denial of the only-begotten, before ages God, as Jews do, be he anathema." Similarly *Philippians* 3, arguing that there are not three Gods, but there are likewise not three Fathers, or three Sons,

[25]Theodor Zahn, *Ignatius von Antiochien* (Gotha: Perthes, 1873), 137.

may be compared to the 23rd anathema of Sirmium, "Whoever shall say that the Father and the Son and the Holy Ghost are three Gods, be he anathema." The fundamental purpose of this council was the condemnation of the views of Photinus, which makes a ready point of comparison with ps-Ignatius, but we may also note that these anathemas espouse a conservative Antiochene theology.

We may also note with Perler the insistence on the sinless nature of the life and conduct of Jesus with the repeated phrase "living in a holy manner" (*Magnesians* 11.2, *Smyrnaeans* 1.2), a phrase appearing in the creed of Antioch (341) and repeated in further creedal formulations in the course of the century.[26]

As a result, it is hard to place with certainty the alignment of the forger within the factional politics of Antioch. Possibly this is part of a deliberate ploy, to appeal to a faith, and a praxis, which is beyond the immediate factional division to which the author is re-addressing Ignatius, a *modus operandi* which points us, once again, in the direction of Meletius' party. Lightfoot describes the *corpus* as an *eirenikon*, intended to bring about reconciliation:[27] here, perhaps, is the reason why it is so difficult to place the author's theology. He opposes the classical and extreme positions of monarchian modalism and psilanthropism, but otherwise, by contrast to the increasing sophistication of the fourth-century debate regarding Christ and God, represents a naïve biblical theology. As such we might do better to abandon the term "Arian" and, with Amelungk, describe him as Eusebian.[28] The choice of Ignatius and the reiteration of Ignatius' appeal to unity and to a gathering around a single bishop are indications that the intent of the writer is conciliatory, and that the long recension is not to be seen as a parting shot from a defeated theological party.[29]

[26]Othmar Perler, "Pseudo-Ignatius und Eusebius von Emesa," *Historisches Jahrbuch* 77 (1958): 73–82, 80–81.

[27]Lightfoot, *Apostolic Fathers* 2.1, 273.

[28]Amelungk, *Untersuchungen,* 24, 71.

[29]So Woollcombe, "Doctrinal Connexions," 273.

This choice also represents a traditionalist Antiochene theology; we have already noted echoes of the Antiochene tradition expressed in various councils, and we may here observe the manner in which ps-Ignatius takes the Ignatian picture of a church gathered around a bishop to make it a much more hierarchical picture, with presbyters subservient to bishops, and deacons to presbyters, etc.[30] This is reminiscent of the statements of the Council of Antioch in 341 which deny that the Antiochene church is Arian on the basis that bishops would not be subservient to Arius, who was merely a presbyter.

In one point, however, his traditionalist theology is seriously defective, namely in his assertions that the *logos* took the place of a human soul within Christ. This led Funk to charge that he was an Apollinarian,[31] but as Woollcombe points out, there is nothing like the complex anthropology of Apollinaris.[32] Rather we should look for the source of this belief once again within the Antiochene tradition: precisely such an assertion is found in the condemnation of Paul of Samosata,[33] and such a Christological formulation is found in the work of Eusebius of Emesa (one of a number of named candidates for the pseudonymous Ignatius).[34]

We thus conclude that the pseudonymous author's intent was fundamentally irenic, to set forth a conservative Antiochene theology as the means of unity between the factions of the Antiochene church. It is this conservative tone which has led him to be considered both an Arian and an Apollinarian, and to be placed by others at the end of the third century, rather than in the fourth.[35] This same irenic purpose is manifest in the passage from *Philadelphians* cited above, in which it is said that heretics should not be persecuted but

[30]Thus, e.g., *Tars.* 7.

[31]Funk, *Apostolischen Konstitutionen*, 305–313.

[32]So Woollcombe, "Doctrinal Connexions," 270.

[33]*Apud* Leontius of Byzantium, *Against the Eutychians and the Nestorians* 3.41 (PG 86a: 1380).

[34]So Perler, "Pseudo-Ignatius."

[35]By, e.g., Harold W. Ford, "A Comparison of the Recensions of the Ignatian Corpus," *Iliff Review* 18 (1961): 21–32.

converted. The arm of the state is not, as it was through the exile of Meletius, to be used to enforce orthodoxy, but orthodoxy should be a matter of the heart. Already recognized as an authority in Christology, the choice of Ignatius as peacemaker is an obvious choice in an Antiochene context.

Ps-Ignatius is a figure of the 360s or 370s, a supporter of Meletius, opposed to imperial intervention in the church, a representative of a conservative strand in Antiochene theology, and an advocate of reconciliation among the warring Christian factions of the city. However, the traditionalist nature of his theology shows the limitations of this approach to reconciliation. Ignatius faced the divisions in the Antiochene Christian community by setting forth a bold vision. With an obvious pastoral intent, ps-Ignatius appeals to tradition and to a naïve hermeneutic; however, this leads him in turn to present a deficient Christology as well as deliberately to turn away from what were real questions.[36]

[36]I write from a Communion of churches which is seriously fractured and cannot see at this point how unity of purpose might be achieved. What I do see is that to appeal to common ground on the basis of naïve biblicism and to a non-dynamic view of tradition is not an answer.

Correspondence between Ignatius and Mary of Cassobola

This fictive correspondence between a Mary, perhaps, on the basis of references to her activities in Rome in Ignatius' reply, to be identified with the Mary to whom Paul makes reference in Romans 16:6, and Ignatius, consists of a request from Mary for clergy for her town of Cassobola, and a response from Ignatius acceding to her request.

The fictive Ignatius is in Antioch, and the correspondence heads up the manuscripts. We can only speculate as to its rationale. Mary raises the matter of youthful clergy, an issue which appears within the church order literature (particularly within the Didascalia, taken up by the Apostolic Constitutions), but there may be some reason for its being raised here. It is also possible, given that the location of Cassobola is apparently in Tarsus, that the extent of metropolitical authority for Antioch in this region is being asserted. Anazarbus, the only place mentioned which can be definitely identified, was under Antiochene authority in a later period, though close to the regions governed by the extended authority of Constantinople, a city given metropolitical authority only in 381 (at the Council of Constantinople). This relates at least approximately to the period to which ps-Ignatius is to be dated, and may provide a significant clue.

To Ignatius, from Mary of Cassobola:

Mary, a proselyte of Jesus Christ, to Ignatius, God-carrier, the most blessed bishop of the apostolic church at Antioch, beloved in God the Father and Jesus. We always pray that you may have joy and health in him.

1 Since Christ, wonderfully, has been made known among us to be Son of the living God, made human in latter times through the virgin Mary, from the seed of David and Abraham, in accordance with the voices which spoke of him in advance in the choir of the prophets, on this account we ask that in your wisdom you send us Maris, our companion, the bishop of our native Neapolis, which is near Zarbus, as well as Eulogius the presbyter of Cassobola,[1] that we be not deprived of people to preside over the divine word, as Moses also says, "Let the Lord God look out for a person who may guide this people, and the congregation of the Lord shall not be as sheep which have no shepherd."[2]

2 Do not be anxious, blessed one, regarding the fact that those we have mentioned above are young. For I would have you know that they are wise regarding the flesh and are insensible to its passions. Although young, recently called to the priesthood, they glisten with the silver hairs of age.[3] So gather up your reasoning through the Spirit which is given you of God through Christ and recollect that Samuel was called a seer whilst a young child and reckoned among the company of prophets, that he rebuked the elderly Eli for transgression, since he had valued his maddened sons above God the author of all things, and had allowed them to go unpunished, when they brought the priestly office into ridicule and abused the people.[4]

3 Daniel indeed was young when he passed judgement on certain crude old men, showing that they were abandoned, and not presby-

---

[1]Some manuscripts add "and Sobelius the presbyter." There are, however, grounds to omit this; it is not present in other manuscripts, but more to the point there is no further reference to this person in subsequent correspondence; in his letter to Mary (3.1) ps-Ignatius refers to two men (namely Maris and Eulogius).

[2]Num 27.16–17.

[3]When the (young) Eleazer b. Azariah is appointed leader of the academy at Yabneh white hairs appear in his beard as a sign of the confirmation of the appointment (TB *Berakoth* 27B).

[4]1 Sam 3.10–14.

ters, being Canaanites in their ways even whilst Jews by race.[5] And Jeremiah heard, when he declined the task of prophecy entrusted to him of God, "Do not say 'I am a young man.' Since you shall go to all to whom I send you, and speak all in accordance with what I direct you, for I am with you."[6] The wise Solomon, at twelve years old, had understanding of the great dispute of the women on the basis of their ignorance regarding their children,[7] so the whole people wondered at such wisdom in a child and honored him as a full-grown man, not a youth. And he solved the puzzles of the queen of the Ethiopians, who had reward like the streams of the Nile, so that she, so wise herself, was amazed.[8]

4   Josiah also, beloved of God, whilst barely able to speak articulately, convicts those possessed of a wicked spirit as false in their speech and deceitful toward the people, uncovering the deceit of the demons and exposing those who are not gods, slaughtering their priests with impunity, overturning their altars, defiling the sanctuaries with the remains of dead bodies, throwing down the temples, cutting down the groves, shattering the pillars, and breaking open the tombs of the ungodly, so that no relic of the wicked might remain.[9] Thus he was zealous for godliness, and for the punishment of the ungodly, even while tongue-tied. David, both prophet and king, the root of our Savior in the flesh, was anointed as king by Samuel while a youth.[10] For he himself says, somewhere, "I was small among my brothers, and the youngest in my father's house."[11]

---

[5] Susanna.

[6] Jer 1.7.

[7] 1 Kg 3.16–27.

[8] Cf. 1 Kg 10.1–13. However, nothing is said in the scriptural source regarding Solomon's age. The same age is given at *Apostolic Constitutions* (=*Didascalia*) 2.1; we may compare the two passages in detail, as both discuss the possibility of younger men being appointed to the episcopate.

[9] 2 Kg 22, 23.

[10] 1 Sam 16.

[11] Ps 151.1 (LXX).

5 But time would fail me if I should endeavor to enumerate all those who in their youth were well-pleasing to God, entrusted by God with prophecy, priesthood, or kingship; those already mentioned are enough as a reminder. But I do not want you to think me presumptuous or ostentatious; I have put down these words not to teach you, but simply to prompt the memory of my father in God. For I know my own position, and do not compare myself with such as you. I greet your holy clergy and the Christ-loving people who are shepherded under your solicitude. All the faithful with us salute you. Blessed pastor, pray that I may be healthy as concerns God.

IGNATIUS TO MARY:

Ignatius, who is also God-carrier, to her who has found mercy through the grace of God the Father most high, and Jesus Christ the Lord, who died for on our account, to my daughter Mary, most faithful, God-worthy, and Christ-carrier, an abundance of happiness in God.

1 Sight is indeed better than writing, as by being one of the company of the senses, it not only honors the recipient, as it reveals friendship, but also is enriched all the more when it receives in return the desire for even better things. But, as they say, the second harbor of refuge is the practice of writing,[12] which, through your faith, we have received as a convenient haven from far away, since through this means we have seen the goodness within you. For, all-wise woman, the souls of the good resemble the purest springs, for they bring passers-by to drink of them through their form, even should they not be thirsty. So your understanding invites us, as though we were commanded, to partake of the divine draughts which are flowing forth in your soul.

---

[12]This idea is a commonplace in the ancient world.

2   But I, blessed woman, not being now so much my own master as in the power of others, am being driven along by the wills of many adversaries, being in one sense in exile, in another in prison, and in a third in chains. But I pay no regard to any of these. Indeed, through these injustices I am becoming more of a disciple, so that I may attain to Jesus Christ.[13] May I delight in the punishments being prepared for me, since "the sufferings of this present time are nothing set against the future glory which is to be revealed."[14]

3   I have gladly brought about what was demanded by you in your letter, since I have no doubt of those whom you have tested and found good. For I know that your witness concerning these two men is made in the judgement of God, and not on the basis of fleshly favor. Also your citation of many passages of Scripture pleased me greatly; when I had read them I had no further doubt concerning the matter. For in receiving such an incontrovertible demonstration from you I did not consider that I should simply glance over them with my eyes. May I be your ransom, because you love Jesus, the Son of the living God. Thus he himself says to me: "I love those who love me, and those who seek me shall find peace."[15]

4   It occurs to me to mention that the report which I heard of you, while you were at Rome with the blessed father Anacletus,[16] whom the most excellently blessed Clement, a hearer of Peter and Paul, has by now succeeded, is true. And now you have increased it a hundredfold, and may you further it yet more. I was greatly desirous of coming to you so that I might be refreshed with you, but "a person's way

[13] Cf. Ign. *Rom.* 5.1–2.
[14] Rom 8.18.
[15] Prov 8.17 (LXX).
[16] One manuscript reads "Linus," which would accord with the succession of Roman bishops given at *Apostolic Constitutions* 7.46, whereas as given here the order is as found in Eusebius (*Ecclesiastical History* 3.21.6). See also the mention of Roman bishops at *ps-Trallians* 7. As noted in the introduction, ps-Ignatius may be identifying his correspondent with the Mary greeted by Paul at Rom 16.6.

is not his own."[17] For the military guard prevents such a proposal, and does not allow me to go beyond it. In my present circumstances I cannot undertake or suffer anything. Thus reckoning writing as a secondary means of encouragement among friends I greet your holy soul, exhorting you further to add to its vigor. For our present labor is slight, but a great reward is anticipated.

5   Flee those who deny the passion of Christ and his begetting in the flesh. There are many at present suffering under this disease. But it would be pointless to instruct you otherwise since you are furnished with every good deed and word, and able to direct others in Christ. Greet all who are of like mind with you and who hold fast to their own salvation in Christ. The presbyters and the deacons, and above all the saintly Hero, greet you. My host Cassian greets you, as well as my sister, his wife, and their dearest children. May the Lord hallow you always in fleshly and spiritual health, and may I see you in Christ attaining to the crown.

---

[17]Jer 10.23.

Trallians

The pseudo-Ignatian letter to the Trallians is an expansion of the authentic Ignatian letter. The main expansion undertaken by the interpolator is to extend the warnings regarding heresy, in particular asserting the true physical reality of Jesus Christ. Whereas this would point to a discussion more relevant to the time of Ignatius than to the latter part of the fourth century, we may see this as part of the interpolator's eirenic process, calling his readers to what is truly significant and truly heretical, namely the denial of Christ, as opposed to the fine detail of anti-heretical discussion in his own period.

IGNATIUS TO THE TRALLIANS:

Ignatius, who is also God-carrier, to the holy Church which is at Tralles, in Asia, beloved of God the Father and Jesus Christ, elect and God-worthy, brought to peace in Jesus Christ's flesh and spirit, our hope in enduring the cross and death and in resurrection, which (church) also I greet in its completeness, in the apostolic manner, and wish abundance of happiness.

1 ₁I came to know that you possess a blameless and unwavering mind in patience that is not by habit but as a possession, just as Polybius, your bishop, has shown me in coming to Smyrna by the will of God the Father and Jesus Christ his Son, with the co-operation of the Spirit. So he rejoiced with me, who am bound in Christ Jesus, so that in him I discerned your whole congregation. ₂I gloried in receiving through him your godly goodwill, discovering that you were imitators of Jesus Christ the Savior.

2 ₁Be subject to the bishop as to the Lord, for he watches for your souls as one who will give an account to God."[1] Thus you seem to me not to be living in a human way but in accordance with Jesus Christ who died for us, so that believing in his death we may, by baptism, have fellowship in his resurrection. ₂So it is required, in whatever you do, to undertake nothing without the bishop, but that you be subject also to the presbytery, as to the apostles of Jesus Christ, our hope, in whom we will be found should we live in him. ₃And it is necessary that the deacons of the mysteries of Jesus Christ should be pleasing to all in every way. For they are not deacons of food and drink, but ministers of the church of God, who should guard themselves against accusations as against burning fire.

3 So let them remain as such. You should respect them as Jesus Christ, of whose place they are guardians, just as the bishop is the representation of the Father of all things, and the presbyters are the sanhedrin of God and company of the apostles of Christ. Apart from these there is no elect church, no holy gathering, no assembly of the sanctified. ₂I am persuaded that you agree in this, for I have received the proof of your love and I have it with me still in your bishop, whose very appearance is highly instructive, whose meekness itself is powerful. I reckon that even the godless respect him. ₃I refrain from writing to you in any more severe manner, so that I should not appear to anyone to be harsh or importunate. Though bound for the sake of Christ, yet I am not yet worthy of Christ. Should I be perfected then perhaps I may become so.

4 ₁I do not rate myself an apostle, but I limit myself so that I should not be destroyed by boasting. It is good to boast in the Lord.[2] Even if I should be vigorous in the things of God, I would have to be all the more fearful and pay no attention to those who would puff me up. For those who speak to me are scourging me. ₂For indeed I am

[1]Heb 13.17.
[2]1 Cor 1.31.

a lover of suffering, but I do not know whether I am worthy. For the envy of the enemy is not visible to many, but it wars against me. I therefore have need of humility, by which the ruler of this age, the devil, is undone.

5 Am I not able to write to you regarding more mystical matters? Yet I am afraid to do so lest, being infants, I should harm you. Forgive me this, lest not being able to take on their import, you might choke. ₂For even I, whilst in bondage, and able to understand heavenly matters, the angelic orders and the various kinds of archangels and armies, the differences between powers and dominions, the distinctions between thrones and authorities, the greatness of the aeons, the pre-eminence of the cherubim and seraphim, the heights of the Spirit and the kingdom of the Lord, and above all the incomparability of Almighty God—knowing all of this, I am not yet perfected thoroughly, nor am I a disciple such as Paul or Peter. For much is still lacking to me, many things are yet wanting to me, but I am not lacking in God.

6 ₁I therefore—yet not I, but the love of Jesus Christ—entreat you "that you should all speak the same thing and there should be no divisions among you. Be joined together with the same understanding and the same mind."[3] ₂For some are vain talkers and deceivers,[4] not Christians but Christmongers,[5] deceitfully carrying around the name of Christ and corrupting the word of the gospel,[6] mixing the poison of their deceit with their sweet talk, as though confecting aconite with honeyed wine so that whoever drinks is deceived in his taste by the pleasant sensation, and unguardedly meets death. One of the ancients advises thus: "Let nobody who mingles good with evil

[3] 1 Cor 1.11; cf. ps-Ign. *Eph.* 2.
[4] Titus 1.10.
[5] Cf. ps-*Magn.* 9; *Didache* 12.
[6] 2 Cor 2.17.
[7] *Apostolic Constitutions* 6.13. Otherwise the source is unknown, though Lightfoot, *Apostolic Fathers* 2.3, 153–154, cites a similar tradition from an "elder" cited by

be called good."[7] For they speak of Christ, not that they may preach Christ, but that they may do Christ down, and they propound the law not that they may uphold the law[8] but so that they can proclaim lawlessness. For they alienate Christ from the Father, and the law from Christ. They deny his birth from a virgin. Ashamed of the cross, they deny His passion and have no faith in the resurrection. They introduce God as an unknown being, they suppose Christ to be unbegotten, and do not make confession of the existence of the Spirit. Some of them say that the Son was simply human, that the Father and the Son and the Holy Spirit are the same being, and that the creation is the work of God, not through Christ but through some other alien power.

7   ₁Therefore defend yourselves against such people so that you do not admit a trap for your own souls, so as not to become a "snare on a watchtower, and like a net spread out."[9] For "whoever does not heal himself in his own deeds is the brother of the one who destroys himself."[10] Thus, if you are able to put away all conceit, arrogance, disdain, and haughtiness you will find it possible to be unseparated from God. For "He is near to those who fear him."[11] And he says, "On whom shall I look but upon the one who is humble and quiet and who trembles at my words."[12] Reverence your bishop like Christ, as the blessed apostles have directed you.[13] ₂Whoever is within the sanctuary is pure. So that person is obedient to the bishop and to the presbyters. Whoever, being outside, undertakes anything apart from the bishop and the presbyters and the deacons has a polluted

Irenaeus *Against the Heresies* 3.17.4.

[8]The phrase "they propound the law" is absent from the Greek manuscripts and is supplied, following Lightfoot, *Apostolic Fathers* 2.3, 154, from the Latin version.

[9]Hos 5.1.

[10]Prov 18.9.

[11]Ps 85.9.

[12]Is 66.2.

[13]A reference to *Apostolic Constitutions*, having in mind *Apostolic Constitutions* 2.20, is possible, though this may also be a reference to the *Didascalia*.

[14]Titus 1.15; 1 Tim 5.8.

conscience and is worse than faithless.[14] For what is a bishop but one who, beyond all other, governs with all authority and power? How is a human being to govern but by becoming an imitator of the Christ of God, insofar as he is able? And what is the presbytery but a sacred conclave, the counsellors and assessors of the bishop? And what are the deacons but imitators of the angelic powers, serving with a pure and blameless service? So was Stephen to the blessed James, Timothy and Linus to Paul, and Anacletus and Clement to Peter.[15] Whoever does not yield to these is altogether godless, and impious, despising Christ and belittling his direction.

8 ₁I am communicating these things to you, not because I am aware that there are any such persons among you; rather I hope that God "who did not spare his Son for the sake of His holy Church"[16] will never permit any such report to reach my ears. But foreseeing the ambushes of the evil one, I am protecting you in advance by my admonitions, as my beloved and faithful children in Christ, providing you with the means of protection against the deathly disease of the unruly. Shun this disease by the good will of Christ our Lord. There-fore, taking on meekness, become imitators of the sufferings of Christ and of his love, with which he loved us when he gave himself a ran-som for us,[17] that He might cleanse us by His blood from our ancient ungodliness, and bestow life upon us, just as we were about to perish through the evil within us. ₂Therefore let none of you hold anything against your neighbor. For our Lord says, "Forgive, and it shall be for-given you."[18] Do not give any entry-point to heathens, lest "by means of a few foolish people the word and the teaching be blasphemed."[19] For the prophet, as though in the person of God, says: "Woe to him by whom my name is blasphemed among the Gentiles."[20]

[15]Cf. *To Hero* 3; *To Mary* 4.
[16]Rom 8.32.
[17]Cf. 1 Tim 2.6.
[18]Mt 6.14.
[19] 1 Tim 6.1; Titus 2.5.
[20] Is 53.5.

9 ₁Be deaf, therefore, when anyone speaks to you apart from of Jesus Christ, who is of the race of David, who is from Mary, who was truly begotten of God and of the virgin, but not in the same way, for God and humanity are not the same.[21] Truly he put on a body; for "the Word was made flesh,"[22] and lived upon earth without sin (for he says, "Which of you convicts me of sin?").[23] Truly he ate and drank. He was crucified and died under Pontius Pilate, was truly, and not in appearance, crucified and died, as those in the heavens, and on the earth, and beneath the earth looked on. Those in heaven are those whose natures are incorporeal. Those on earth are the Jews and Romans, and such persons as were present at that time when the Lord was crucified. Those beneath the earth are the multitude that arose together with the Lord (for the Scripture says, "Many bodies of the saints that slept arose,"[24] as their graves were opened). Alone he descended to Hades, but he arose with a multitude,[25] and split apart that fence that had existed from the beginning of the world, and cast down its partition-wall.[26] ₂He rose again in three days, raised by his Father, and spending forty days with the apostles was received by the Father. And he sat down at his right hand, "remaining until his enemies are placed under his feet."[27] He received the sentence from Pilate on the day of preparation, at the third hour, as the Father allowed. He was crucified at the sixth hour, he breathed his last at the ninth, he was buried before the setting of the sun, he remained under the earth in the tomb in which Joseph of Aramathea had laid him on the Sabbath, he arose from the dead at the dawning of the Lord's day, in accordance with what he had said:[28] "As Jonah was

[21]The idea of the Father's begetting of the Son was opposed by the Arians on the basis that this seemed to attribute a human activity to God.

[22]Jn 1.14.

[23]Jn 8.46.

[24]Mt 27.52.

[25]This statement is found in the *Teaching of Addai*, which is cited by Eusebius in *Ecclesiastical History* 1.13.19.

[26]Cf. Eph 2.14.

[27]Heb 10.12–13.

[28]Lightfoot, *Apostolic Fathers* 2.3, 159, compares *Apostolic Constitutions* 5.14.

three days and three nights in the whale's belly, so the Son of Man shall also be three days and three nights in the heart of the earth."[29] The day of the preparation, then, contains the passion; the Sabbath the burial; the Lord's Day the resurrection.[30]

10 Thus if some people, atheists—that is, unbelievers—say that he became man in appearance only, that he did not truly put on a body, that he appeared to have died, and did not suffer in reality, why am I bound? Why do I beg to fight the wild beasts? Am I therefore dying in vain? Am I, even more, lying about the Lord? Also the prophet states in vain, "They shall look on him whom they have pierced, and mourn over themselves as over one beloved."[31] These people, therefore, are unbelievers no less than those who crucified him. I, however, do not place my hopes in one who died for me in appearance, but in reality. For falsehood is totally foreign to the truth. So Mary truly conceived a body which God inhabited. And God the Word was truly born of the Virgin, clothing himself with a body of sufferings like ours. The one who forms all in the womb was himself truly in a womb, and made himself a body from the seed of the Virgin, but without any intercourse with a man. He was carried in the womb, even as we are, for the usual period of time; and was truly born, even as we are; and was in reality nourished with milk, and partook of common food and drink, even as we do. And when he had lived for thirty years, he was baptized by John, in truth and not in appearance. And when he had proclaimed the gospel three years, and done signs and wonders,[32] the judge was judged by the false Jews and by Pilate the governor. He was scourged, he was struck on

[29] Mt 12.40.

[30] There are a number of similarities between this passage and the passion chronology found in the *Didascalia,* followed by the *Apostolic Constitutions.* A literary dependence cannot be ruled out, though it is equally possible that there are common exegetical traditions underlying the similarities.

[31] Zech 12.10. Cf. also Jn 19.37.

[32] Lightfoot, *Apostolic Fathers* 2.3, 160, compares Melito fragment 6 for the juxtaposition of the thirty years and the three. However, this fragment is not authentic but from christological controversy in the fourth century.

the cheek, he was spit upon, he wore a crown of thorns and a purple robe, he was condemned. He was truly crucified, not in appearance, not in imagination, not in deceit. He truly died, and was buried, and rose from the dead, just as he prayed somewhere, saying, "Raise me up again, O Lord, and I will repay them."[33] And the Father, who always hears him, answered and said, "Arise, O God, and judge the earth; for you shall receive all the nations for your inheritance."[34] The Father, therefore, who raised him up, will also raise us up through him, apart from whom we do not have true life. For he says, "I am the life; whoever believes in me shall live, even if he die, and everyone who lives and believes in me shall live for ever, even if he die."[35] Therefore flee these ungodly heresies; for they are the inventions of the devil, that serpent who was the author of evil who, by means of the woman, deceived Adam, the father of our race.

11   ₁Flee him, and his wicked offshoots, Simon his first-born son, and Menander and Basilides and his whole babble of wickedness,[36] the human-worshippers, whom Jeremiah the prophet calls accursed.[37] Also flee the impure Nicolaitans, falsely so-called,[38] who are lovers of pleasure, and slanderers. Also flee the children of the

[33]Ps 51.10.

[34] Ps 82.8.

[35]Jn 11.25–26.

[36]Simon is identified in a number of patristic texts as the originator of heresy. Perhaps most relevant is *Apostolic Constitutions* 6.8. Menander and Basilides were gnostic teachers of the second century. There is a clear resemblance here to *Apostolic Constitutions* 6.8, though the connection need not be a matter of direct literary dependence.

[37]Jer 17.5: "Accursed is the one who puts hope in a human being." The reference to "human-worshippers" might refer to a number of heretical groups, in particular any who deny the divinity of Christ. The term is used in the fourth century by Athanasius (*Against the Arians* 2.16), as Apollinarians laid the same charge against Catholic Christians (Gregory Nazianzen *Letter* 101); the charge was subsequently laid against the Nestorians (Cyril *Letter* 20).

[38]Lightfoot. *Apostolic Fathers* 2.3, 161, suggests that the term is borrowed from *Apostolic Constitutions* 6.8. See, however, the brief discussion in the introduction above.

evil one, Theodotus[39] and Cleobulus,[40] who produce death-dealing fruit; anyone who tastes of it dies instantly, not just a temporary death but one which is eternal. These are not of the Father's planting but are an accursed brood. The Lord says, "Let every plant which my heavenly Father has not planted be extirpated."[41] ₂If they were stems of the Father, they would not have been "enemies of the cross of Christ"[42] but of those who "killed the Lord of glory."[43] Denying the cross and being ashamed of the passion, they are covering up the transgression of the Jews, those who fight against God, those who murdered the Lord, for it is too slight to term them murderers of the prophets. But Christ invites you to incorruption, through his passion and his resurrection, as you are parts of his body.

12 ₁I greet you from Smyrna, along with the churches of God which are present with me, whose leaders in all manner of ways have refreshed me, both in body and in spirit. ₂My chains, which I wear on account of Jesus Christ, are exhorting you, as I ask that I may attain to God. Remain in your concord with one another and in prayer. For it is proper that every one of you, and especially the presbyters, should refresh the bishop for the honor of the Father and Jesus Christ and the apostles. ₃I pray that you hear me in love, and that my writing should not stand as a witness against you. And pray for me, in need of your love through the mercy of God, that I be found worthy of the lot which is to fall to me, lest I be found undeserving.

[39]Theodotus is probably the leatherseller of Byzantium, mentioned by Eusebius *Ecclesiastical History* 5.28. It is to be noted that the mention of this figure is a gross anachronism. It is also to be noted that Theodotus does not appear in the parallel passage of the *Apostolic Constitutions*.

[40]Cleobulus, also called Cleobius, first appears in a citation of Hegesippus in Eusebius, *Ecclesiastical History* 4.22. He is found in *Apostolic Constitutions* 6.8 as a successor to Simon.

[41]Matt 15.13.

[42]Phil 3.18.

[43]1 Cor 2.8.

Magnesians

The pseudonymous letter to the Magnesians is, once again, an expansion of an original Ignatian letter. The interpolator expands the passages regarding heresy as he had in the expansion of the letter to the Trallians. However, he also expands the passage regarding Judaizing. That Christians in the Antioch of the fourth century continued to be attracted to Judaism and to retain a number of Jewish practices, is clear from the preaching of John Chrystostom; the Didascalia and the Apostolic Constitutions are likewise much exercised by the issue. Thus the Ignatian original provides a ready springboard for the interpolator to expand this polemic. It is also to be noted that the discussion of young bishops, already undertaken in the fictive letter from Mary to Ignatius, is picked up once again on the basis of Ignatius' discussion of the young Magnesian bishop. We are led to wonder to what extent this might have been a real issue in the community of the interpolator, or whether this is simply the reproduction of traditional material.

Ignatius to the Magnesians:

Ignatius, who is also God-carrier, to the one blessed in the grace of God the Father, in Christ Jesus our Savior, in whom I greet the church which is in Magnesia, on the Meander, for which I pray in God the Father and the Lord Jesus Christ. May you enjoy utmost rejoicing in him.

1 ₁Being aware of the well-ordered nature of your godly love, rejoicingly I determined to address you in the faith of Jesus Christ. ₂For being thought worthy of a divine and desirable name, in the

chains which I carry around, I sing the churches, in which I pray that there may be the unity of flesh and spirit from Jesus Christ, "who is the Savior of all people, especially of those who believe;"[1] by whose blood you were redeemed, by whom you have come to know God, or rather have come to be known by him.[2] Abiding in him you may escape all the abuse of the ruler of this age, for "he is faithful, who will not allow you to be tested more than you may bear."[3]

2   Since, therefore, I have been deemed worthy to behold you through Damas, your God-worthy bishop, and your God-worthy presbyters Bassus and Apollonius, and my companion, the deacon Zotion, in whom may I delight, because he is subject to the bishop and to the presbytery by the grace of God in the law of Jesus Christ.

3   ₁It is proper that you should not think ill of the age of the bishop, but in accordance with the knowledge of God you should yield every respect to him, as I am aware that the holy presbyters have not had regard to apparent youth but to understanding in God, since "those of many years are not wise, nor do old men have knowledge of prudence, but there is a spirit in mortals."[4] For at twelve years old Daniel was possessed of the divine spirit, and refuted the elders who were making accusations and lusting after the beauty of another's wife, wearing grey hairs in vain.[5] And Samuel, a little lad, reproved Eli, being ninety years old, for giving preference to his sons over God.[6] Similarly Jeremiah heard from God, "Do not say 'I am young.'"[7] Solomon and Josiah also. One at twelve years of age was king, and gave the terrifying and complex judgement in the case of the women

[1] 1 Tim 4.10.
[2] Cf. Gal 4.9.
[3] 1 Cor 10.13.
[4] Job 32. 8, 9
[5] Susanna. Nothing is said, here, however, of Daniel's age, though the tradition that he was a youth at the time is found elsewhere.
[6] 1 Sam 3.11–18.
[7] Jer 1.7.

and their children,[8] the other, governing at eight years of age,[9] tore down the altars and the temples, and burnt down the groves, for they were dedicated to demons and not to God. And he slaughtered the false priests as corrupters and deceivers of people who did not worship the Godhead. Thus youth, when devoted to God, is not to be despised, but any corrupt mind, even though "aged in evil days."[10] The Christ-carrier Timothy was young, but listen to what his teacher writes to him: "Nobody should despise your youth, but be an example of the faithful in word and in conduct."[11] 2Therefore it is proper that you should be obedient to your bishop and contradict him in nothing, for it is fearful to contradict one such. One does not do it to the visible, but gives a false account to the one who is invisible, who is incapable of being deceived by anyone. Such an act is not directed towards any human being, but towards God. For God says to Samuel: "Their false account is not to you but to me."[12] And Moses says: "The grumbling is not against us, but against the Lord God."[13] None of those who rose up against their superiors remained unpunished, for Dathan and Abiram spoke not against the law but against Moses, and were cast down into Hades alive.[14] Korah, and those two hundred and fifty who conspired with him against Aaron, were destroyed by fire.[15] Absalom, being a fratricide, was hanged on a tree and his evil-scheming heart was pierced with darts.[16] Likewise Abeddadan lost his head on a similar account.[17] Uzziah, when he dared to oppose the priests and the priesthood, was struck

[8] 1 Kg 3.16.
[9] 2 Kg 22, 23; cf. *From Mary* 4 above.
[10] Susanna 52.
[11] 1 Tim 4.12.
[12] 1 Sam 7.7.
[13] Ex 16.8
[14] Num 16.31–32.
[15] Num 16.35.
[16] 2 Sam 18.9, 14.
[17] 2 Sam 20.22. This is, however, an error, as it was Sheba, and not Obededom, who was beheaded in this manner. See the discussion of this point in the introduction, as the same error is found in the *Apostolic Constitutions*.

with leprosy.[18] Saul was dishonored for not awaiting the high priest Samuel.[19] Therefore you should reverence your superiors.

4   So it is proper not only to be called Christians but to be such as well, for one is rendered blessed not by speaking but by being. Should any speak of a bishop, yet do everything without him, so shall he, who is the true and first overseer, and is alone the high priest by nature, say to such as these, "Why do you call me 'Lord, Lord' and not do what I say?"[20] Such persons do not seem to me to have a good conscience, but seem to me to be dissemblers and pretenders.

5   Thus, since there is an end to things, and there is laid out life (from observance) and death (from disobedience), and each of us is to go the place we have chosen, let us flee death and make the choice of life. ₂For I say there are two imprints to be found among people, the one a true coin, the other a forgery. The devout person is a coin imprinted by God, the ungodly a coin with false value, debased, counterfeit, forged, minted not by God but by the devil. I do not say that there are two human natures but that there is one humanity, some of whom are of God and some of the devil. If somebody is devout he is a person of God. If ungodly, a person of the devil, being so not out of nature but by individual choice. The faithless have the image of the ruler of evil, the faithful have the image of God the Father, who rules, and of Jesus Christ, whose life, if we do not choose willingly to die for truth in likeness of his passion, is not in us.

6   Therefore, since I have in faith discerned the entire congregation, and loved it, in the persons of whom I have already written, I urge you to be anxious to do everything in the concord of God, as the bishop is seated first, in the place of God,[21] and the presbyters in the

[18]2 Chr 26. 20.
[19]1 Sam 13.11.
[20]Lk 6.46.
[21]Here, by contrast to the *typos* of the middle recension, I have allowed *topos* to stand as the reading.

place of the council of the apostles, and the deacons, especially dear to me, entrusted with the ministry of Jesus Christ, who, begotten of the Father before the ages, was the Word of God, the only-begotten Son, and at the consummation of the ages will remain so, for Daniel the prophet says "of his kingdom there will be no end."[22] Therefore let us all love one another in concord, and let nobody look upon a neighbor in a fleshly manner but in Christ Jesus. There should be nothing among you which is capable of dividing you, but be united with the bishop, being subject to God in Christ through him.

7 Therefore, just as, without regard to the Father, the Lord does nothing, for, he says, "I can do nothing of myself,"[23] so you, without regard to the bishop, neither a presbyter, nor a deacon, nor a layperson. Nor should you consider anything reasonable which is contrary to his knowledge, for anything such is a transgression and opposed to God. You should all be one in prayer as you come together. There should be one common petition, one mind, one hope in love, in a blameless faith in Christ Jesus, to whom nothing is superior. You should all run together to the temple of God, as upon one altar, upon one Jesus Christ, the high priest of the unbegotten God.

8 Do not be deceived by strange opinions, nor "hold to fables and to endless genealogies,"[24] or Jewish delusions: "The things of old have passed away; look, everything is become new."[25] For if, even now, we live in accordance with the Jewish law and the circumcision of the flesh, we should be denying that we had received grace. For the most godly prophets lived in accordance with Jesus Christ. On this account they were persecuted, being inspired by grace fully to

[22]Dan 2.44. The insistence on the continuing kingdom of Christ would seem to be prompted by the idea of Marcellus of Ancyra that the kingdom would be given up to the Father at the end of all things. The same motivation prompted the insertion of this clause into the Nicene creed at its revision at Constantinople.

[23]Jn 5.30.

[24]1 Tim 1.4.

[25]2 Cor 5.17.

convict the unpersuaded that there is one almighty God, who made himself manifest through Jesus Christ his Son, who is his Word, not spoken, but of his essence.[26] For he is not the sound of an articulate statement, but is essence begotten of divine activity, who is well pleasing in everything to the one who sent him.

9 Therefore, if those who conducted themselves in accordance with the ancient writings came to a newness of hope in understanding Christ, as the Lord teaches, saying: "If you believed Moses you would believe in me, for he it is who wrote of me,"[27] and "Abraham, your father, exulted to see my day, and he saw it and rejoiced," since "Before Abraham, I am,"[28] 2how then could we live without regard to him? It is of him that the prophets were slaves, foreseeing him in the Spirit, and awaiting him as their teacher, and expecting him as Lord and Savior saying: "He himself will come and save us."[29] No longer, therefore, should we keep the Sabbath in a Jewish manner and rejoice in lazy days. For "Whoever does not work should not eat."[30] For "in the sweat of your brow shall you eat your bread," say the oracles.[31] Each of you should keep the Sabbath in a spiritual way, rejoicing in meditation on the laws, not in bodily relaxation, wondering at the workmanship of God, not in eating food a day old, and lukewarm drinks, and walking for a prescribed distance, and

[26]Lightfoot, *Apostolic Fathers*, 2.3, 170–171, suggests that the alteration to Ignatius' original text is undertaken because Ignatius' original statement might seem to imply the doctrine taught by Marcellus of Ancyra, who held that the Son did not have personhood as such, but that he was simply an expression of the Father. Amelungk, *Untersuchungen über Pseudo-Ignatius*, 26–27, makes substantially the same point. Although many make the same denial as ps-Ignatius here we may particularly observe a citation from the sermon of Meletius of Antioch preserved in Epiphanius, *Medicine Chest*, 73.30: "Because he is the Word, and is referred to as Son, he should not be considered the voice of the Father, nor a statement, for he subsisted and acted in himself."

[27]Jn 5.46.
[28]Jn 8.56, 58.
[29]Is 35.4.
[30]2 Thess 3.10.
[31]Gen 3.19.

rejoicing in dancing and in senseless applause.[32] And after keeping the Sabbath every friend of Christ should keep the Lord's day as a festival, the day of resurrection, the queen, the chief of all days, of which the prophet stated, as he looked for it, "To the end, for the eighth day,"[33] on which our life appeared, and victory in Christ was given over death. The "children of perdition,"[34] who are "enemies of the cross, whose god is the belly, whose thoughts are fixed on earth,"[35] who are lovers of pleasure and not lovers of God, who have the appearance of piety whilst denying its power,[36] deny him. They are traders in Christ, "huckstering the Word"[37] and selling Jesus, corrupters of women and covetous of others' goods, tornadoes sucking up money. By the mercy of God may you be delivered from them through the Lord Jesus Christ.

10 1Therefore we should not be imperceptive of his kindness. For if he were to act in imitation of our actions, we would not still exist. For, "if you, Lord, should mark our guilt, who would survive?"[38] Therefore let us be worthy of the name which we have received, for whoever is known by a name other than this, this person is not God's. He has not received the prophecy which is spoken concerning us: "He will be called by a new name, with which the Lord will name him" and will be "a holy people."[39] And first this was fulfilled in Syria,

---

[32]Here are a number of references to contemporary Jewish Sabbath practices. Thus the drinks are lukewarm, and the food a day old, because fire cannot be kindled, though items may be kept warm through a fire lit the previous day. There are restrictions on the distance which might be walked, but also evidence that the Sabbath was kept as a festival, and hence the reference to dancing and applause. The polemic against keeping the Sabbath in a Jewish manner is commonplace in the fourth century; Christians in Syria kept the Sabbath, but as a day of study and instruction.

[33]Ps 6.1, 11.1.
[34]Is 57.4.
[35]Phil 3.18, 19.
[36]2 Tim 3.4.
[37]2 Cor 2.17.
[38]Ps 129.3.
[39]Is 62.2, 12.

in Antioch, for "the disciples were termed Christians,"[40] when Paul
and Peter were laying the foundations of the church.

₂Therefore put aside the evil yeast, which is aged and soured,
and be changed into new yeast of grace. Abide[41] in Christ, so that
no stranger may exercise dominion over you.

₃It is outlandish to speak of Jesus Christ with the tongue and
mentally cleave to the Judaism which ceased to be, for Christianity
did not put its faith in Judaism but Judaism in Christianity. For in
Christianity every nation which believes and every tongue which
confesses is gathered together into God, and those of stony heart
are children of Abraham,[42] the friend of God, and in his seed are all
those who have been blessed,[43] "who are ordained to eternal life"[44]
in Christ.

11   My beloved, these are (written) not as knowing that any of you
are acting thus, but I wish to put you on your guard, as one who is less
than you, so that you should not be hooked by the barbs of vain doctrine but that you should have the fullest conviction in Christ, who,
begotten of the Father before all the ages, was afterwards begotten
more recently from Mary the virgin regardless of any involvement
with a man, and who, living in a holy manner, and healing every disease and weakness among the people, and doing signs and wonders
for human benefit, and proclaiming the one true God, his Father, to
those who had fallen into polytheism, and undergoing the passion,
enduring the cross, when Pontius Pilate was governor and Herod the
king, at the behest of the Christ-killing Jews, dying, and rising and
ascending into the heavens to the one who sent him, taking his seat
at his right hand, and who is to come again at the completion of the
ages with his Father's glory to judge the living and the dead and to
reward each person in accordance with his or her deeds. Whoever

[40] Acts 11.26
[41] *Aulisthēte*, cf. Ignatius *halisthēte*.
[42] Cf. Mt 3.9; Is 41.8; Jas 2.23.
[43] An allusion to Gen 22.18.
[44] Acts 13.48.

knows and believes in the fullest conviction is blessed, even as now you are God-lovers and Christ-lovers in the fullest conviction of our hope, from which may none of us turn aside.

12 May I delight in you in every way, should I prove worthy. For although I am enchained, I am nothing compared to any of you who are freed. That you are not haughty, I know, for you have Jesus Christ among you. When I praise you, moreover, I know that you feel compunction: as it is written, "The just person is his own accuser,"[45] and, "Speak of your own sins first, so that you may be justified,"[46] and, "When you have performed all that was directed of you, say 'We are useless servants.'"[47] Because "what is highly esteemed in human company is an abomination to God," for it says "God, be merciful to me a sinner."[48] For this reason those who were great, Abraham and Job, styled themselves "dust and ashes" before God,[49] and David says "Who am I before you, Lord, that you have glorified me until now,"[50] and Moses, of all people the meekest,[51] says to God "I am of a feeble voice and tongue-tied."[52] So be humble in spirit yourselves, so that you may be exalted." For "whoever humbles himself shall be exalted, and whoever exalts himself will be humbled."[53]

13 Therefore be keen to stand strong in the opinions of the Lord and the apostles, so that all that you undertake may be prospered, in flesh and spirit, in faith and love, in the Son and the Father and in the Spirit, in the beginning and the end, together with your most worthy bishop and your presbytery, well woven into a spiritual

[45]Prov 18.17.
[46]Is 53.26.
[47]Luke 17.10.
[48]Luke 18.13.
[49]Gen 18.27; Job 30.19.
[50]1 Chr 17.16.
[51]Num 12.3.
[52]Ex 4.10.
[53]Lk 14.11. Lightfoot, *Apostolic Fathers* 2.3, 179, points out that 1 Clement 17–18 similarly links Abraham and Job, Moses and David as examples of humility.

crown, and your godly deacons. ₂Be subject to the bishop and to each other, as Christ was to the Father,[54] so that there may be godly unity among you.

14   Knowing that you are filled up with all that is good I have exhorted you concisely in the love of Jesus Christ. Remember me in your prayers so that I may attain to God, and the church in Syria, of which I am not worthy to be called bishop. For I am in need of your unified prayer and love in God, so that the church in Syria may prove worthy, through your good order, to be pastured in Christ.

15   The Ephesians greet you from Smyrna, from where I am writing to you, They are here for the glory of God, as are you. In every way they have refreshed me, as has Polycarp. The rest of the churches also greet you in the honor of Jesus Christ. Fare well in concord to you who have obtained an undivided spirit in Jesus Christ through the will of God.

[54]Cf. the authentic Ignatius.

Tarsians

The pseudonymous letter to the Tarsians is one of a number which fundamentally set out the forger's theological position with regard to the disputes over the faith which characterized the fourth century. The choice of Tarsus as a destination seems to be motivated by the fact that Paul is from Tarsus, as the pseudo-Ignatius, as much as the authentic, sees the Ignatian tradition as a continuation of the Pauline; nonetheless it is also interesting as it seems to exhibit an assertion that Tarsus should be within the ambit of the Antiochene metropolitan see. The doctrinal section is followed by a brief, and largely conventional, ethical exhortation.

IGNATIUS TO THE TARSIANS:

Ignatius, who is also God-carrier, to the church with is saved in Christ, worthy of praise and worthy of mention and worthy of love, which is in Tarsus. Mercy, peace from God the Father and the Lord Jesus Christ be amplified always.

1   I fight wild beasts from Syria, all the way to Rome.[1] I am not devoured by unreasoning beasts, for as you know they spared Daniel, as God willed, but by those in human form, in which the merciless beast has hidden himself, pricking and wounding me daily. But I make nothing of these hardships nor "do I hold my life worthwhile"[2] so as to love it more than the Lord. So I am prepared for fire, for wild beasts, for the sword, for the cross, as long as I can see Christ, my

[1]Ign. *Rom.* 5.
[2]Acts 20.24.

Savior and my God,[3] who died for me. As a "prisoner for Christ,"[4] driven across land and sea,[5] I exhort you: "Stand firm in the faith,"[6] because "the righteous one will live by faith."[7] Be unwavering, because "The Lord makes those of one character to dwell in a house."[8]

2 I am aware that some of Satan's servants desire to trouble you. Some state that Jesus was begotten in appearance and crucified in appearance and died in appearance,[9] some that he is not the Son of the Creator, some that he is himself God over all, some that he was simply a human being. Others say that this flesh will not be raised and that it is necessary to participate in a life devoted to enjoyment, for this is the chief good for those who are to perish in a short while. A swarm of such evils has burst in upon us, but "not for one hour" have you "yielded in subjection" to them.[10] For you are fellow-citizens with Paul[11] as well as disciples of him who "fully proclaimed the gospel from Jerusalem around as far as Illyricum"[12] and who carried around the wounds of Christ in his flesh.[13]

3 Mindful of him, be completely aware that the Lord Jesus was truly begotten of Mary, "born of a woman," and was truly crucified. For he says: "May I not boast at all, except in the cross of the Lord."[14] And in truth he suffered, and died, and arose. For, he says, "If Christ is capable of suffering, if he is the first of the resurrection of the dead,"[15] and "He died, he died to sin once and for all. He lives, he lives

[3] A combination of Ign. *Smyrn.* 4 and Ign. *Rom* 5.
[4] Eph 4.1.
[5] Ign. *Rom.* 5.
[6] 1 Cor 16.13; Ign. *Eph.* 10.
[7] Hab 2.4; cited by Paul at Rom 1.17, Gal 3.11.
[8] Ps 67.6.
[9] This last clause is not found in all texts.
[10] A reference to Gal 2.5.
[11] Cf. Ign. *Rom.* 12.
[12] Rom 15.19.
[13] An allusion to Gal 6.17.
[14] Gal 6.14.
[15] Acts 26.23.

for God."[16] Had Christ not died, what advantage would there be in chains? What advantage in patience? What advantage in whippings? Why otherwise would Peter be crucified, Paul and James felled with the sword, John exiled to Patmos, Stephen done away with stones by the Lord-killing Jews? But none of this was purposeless, for the Lord was in truth crucified by the ungodly.

4 (Likewise be aware) that he, begotten of a woman, is the Son of God, and he, "the firstborn of all creation"[17] and God the Word, the one who made all things, was crucified. For the apostle says: "There is one God, the Father, from whom are all things, and one Lord Jesus Christ, through whom are all things."[18] And again: "For there is one God, and one mediator for God and humanity, Jesus Christ the human being."[19] And: "All things were created in him, in heaven and on the earth, visible and invisible. And he himself is before all things, and everything consists in him."[20]

5 And that this is not God over all but his Son. He says: "I ascend to my Father and your Father and to my God and your God." And "When he has made everything subject, then he will himself be subjected to the one who subjected all things to him, so that God might be all in all." Thus the one who does the subjecting, and who is all in all, must be different from the one to whom they are subjected, who then becomes subject together with everything else.

6 Nor was the one through whom and in whom everything came to be, simply human. For "through him everything came into being." "When he made heaven I was with him, and I was there with him with him, setting it in order, and he rejoiced in me daily."[21] How

[16]Rom 6.10.
[17]Col 1.15.
[18]1 Cor 8.6.
[19]1 Tim 2.5.
[20]Col 1.16–17.
[21]Prov 8.27, 30.

might a simple human being hear "Sit at my right hand"?[22] How might he say: "Before Abraham was, I am,"[23] and "Glorify me with the glory I had before the world came to be"?[24] How does a human being say: "I have come down from heaven not to do my own will but the will of the one who sent me"?[25] About what kind of man does it say: "He was the true light, which illuminates everyone who comes into the world. He was in the world, and the world came to be through him, and the world did not know him. He came to his own, and his own did not receive him"?[26] How could anyone like this be simply human, taking the origin of his existence from Mary, but not rather God the Word and only-begotten Son? For "in the beginning was the Word, and the Word was with God, and the Word was God."[27] And elsewhere: "The Lord created me as the beginning of his ways for his work. He established me before the age, before all the hills he begot me."[28]

7   And that our bodies also shall rise. He says: "Truly I say to you, that the hour is coming when all who are in their tombs will hear the voice of the Son of God and those who hear shall live."[29] And the apostle: "This corruptible must put on incorruption, and this mortal put on immortality."[30] And that we should live soberly and justly. He says: "Do not be fooled. Neither adulterers, nor effeminate men, nor homosexuals nor fornicators nor abusers nor drunkards nor thieves are able to inherit the kingdom of God,"[31] and "If the dead are not raised, Christ is not raised. So our proclamation is pointless, and

[22]Ps 110.1.
[23]Jn 8.58.
[24]Jn 17.5.
[25]Jn 6.38.
[26]Jn 1.9–11.
[27]Jn 1.1.
[28]Prov 8.22, 23, 25. This passage was much discussed and cited in the Arian controversies. In particular we may note its appearance in the long-lined creed, briefly discussed in the introduction.
[29]Jn 5.25, 28.
[30]1 Cor 15.53.
[31]1 Cor 6.9.

your faith is pointless. You are still in your sins. So those who lie in Christ are lost. If we put our hope in Christ for this life alone, we are the most pitiable of all people. If the dead are not raised, we should eat and drink, for tomorrow we die."[32] Should we dispose ourselves thus, how should we differ from asses and dogs, who give no thought to what is to occur in the future but whose appetite is only for eating and for whatever follows on from eating, for they are ignorant of any mind moving within themselves?[33]

8 May I delight in the Lord on your account! Be wary: You should keep yourselves—each of you—from any evil, bestial rage, gossip, falsehood, disgusting words, vulgarity, whispering, arrogance, drunkenness, lust, avarice, vainglory, envy, and anything that goes along with these. "Put on our Lord Jesus Christ and make no provision for the demands of the flesh."[34] The presbyters should be subordinate to the bishop, the deacons to the presbyters, the people to the deacons. I am the ransom for those who maintain this good order.[35] And may the Lord be perpetually with them.

9 Men, love your wives, women your husbands. Children, reverence your parents. Parents, "raise your children in the training and the admonition of the Lord."[36] Honor those who are in virginity as priestesses of Christ, those widows who are in continence as the altar of God.[37] Masters, direct your slaves sparingly. Slaves, wait upon your masters with fear. Let nobody among you be idle, as idleness is the mother of want. I do not direct you as though I were a

[32] A catena of passages from 1 Cor 15.

[33] Or, if Lightfoot's text is followed: "They have no director for the mind which is moving within themselves."

[34] Rom 13.14.

[35] Cf. Ign. *Pol.* 6.1.

[36] Eph 6.4.

[37] The image of the widow as an altar is found in Polycarp's letter to the Philippians 4, and is found widely in the church order literature, thus note *Didascalia* 2.26 and 3.6 with the parallel passages in *Apostolic Constitutions*.

somebody,[38] even though I am bound, but I remind you as a brother. May the Lord be with you.

10 I delight in your intercessions. Pray that I may attain to Jesus. I commend to you the church in Antioch. The churches of Asia and Polycarp the man of God, to whom I now commend the church of Syria, greet you. The church of the Philippians, from which I write to you, greets you. Philo your deacon, for whom I give thanks as in all manner of ways he has served me zealously, greets you. Agathopus, the deacon from Syria who follows me in Christ, greets you. "Greet one another with a holy kiss."[39] I greet one and all who are in Christ. Be well in body and soul and spirit, and do not forget me. May the Lord be with you.

[38]Cf. Ign. *Eph*. 3.
[39]Rom 16.16, etc.

Philippians

Like the letter to the Tarsians, the pseudonymous letter to the Philippians is fundamentally concerned to set out the doctrinal position of the forger. Here, however, in an apostrophe to Satan (reminiscent of the passage in the letter to the Ephesians) there is a more constructive approach, insofar as the pseudonymous author's Christology is set out in more detail; rather than simply denying the extreme positions of psilanthropism and Docetism as elsewhere, the author suggests explicitly that the Word took the place of a human soul in Christ.

IGNATIUS TO THE PHILIPPIANS:

Ignatius, who is also God-carrier, to the church which is in Philippi, having obtained mercy from God in faith and patience and unfeigned love. Mercy, peace from God the Father and the Lord Jesus Christ, "who is the Savior of all, especially of the faithful."[1]

1   Recollecting your love and zeal in Christ, which you have shown forth among us, I considered it appropriate to write on account of your brotherly affection, which is godly and spiritual, to remind you of your path in Christ, "so that you might all speak the same thing, should be of one mind, thinking the same thing, and acquiescing in the same rule" of faith, as Paul admonished you. For if there is one God of all, the Father of Christ, from whom is everything, and one Lord Jesus Christ, the only-begotten Son of God, the Lord of all, through whom is everything, and one Holy Spirit, who was active

---

[1] 1 Tim 4.10.

in Moses and the prophets and apostles, and one baptism which is administered on the basis of the Lord's death, and one chosen church, it seems that there should be one faith regarding Christ. For there is "One Lord, one faith, one baptism, one God and Father of all and through all and in all."[2]

2   Therefore there is one God, and not two or three. There is one, "Who was and who is," and there is none other than he, who alone is true. For the Lord says: "The Lord your God is one,"[3] and again "Did not one God create us? Is there not one Father of us all?"[4] There is one Son, the Word of God. For it says: "the only-begotten Son, who was in the bosom of the Father,"[5] and again "One Lord Jesus Christ."[6] And elsewhere: "What is his name, or what is the name of his Son, that we may know."[7] And there is one Paraclete. For it also says "there is one Spirit, since we were all called in one hope in our calling,"[8] and again, "we have drunk of one Spirit,"[9] with what follows on. "One and the same Spirit performs all of these"[10] spiritual gifts, as is manifest. Therefore there are not three fathers, nor three sons, nor three para-cletes, but one Father and one Son and one Paraclete. Therefore the Lord, sending the apostles "to teach all nations" enjoined them to baptize "in the name of the Father and of the Son and of the Holy Spirit."[11] Not in one with three names, nor in three in human form, but into three of equal honor.[12]

[2]Eph 4.5.
[3]Deut 6.4.
[4]Mal 2.10.
[5]Jn 1.18.
[6]1 Cor 8.6.
[7]Prov 30.4.
[8]Eph 4.4; 1 Cor 12.13.
[9]Eph 4.4.
[10]1 Cor 12.11.
[11]Mt 28.19.
[12]So the text. However, given that the path is one of denial, and a refusal to go beyond the statement of Scripture, we should give serious consideration to the possibility that the text is corrupt and should read at this point "nor into three of equal honour."

3 For one was in human form, not the Father, nor the Paraclete, but only the Son. Not in appearance, not in imagination, but in reality. For "the Word became flesh." For "Wisdom built a house for herself," and God the Word was born as a human, with a body from the virgin, without the intervention of a man. For "the virgin shall conceive in her womb and give birth to a son."[13] Therefore he was truly born, truly grew, truly ate and drank, was truly crucified and died and rose.[14] Whoever believes all this, as they were and as they so occurred, is blessed. Whoever does not believe is accursed no less than they who crucified the Lord. For the ruler of this world rejoices when anyone denies the cross, for he knows that the confession of the cross is his own destruction, as this is the trophy which gainsays his power, on seeing which he shudders and on hearing of which he takes fright.

4 Even before the cross he was anxious lest it should occur. And "he was active in the sons of disobedience."[15] He was active in Judas, among the Pharisees, among the Sadducees, among the elders, among the young, among the priests. When it was about to occur he was troubled, and introduced regret into the betrayer, and showed him a rope and taught him strangulation. He also put fright into the weak woman, disturbing her in her dreams, and sought to prevent what would happen on the cross, having made every move towards its preparation. Not that he repented of such great evil, for were this so he would not be utterly wicked, but he perceived his own destruction, for the cross of Christ is the beginning of his condemnation, the beginning of his death, the beginning of his destruction. Therefore he is active among some people so that they deny the cross, are ashamed of the passion, call his death an appearance, trim the birth from a virgin, and reject his nature as corrupt. He battles alongside the Jews in their denial of the cross, alongside the Greeks

[13] Is 7.14.
[14] Cf. Ign. *Trall.* 9.
[15] Eph 2.2.

in the false charge of sorcery, alongside the heretics in their imaginations. For the leader of wickedness takes on many forms, confusing the mind, inconsistent, self-contradictory, propounding first one thing and then another. At evildoing he is a savant, though ignorant of anything that is good. He overflows with ignorance through his voluntary derangement, for how can anyone who fails to see reason lying at his own feet be otherwise?

5   For if the Lord were simply human, of a soul and a body, why do you trim the birth which is of common human nature? And why, as though it were something extraordinary to happen to any human being, do you term his suffering an illusion, and consider the death of a mortal simply apparent? If he is God and human, why do you consider that it is unlawful to say "the Lord of glory," who is by nature unalterable? Why do you call the lawgiver, not having a human soul, unlawful? "The Word became flesh,"[16] the Word was human, not just dwelling in a human. How can he be a sorcerer, who in accordance with the Father's knowledge prepared beforehand every nature perceptible by feeling or intellect, who, in becoming human, "healed every disease and weakness."[17]

6   How can he who raises the dead, who sends the lame away made whole, who cleanses lepers, who gives sight to the blind, who increases or transforms substances such as the five loaves and the two fish and the water into wine, who puts your army to flight simply with a Word, not be God? Why do you vilify the virgin's nature and disdain her body-parts as disgusting things, when formerly you would exhibit such things in processions, and ordered males to be naked in the view of females, and females to excite the disordered lust of males? Now, indeed you consider all this disgusting, and make yourself out to be modest, you spirit of fornication, unaware that only when polluted by lawlessness does anything become

[16] Jn 1.14.
[17] Mt 4.23 etc. Also cited at ps-*Magn.* 11.

disgusting. Nothing is disgusting, nothing is vile, but everything is very good when not tainted by sin. But you fail to observe this, and so vilify them.

7   And again, how is it that Christ does not seem to you to be of the virgin, but yet to be God over all, the One-who-Is, the Almighty? Tell me then, who sent him? Who was his lord? To whose will was he subservient? And of what laws was he the completion, if he was subject to no will or authority? Even as you deny the birth of Christ you affirm that the unbegotten was begotten, and that the one with no beginning was nailed to the cross, though I am unable to say with whose agreement. But your changeability does not elude me, nor am I unaware that you walk crookedly and uncertainly. Pretending to know everything you are ignorant of the one who was begotten.

8   For much eludes you:[18] the virginity of Mary, the wonderful birth, the identity of the one who was embodied, the star directing the magi from the east who presented gifts, the archangel's greeting to the virgin, the marvellous conception of the betrothed virgin, the announcement of a child who would proceed in front of the one who was from the virgin as he skipped in the womb at what was foreseen, the angels' hymns for the one who was born, the good news to the shepherds, the fear of Herod at the loss of his kingdom, the command to kill the infants, the removal into Egypt and the return from there to the previous place, the Infant's swaddling bands, the human registration, the feeding with milk, the paternity ascribed to him who had no child, the manger as there was no place, the lack of any human preparation, the gradual growth, human speech, hunger, thirst, travelling, toil, the offering of sacrifices, the circumcision following, the baptism, the voice of God over the one baptized regarding his identity and origin, the witness of the Spirit and the voice of the Father[19] from on high, the prophecy of John pointing out the

[18]Cf. Ign. *Eph*. 19.
[19]Many mss read "of God" at this point.

passion by referring to him as a lamb, the working of various signs, diverse healings, the masterly warning governing both the sea and the winds, the expulsion of evil spirits, your own torture and your inability to do anything when afflicted by the power of the one who was made manifest.

9   You were dizzy when you saw these things. You did not know that it was a virgin who would bear a child, but the hymns of the angels struck you with astonishment, as did the worship of the magi and the appearance of the star.[20] You reverted to your ignorance as though these were trifling matters. For the swaddling bands, the manger, the circumcision, the feeding with milk, seemed to you as unworthy of God. Again, you saw somebody without human nourishment for forty days and forty nights, whilst angels ministered and you shuddered at their presence, though first you saw him baptized as a common human being, whilst knowing not the cause. But you took courage again after the fast, when he was hungry, and tempted him like a common human being, not knowing his identity. For you said, "If you are the Son of God, say that these stones should become bread." This "if you are" betrays ignorance; had you any true knowledge you would be aware that the Creator is equally capable of making something which does not exist already and changing something which exists already. And, through hunger, you tempted the one who gives nourishment to all who need to be fed, and you tempted the Lord of glory, as in your malice you forgot that a person should not live from bread alone but from every word proceeding through the mouth of God. For had you known that he was the Son of God you would have recognized that one who kept his body free of want for forty days and an equal number of nights was capable of doing so indefinitely. Why then was he hungry? So that he might demonstrate that he had, in truth, taken a body subject to the same human feelings. By the first means he demonstrated that he was God, through the second that he was human.

[20]Cf. Ign. *Eph.* 19.2.

10   Did you, who fell like lightning from the most exalted glory, dare to say to the Lord: "Throw yourself down from here," speaking to the one for whom things that exist are reckoned as though they did not, and provoking one without ostentation into vainglory? And you pretended to read the Scripture concerning him: "Because I will put him into the charge of the angels, and they will bear you up on their hands, so that you do not dash your foot against a stone"? And you pretended to be ignorant about the rest, concealing what was prophesied regarding you and your attendants: "You shall walk over the adder and the basilisk, and you shall tread down the lion and the dragon."

11   Now if you are a path for the feet of the Lord, how could you tempt the untemptable, forgetting what was demanded by the law-giver, that "you shall not put the Lord your God to the test"?[21] But you dared, most accursed one, to appropriate the works of God to yourself and to state that the authority over them had been delivered to you.[22] And you enticed the Lord to a downfall like your own,[23] and promised to grant him what was his own, if he fell to the ground to worship you. And how did you not shudder at addressing the Master in such a tone, most wicked of wicked spirits in your malevolence? You were overcome through your appetite and you were dishonored through your vainglory. Through love of money and love of power you draw others on to impiety. You, Beliar, apostate dragon, twisted serpent, distant from God, separated from Christ, alien to the Holy Spirit, exiled from the company of angels, resister of the laws of God, adversary of all that is lawful, taking your stand against the first formed people, distant from the commandment, harming the one who never did you injustice, who set the homicidal Cain against Abel, who took up arms against Job, do you say to the Lord, "If you fall down to worship me?" Such effrontery! Such madness! Runaway

[21]Deut 6.16.
[22]Luke 4.6.
[23]Lightfoot, *Apostolic Fathers* 2.3, 199, observes here a similar passage in Eusebius, *Preparation for the Gospel*, 7.16.

slave, worthless slave, do you rebel against the worthy Master? To such a Master, to the God of all thoughts and feelings, do you say, "If you fall down to worship me"?

12   The Lord is very patient, and does not reduce to nothing the one who in ignorance was so defiant, but gently replies: "Satan, depart."[24] He did not say "get behind me," for he is incapable of conversion, but "Satan, depart" to the ways you have chosen, depart to whatever you have incited in malevolence. For I know who I am, and by whom I have been sent, and I am aware whom I should worship. For, it says "you shall worship the Lord your God, and him alone should you serve."[25] I know the one, I have knowledge of the unique one from whom you have distanced yourself. I am not God's opponent, I confess his pre-eminence, and I do not shrink from worshipping the one whom I know, the cause of my own begetting, for "I live through the Father."[26]

13   I have felt compelled to send this to you, brothers, through the affection which I have for you. I have encouraged you to the glory of God, not as though I were a somebody, but as a brother. Be subject to the bishop, to the presbyters, to the deacons. Love one another in the Lord as images of God. Husbands see that you love your wives as your own members. Wives, love your husbands as you are one with them through your union. Anyone who is continent or chaste should not be exalted, so that he does not lose his reward. Do not disparage the festivals, do not ignore the forty days, for they comprise an imitation of the Lord's conduct. After the week of the passion, do not overlook the fasting on the fourth day and the Friday, distributing your surplus to the poor. Anyone who fasts on the Lord's day or the Sabbath, apart from the one Sabbath,[27] is a Christ-killer.

[24]Mt 4.10.

[25]Mt 4.10; Deut 6.13.

[26]Jn 6.57. The first part of this phrase is hopelessly corrupt.

[27]Namely the Saturday of Great Week.

14 May your prayers reach the church of Antioch, from which I am being led off to Rome as a prisoner. I greet the saintly bishop Polycarp. I greet the saintly bishop Vitalius, and the sacred presbytery, and my fellow-slaves the deacons. I am become a sacrifice for them, because they are subject to the bishop and to the presbyters in the Lord. Anyone who keeps the Pascha with the Jews, and receives the tokens of their feast, is a companion of those who murdered the Lord and his apostles.

15 The deacons Philo and Agathopus greet you. I greet the company of virgins and the order of widows, in whom I delight. I greet the people of the Lord, the least and the greatest. I send you these writings through Euphanius the reader, who is honored by God and is very faithful. I met him by Rhegium, as he was getting into the boat. Remember my chains, that I may be perfected in Christ. Fare well in the flesh, in the soul, in the spirit, thinking of perfection, rejecting all workers of lawlessness and anyone who corrupts the word of truth, and be empowered in the grace of our Lord Jesus Christ.

Philadelphians

The Ignatian letter to the Philadelphians centres on the importance of the unity of the Christian assembly gathered around the bishop. In the hands of the interpolator the letter becomes even more an appeal for unity and peace on the basis of the recognition of a single bishop and a single Eucharist, as the church worships one Lord, an appeal with a degree of forlorn sadness when faced with the reality of a divided Antiochene church.

IGNATIUS TO THE PHILADELPHIANS:

Ignatius, who is also God-carrier, to the church of God the Father and the Lord Jesus Christ which is in Philadelphia of Asia, which has received mercy and is established in the agreement of God and which rejoices in the passion of our Lord without distinction, as in his resurrection, which is fully satisfied in all mercy, which I greet in the blood of Jesus Christ, which is an eternal and lasting joy, especially if they are at one with the bishop and those with him, the presbyters and deacons who are appointed by the will of God the Father through the Lord Jesus Christ, who in accordance with his own will set them in place firmly, the church upon a rock, a spiritual building not made with hands, which the swirling winds and rivers were unable to overthrow[1]—indeed may spiritual forces of wickedness never prevail, rather let them be enfeebled through the power of Jesus Christ our Lord.

[1] Cf. Mt 7.25.

1   ₁Looking upon your bishop I am aware that he was not selected to have entrusted to him the ministry to the community which is his from himself, nor through any human agency, nor on account of vainglory, but in the love of Jesus Christ and God the Father who raised him from the dead. I have been astonished by his fairness, as being silent he can achieve more than those who speak. ₂For he is attuned to the commandments of the Lord and to his ordinances like the strings to a harp, and is no less blameless than Zachariah the priest. So my soul blesses his understanding of God, knowing it to be virtuous and perfect, together with his calm and composed nature, in all fairness, deriving from the living God.

2   Therefore, as children of the light of truth, avoid the division of your unity and the evil teachings of the heretics, from whom "a defiling influence has gone forth on all the earth."[2] Where the shepherd is, there you, the sheep, should follow. ₂For many wolves, wrapped in fleeces, imprison, by means of wicked pleasure, those who go the way of God, but in your unity shall they have no place.

3   Therefore stay away from the wicked plants, those which Jesus Christ does not cultivate, but the homicidal beast, since they are not a planting of the Father but a seed of the evil one. Not because I have found division among you do I write, but to set you on guard in advance as children of God. ₂Those who are of Christ are with the bishop, but those who incline away from him, and embrace the communion of the accursed, will be pruned away with them, for they are not the cultivation of Christ but the seed of the enemy. May you always be rescued through the prayers of the shepherd who is set at your head, who is most faithful and most gentle. Therefore I exhort you in the Lord to receive with all gentleness those who are repentant and who come into the unity of the church, that through your kindness and your goodness they will escape the devil's trap, becoming worthy of Jesus Christ, attaining eternal salvation in the

[2]Jer 23.15.

kingdom of Christ. ₃Do not be deceived, brothers. Anyone who follows the one who separates from the truth shall not inherit the kingdom of God. And anyone who does not distance himself from the preacher of falsehood shall be condemned to Gehenna. One should neither distance oneself from the godly, nor should one consort with the ungodly. Anyone who acts in accordance with an alien opinion is not of Christ, and is not a participant in his passion, but is a fox, a trampler of Christ's vineyard.[3] Have no relations with anyone like this, so that you do not perish together, even if he is your father, your son, your brother, or a member of your family. For it says: "Your eye shall not spare him."[4] You should therefore hate those who hate God[5] and waste away on account of his enemies. I do not mean that you should beat them or persecute them, as do the Gentiles who "know not the Lord and God,"[6] but you should consider them your enemies and keep away from them, whilst warning them and exhorting them to repentance, as it is possible that they may hear, and possible that they may submit themselves. For our God is a lover of humanity, and desires that "all people should be saved and should come to knowledge of the truth."[7] So "he causes the sun to rise on the wicked and the good, and sends rain on the just and the unjust."[8] Desiring that we should be imitators of his kindness the Lord says: "Be perfect, just as your heavenly Father is perfect."[9]

4 In the Lord I am confident in you, that you would think no other way. Therefore I have taken courage to write to your God-worthy love, exhorting you to celebrate one faith and one proclamation and one Eucharist. For there is one flesh of the Lord Jesus and his blood, which is poured out for us, is one. There is one bread which is broken for all, and one cup which is shared with the whole congregation.

[3]Cf. Song 2.15.
[4]Deut 6.13, 18.
[5]Cf. Ps 138 (139).21.
[6]1 Thess 4.5.
[7]1 Tim 2.4.
[8]Mt 5.45.
[9]Mt 5.48.

There is one altar for the entire church, and one bishop together with the presbytery and the deacons, my fellow-slaves. Since, also, there is but one who is unbegotten Being, one God and Father, and one only-begotten Son, God, the Word and human being, and one Paraclete, the Spirit of truth. And one proclamation, and one faith, and one baptism, and one church which the sainted apostles founded from one end of the earth to the other, in the blood of Christ and through the sweat of their own brows and their labor. And you should therefore be a "people set apart" and "a holy nation,"[10] in agreement in doing everything in Christ.

Wives, be subject to your husbands in the fear of God, and you virgins to Christ, in incorruption, not despising marriage, but desiring that which is better, not to reject wedlock, but for the sake of meditating on the law. Children, show obedience to your parents, and love them as fellow-workers with God in your birth. Slaves, be subject to your masters in God so that you may be the freedmen of Christ. Husbands, love your wives, as co-slaves of God, as your own body, as companions in life, and your co-workers in the procreation of children. Virgins, have Christ alone before your eyes, and His Father in your souls, being enlightened by the Spirit. May I delight in your sanctity, like that of Elijah, of Joshua son of Nave, of Melchizedek, of Elisha, of Jeremiah, of John the Baptist, of the beloved disciple, of Timothy, of Titus, of Euodius, of Clement, each of whom departed this life in chastity.[11] I do not blame the other blessed ones for contracting marriages, of which I was just speaking. For I pray that, being found worthy of God, I may follow their footsteps into the kingdom, following Abraham, and Isaac, and Jacob, and Joseph and Isaiah and the other prophets, and Peter and Paul[12] and the other apostles who contracted marriages.

[10]1 Pet 2.9.

[11]Chastity is attributed to a number of these figures in the pseudo-Clementine *On Virginity* 1.6. This work of Clement may be the basis for the attribution of chastity to Clement himself. Of Euodius nothing is known, so this may be a guess on the part of the pseudonymous author.

[12]Clearly 1 Cor 9.5, Phil 4.3 have been misread.

They did not do so out of desire, but did so with a mind to the human race. Fathers, raise your children in discipline and direction to the Lord,[13] and teach them the sacred Scriptures, as well as trades, so that they should not rejoice in idleness. For it says: "A righteous father raises his children well, and in an understanding son will his heart rejoice."[14] Masters, act kindly towards your servants, as the sainted Job taught.[15] For there is one nature and one race of humanity. For "in Christ there is neither slave nor free."[16] The governors should show obedience to Caesar, the soldiers to their commanders, deacons to the presbyters, presbyters to the high priests. And the deacons and the rest of the clergy, as well as all the people, and the soldiers and the governors and Caesar to the bishop. The bishop is to Christ as is Christ to the Father. And so unity is preserved throughout. The widows should not wander about, nor be inquisitive, nor gadabouts,[17] but should be like the most serious Judith, or like Anna, profoundly reverent. Not as an apostle do I lay any of this down, for "Who am I, or what is my father's house?"[18] that I should suppose myself to be equal to them in honor, but in the rank of your fellow soldier do I call out to you.

5 [1]My brothers, in loving you I am overflowing greatly, and rejoicing exceedingly I safeguard you. Rather, not I, but the Lord Jesus through me. Although I am bound in him my fear is greater, as I am still incomplete. But your prayer to God will complete me, so that I may attain to the lot which I have received in mercy, as I flee to the gospel as to the flesh of Jesus and the apostles as to the presbytery of the church. [2]And I also love the prophets, as those who proclaimed Christ, as partakers of the same Spirit as the apostles. For as the false prophets and the false apostles inhaled one and the same wicked

[13]Eph 6.4.
[14]Prov 23.24.
[15]Job 31.13, 15. See also *Antiochenes* 10.
[16]Gal 3.28.
[17]On wandering widows see *Didascalia/Apostolic Constitutions* 3.6
[18]1 Sam 18.18.

and beguiling and deceptive spirit, the prophets and the apostles received from God, through Jesus Christ, one and the same Spirit, good and sovereign, true and instructive, a straightforward spirit. For there is one God of the old and the new testament. There is "one mediator of God and humanity,"[19] one creation of intelligent and sentient beings, a beneficent and suitable providence. And there is one Paraclete, which operated in Moses and the prophets and the apostles.Therefore all the saints are saved in Christ, hoping in him and awaiting him. And through him they attained to salvation, as they were saints deserving of love and deserving of admiration, receiving the testimony of Jesus Christ in the gospel of the hope we hold in common.

6   [1]Anyone who should proclaim that the God of the law and the prophets is one, whilst denying that Jesus Christ is God, is a liar, as also his father the devil. And anyone like this, with the circumcision of below, is a false Jew. If anyone confesses that Jesus Christ is Lord, denying the God of the law and the prophets, saying that the maker of heaven and earth is not the Father of Jesus, such a person is not standing in the truth, as also his father the devil. Such a person is a disciple of Simon the Magus, not of the Holy Spirit. If anyone speaks of one God, and confesses Jesus Christ, considering the Lord to be simply human, and not the only-begotten God,[20] and the Word and Wisdom of God, but considers him to be a soul and body, such a person is a serpent, proclaiming deceit and error for human destruction. Anyone like this is poor in understanding, as his name, Ebion, indicates.[21] If anyone confesses these things, yet calls lawful intercourse and the begetting of children destruction and pollution, or certain foods abominations, such a person has the apostate dragon dwelling within. If anyone confesses the Father and the Son and the Holy Spirit and praises the creation, yet states that the

[19]1 Tim 2.5; cf. Ign. *Tars.* 4.
[20]So the mss; perhaps "of God" would be better?
[21]The name "Ebion" is here derived from the Hebrew word for "poor," in common with, e.g., Eusebius *Ecclesiastical History* 3.27.6.

embodiment and the passion are shameful, such a person is denying the faith no less than the Christ-killing Jews. If anyone confesses
these things, and also that God the Word was dwelling in a human
body, the Word being within him like a soul within a body, because
God was indwelling, and not a human soul, yet says that unlawful
intercourse is good, and holds that the goal of happiness is pleasure,
like the falsely-named Nicolaitans,[22] such a person can be neither
a lover of God nor a lover of Christ, but is a corruptor of his own
flesh and thus is empty of the Holy Spirit, and a stranger to Christ.
All such persons are headstones and tombs for the dead, on which
simply human names are written. ₂Therefore flee the evil arts and the
snares of the spirit which is now operating in the sons of this age, so
that you are not weakened in your love through his oppression. But
all of you should stand in agreement with an undivided heart and a
willing soul, "being of one mind and of one judgement,"[23] holding
always the same opinions regarding the same matters, at ease and in
danger, in woes and in delights.

₃I thank God through Jesus Christ that I am of a clear conscience
in regard to you, and that nobody has cause to boast, whether privately or publicly, that I weighed anyone down in any matter, small
or great, and I pray that all with whom I conversed should not find
it a witness against themselves.

7 For even if some people desired to deceive me in the flesh, my
spirit is not deceived, for it comes from God, for it knows whence it
came and where it is going, and it exposes what is hidden.[24] Amongst
you I cried out, I spoke with a great voice, not my own voice but
that of God: "Give mind to the bishop and to the presbytery and to
the deacons." There were some who suspected me of having learnt
beforehand of the division among you when I said this, but the one
in whom I am bound bears witness to me that I knew this not from

[22]See the note on this subject at ps-*Trallians* 11.
[23]Phil 2.2.
[24]Cf. Jn 3.8; 1 Cor 2.10.

any human mouth but the Spirit was proclaiming in speaking thus. "Do nothing apart from the bishop, keep your flesh as a temple of God, love unity, shun divisions, be imitators of Paul and the other apostles, as they were of Christ."

8   I, therefore, was acting of my own accord as a person fixed on unity. And I add this, God does not dwell where there is difference of opinion and anger and hatred. God forgives all who repent if they come together in the unity of Christ and the council of the bishop. I have faith in the grace of Jesus Christ, because he will release you from all your chains of unrighteousness. I exhort you: do nothing in a discordant manner, but in accordance with the teaching of Christ. For I heard some saying "If I do not find it in the archives, I do not believe it in the gospel." To such as these I say that for me the archives are Jesus Christ, and it is evidently destruction to disobey him. To me the sacred archive is his cross and death and his resurrection and the faith which bears on these things, by which I desire, by your prayer, to be made righteous. Whoever disbelieves the gospel disbelieves everything along with it. For the archives ought not to be preferred to the Spirit. "It is hard to kick against the goad,"[25] it is hard to disbelieve Christ, it is hard to reject the proclamation of the apostles.

9   ₁Whereas the priests are good, as well as the ministers of the Word, better is the high priest who is entrusted with the holy of holies, who alone is entrusted with the secrets of God. The ministering powers of God are good. The Paraclete is holy, and the Word is holy, the Son of the Father, through whom the Father made all things and watches over them all. He is the way which leads to the Father,[26] the rock,[27] the defensive wall, the key, the shepherd,[28] the sacrifice, the door of knowledge through which enter Abraham and

[25]Acts 26.14.
[26]Jn 14.6.
[27]1 Cor 10.4.
[28]Jn 10.11.

Isaac and Jacob, Moses and the entire company of prophets, and the pillars of the world, the apostles, and the bride of Christ for whom he poured out his own blood as a wedding gift so that he might redeem her. All these are of the unity of the one and only true God. ₂Yet there is something distinct in the gospel, the presence of the Savior, Our Lord Jesus Christ, his passion and the resurrection itself. The proclamation of the prophets, when they said: "Until he for whom it is laid aside shall come, and he is the expectation of the Gentiles,"[29] is fulfilled in the gospel. "Go out and teach all the nations, baptizing them in the name of the Father and of the Son and of the Holy Spirit."[30] All things together are good, the law, the prophets, the apostles, the whole company of those who believed through them, only if we love one another.

10 ₁Since, in accordance with your prayers and the compassion which you possess in Christ Jesus, it is reported to me that the church which is in Syrian Antioch is at peace, it would be fitting for you, as the church of God, to elect a bishop to be delegated as God's ambassador there, to gather with them in a common purpose and glorify the name of God. ₂Whoever is found worthy of such a ministry is happy in Jesus Christ, and being zealous you will yourselves be glorified in Christ. For you who desire to do this, for the name of God, this is not impossible, as the closer churches have already sent bishops, and others presbyters and deacons.

11 ₁Now regarding Philo, a man from Cilicia who has received a good testimony, who even now serves me in the Word of God, alongside Gaius and Agathopus, a chosen man, who follows me from Syria, bidding life farewell, who also bears witness to you, as indeed I thank God on behalf of you, because you received them, and the Lord will also receive you. May those who dishonored them

---

[29]Gen 49.10. The text is cited in a form different from LXX, though the same reading is found at *Apostolic Constitutions* 6.11 and 23.

[30]Mt 28.19.

be redeemed in the grace of Jesus Christ, who does not desire the death of a sinner but repentance.

₂The love of the brothers in Troas greets you. I write to you from there through Burrhus, who has been sent alongside me from the Ephesians and the Smyrneans as a pledge of honor. The Lord Jesus Christ will requite them; they hope in him in flesh, in soul, spirit, faith, love, concord. Fare well in Christ Jesus, who is our common hope, in the Holy Spirit.

Smyrneans

The particular concern of the authentic Ignatius in addressing this church was to warn of the dangers of Docetic teachers; the forger expands the warnings regarding Docetism. In picking up Ignatius' comments on episcopal order, moreover, he also takes time to discuss the relative place of imperial and ecclesiastical power, a more pressing reality in his day.

IGNATIUS TO THE SMYRNAEANS:

Ignatius, who is also God-carrier, to the church of God the most high Father and his beloved Son Jesus Christ, which has received mercy in every good gift, which is filled in faith and love, which is second to none in every good gift, which is most worthy of God and carries sanctification, which is in Smyrna of Asia, many greetings in the spotless Spirit and the Word of God.

1 ₁I glorify the God and Father of our Lord Jesus Christ who, through him, has given you such wisdom. I am aware that you have been equipped in an unmoving faith, just as if you were nailed to the cross of the Lord Jesus Christ in both flesh and spirit, settled in love in the blood of Christ, and fully, and truly, convinced with regard to our Lord Jesus Christ, the Son of God, the firstborn of all creation, God the Word, the only-begotten Son. He was of the race of David in the flesh, of Mary the virgin, baptized by John so that all righteousness might be fulfilled by him. ₂Living in a holy and sinless manner, he was nailed for us truly in the flesh, under Pontius Pilate and Herod the tetrarch, as we ourselves derive from him, from his divinely blessed passion, so that through the resurrection he could lift up the standard for his holy and faithful ones for ever, whether among Jews or among Gentiles, in the single body of his church.

2   For he suffered all this for our sake, and truly he suffered, and not in appearance, as also he was truly raised. And not, as some of the unbelievers, who are ashamed of the human creation and of the cross and of death itself, state, that in appearance and not in truth did he receive a body from the virgin and that he suffered in appearance. They forget the one who said: "The Word was made flesh,"[1] and, "Destroy this temple and in three days I shall raise it,"[2] and, "If I am lifted from the earth I shall draw all people to myself."[3] Therefore the Word dwelt in flesh indeed, for "Wisdom has built a house for herself."[4] The Word raised up its own temple on the third day, when it had been destroyed by the Jews who were hostile to Christ. The Word, when his flesh was lifted up, after the manner of the bronze serpent in the wilderness, drew all people to himself for their eternal salvation.

3   ₁Indeed I know that not only in being begotten and crucified he was in a body, but that even after the resurrection he was in the flesh, and I believe that it was so. ₂And when he came to those who were with Peter he said to them: "Reach out, touch me and see that I am no bodiless demon. For a spirit does not have flesh and bones, as you see that I have."[5] And he says to Thomas: "Put your finger into the mark of the nails, and put your hand out, putting it into my side." And straightaway they believed that he was the Christ. And so Thomas said to him: "My Lord and my God."[6] It was on this account that

[1] Jn 1.14.

[2] Jn 2.19.

[3] Jn 12.32.

[4] Prov 9.1.

[5] On the source for this saying see the note to Ignatius ad loc. It appears that ps-Ignatius has conformed it to Lk 24.39.

[6] Jn 20.27–28.

they too despised death and considered indignities and floggings even less. ₃Not only this, but after he had demonstrated to them that he was truly raised up, and not simply in appearance, he even ate together with them and drank with them throughout the entire forty days. And so it was, together with his flesh, that he was taken up by the one who had sent him, as they looked on, and with it he is coming again with glory and power. For the oracles say: "This Jesus who was taken up from you into the heaven will come in the same way as you saw him go into heaven."[7] If they say that he is to come without the body at the consummation of the age, how shall they see him whom they had pierced, and how mourn for themselves in recognizing him? For bodiless beings have neither form nor figure, nor, because of the simplicity of their nature, do they have the outline of an animal which is possessed of shape.

4 ₁I am encouraging you in these matters, beloved, whilst aware that you are in agreement. I am putting you on your guard in advance against the wild beasts in human guise. Not only should you turn away from them, but you should actually flee them. Simply pray for them, that somehow they might repent. ₂If the Lord was in the body in appearance, and was crucified in appearance, then I am chained up in appearance! Why indeed have I totally given myself up to death, to the fire, to the sword, to wild beasts? But it is not in appearance but in reality that I am bearing all this through Christ, so that I may suffer with him, while he empowers me; I have no such strength.

5 ₁Some, denying him out of ignorance, are advocates of falsehood rather than the truth. Neither the prophets, nor the law which is of Moses have persuaded them, nor even now, have either the gospel, or our own individual sufferings. ₂Indeed, they think the same regarding ourselves. For what does it benefit me if anyone praises me yet insults my Lord, not admitting that he bore flesh as

[7]Acts 1.11.

God? Whoever fails to say this denies him completely as one who bears a corpse. ₃There seems no reason to catalogue their names, which are faithless, indeed I would rather not bear them in mind until they repent.

6 ₁Let nobody be deceived. Anyone who does not believe that Christ lived in the flesh, and who does not confess his cross and his passion and his blood which is poured out for the salvation of the world, shall not attain to everlasting life, whether a king or a priest, or a ruler, or a private citizen, or a master, or a slave, or a man, or a woman. Let the one who can receive this, receive it. Let the one who can hear this, hear it.[8] Let position and honor and wealth puff up nobody, let dishonor or poverty put nobody to shame; faith in God and hope in Christ, the enjoyment of the good things to which we look forward, and love towards God and our neighbor are everything, for "You shall love the Lord your God with your whole heart, and your neighbor as yourself."[9] The Lord also said: "This is eternal life: to know the only true God, and Jesus Christ whom he sent."[10] And, "I give you a new commandment, that you love one another."[11] "The law and the prophets depend on these two commandments."[12] ₂Therefore take note of those whose opinions are false, how they hold that the Father of Christ is unknowable, how they are faithless and hostile towards each other. Love is of no interest to them, they pay no regard to what has been promised, they consider the present reality to be permanent, they overlook the commandments, they disregard the widow and the orphan, they despise those who suffer, they ridicule those who are in chains.

7 ₁They are ashamed of the cross, they scoff at the passion, they treat the resurrection as a joke. They are the offspring of the spirit

[8]Cf. Mt 19.12.
[9]Deut 6.5.
[10]Jn 17.31.
[11]Jn 13.34.
[12]Mt 22.40.

which is the source of evil, who led Adam away from the commandment, by means of his wife, who slew Abel, by means of Cain, who
took up arms against Job, who accused Joshua the son of Josedek,[13]
who sought to sift the faith of the apostles,[14] who stirred up the Jewish mob against the Lord, who even now "works among the children
of disobedience,"[15] from whom the Lord Jesus Christ will rescue us.
He prayed that the faith of the apostles should not fail, not because
he was unable himself to keep it safe, but because he rejoiced in the
Father's pre-eminence. ₂It is right, therefore, to keep away from such
people, and not to speak of them[16] either on one's own or in company, but to give heed to the law and the prophets and to those who
have given us the word of salvation in the gospel. Flee the offensive
heresies, and those who cause schisms, as the origin of evils.

8   ₁Follow the bishop, all of you, as Jesus Christ the Father, and
the presbytery as the apostles. Respect the deacons as those who
administer the commandment of God. Without the bishop, nobody
should do anything relating to the church. That Eucharist which is
under the bishop, or the one to whom he has entrusted it, should be
considered sound. ₂The congregation should be wherever the bishop
is, just as wherever Christ, the commanding general of the Lord's
power, and the agent of every intelligent nature, may be, the heavenly
host stands by. Apart from the bishop it is not permissible to baptize,
or to offer, or to present sacrifice, or to provide an entertainment, but
whatever you do, do whatever seems to him to be pleasing to God,
so that everything is secure and sound.

9   ₁Moreover, it is sensible that we should recover our sobriety
whilst we still have time to turn again to God. For "There is nobody
who can make a confession in Hades."[17] For "Look, there is the man,

[13]Zech 3.1.
[14]Cf. Luke 22.31.
[15]Eph 2.2.
[16]Some mss have "speak with them."
[17]Ps 6.5.

and his work is before his face."[18] And "My son, God and the king."[19] For myself I say, honor God indeed, as the origin of all things and the Lord, the bishop as the high-priest, as one who bears the image of God. Of God in terms of governance and, in terms of priesthood, of Christ. It is after this that we should honor the emperor. For there is nobody superior to God, or who even approaches him, among all the beings that exist. Nor is there anyone in the Church greater than the bishop, who ministers as a priest to God for the salvation of the whole world. Nor, again, is there anyone among rulers who approaches the emperor, who secures peace and good order to those over whom he rules. Whoever honors the bishop will be honored by God, just as anyone who disrespects him will be punished by God. For if anyone who rises up against emperors is justly held worthy of punishment, as one who undoes public order, of how much worse punishment, do you think, should anyone who presumes to do anything without the bishop, destroying concord and confusing good order, be held to deserve? For the priesthood is the very highest point of all that is good in the human realm; anyone who is crazy enough to oppose it is not disrespecting a [mere] human being but God, and Christ Jesus, the first-born, and the sole High Priest, by nature, of the Father. 2Therefore let everything undertaken by you be performed with good order in Christ. Let the laity be subject to the deacons, the deacons to the presbyters, the presbyters to the bishop, the bishop to Christ, even as he is to the Father. As you, brothers, have refreshed me, so will Jesus Christ do to you. In my absence and in my presence have you loved me. God will reward you, since for his sake you have shown such kindness towards his prisoner. For even if I am not worthy of it, yet your zeal is a great thing. For "whoever honors a prophet in the name of a prophet, shall receive a prophet's reward."[20] It is manifest also, that whoever honors a prisoner of Jesus Christ shall receive the reward of the martyrs.

[18]Is 62.11.
[19]Prov 24.21.
[20]Mt 10.41.

10 ₁You did well to receive Philo and Rheus and Agathopous, who have followed me in the Word of God, being deacons of Christ. They also give thanks greatly to the Lord for you because, in every manner, you refreshed them. Nothing of what you have done for them will fail to be accounted for. "May the Lord grant that you find mercy from the Lord on that day."²¹ ₂My spirit is your ransom, as are my chains, of which you showed neither haughtiness nor shame. So the perfect hope, Jesus the Christ, will not be ashamed of you.

11 ₁Your intercessions have come close to the church of the Antiochenes, and it is at peace. From there I came bound, where I greet everyone, not being worthy to be one of them, being the least of them. In accordance with the will of God, not in my own conscience but out of the good gift of God, I pray that I may receive the perfect gift, that I attain to God by your intercession. ₂It is fitting for the honor of God that your church appoint an ambassador for God, to go to Syria and rejoice with them, so shall your task therefore be perfected both on earth and in heaven. Because they are at peace and have taken back their proper greatness, and their proper constitution has been restored to them. ₃What seems to me worthy is this: that you send one of your own with a letter, so that he may rejoice with them in the tranquility which is theirs in God, and that I have attained a safe harbor, Christ, through your intercession. Being perfect, you should also give consideration to what is perfect. God is prepared to supply you who wish to do good.

12 ₁The love of the brothers who are in Troas greets you. I am writing to you from there through Burgus, whom you, together with your co-brothers, the Ephesians, sent alongside me. He has refreshed me in every way. Indeed, would that everyone imitated him as exemplary in the ministry of God. The grace of God will reward him in everything. ₂I greet your God-worthy bishop Polycarp, the presbytery which God approves, and the Christ-carrying deacons,

²¹2 Tim 1.18.

my fellow slaves, and everyone both individually and collectively in Jesus Christ, both in his flesh and in his blood, in his passion and resurrection both fleshly and spiritual, in the unity which is God's and yours. Grace to you, mercy, peace, endurance, at all times in Christ.

13   ₁I greet the households of my brothers together with their wives and children and the perpetual virgins and the widows. Fare well in the power of the Father. Philo, the fellow-deacon, who is with me, greets you. ₂I greet the household of Gavia, which I pray shall remain steadfast in faith and love, both fleshly and spiritual. I greet Alce, a name dear to me, and the incomparable Daphnus, and Eutecnus, and all by name. Fare well in the grace of God and our Lord Jesus Christ, being filled by the Holy Spirit and divine and sacred wisdom.

To Polycarp

The long recension of Ignatius' letter to Polycarp is little different from the original, the changes consisting solely of some slight expansions, including some scriptural citations.

Ignatius to Polycarp:

Ignatius, bishop of Antioch, who is also witness to Jesus Christ, to Polycarp, bishop of the church of the Smyrneans, or rather to him who has God the Father and the Lord Jesus Christ as bishop, abundance of happiness.

1   ₁Welcoming your outlook in God, fixed as upon an immovable rock, I rejoice all the more as I was found worthy to look upon your blameless character, in which, in God, I would delight. ₂I exhort you in the grace with which you are clothed, to progress in your course and to exhort everyone, so that they may be saved. Claim your proper place with every effort, both fleshly and spiritual. Give consideration to unity, for there is nothing better. Bear with all people, just as does the Lord with you. Tolerate everybody in love, as indeed you do already. ₃Be assiduous with constant intercession, asking for an understanding greater than you have. Be alert, in possession of an unsleeping spirit. Address everyone in conformity with the manner of God. Bear the diseases of all as a perfect athlete, like the Lord of all. For it says: "He himself took our weaknesses and he bore our diseases."[1] Where there is more labor, there is great gain.

[1]Mt 8.17.

2 ₁You obtain no merit if you love the good disciples; rather bring the more troublesome to order in compliance. Not every wound is healed by the same plaster; treat irritations with lotions. ₂In every matter be as wise as a serpent, and at all times as pure as a dove. It is for this reason, namely so that you can be gentle with what is apparent to you, that you are of soul and body, fleshly, as well as spiritual; yet pray that what is invisible may also be apparent to you, so that you lack nothing and overflow in every good gift. ₃The occasion is calling on you to pray; for just as the wind aids the helmsmen and as harbors grant safety to a storm-tossed vessel, so is the attainment of God to you. As God's athlete, be wary. Your desire[2] is incorruption and eternal life, of which you are already convinced. In everything I am your ransom, as are my chains, which you have loved.

3 ₁Do not let those who appear trustworthy and who teach strange doctrines browbeat you. Stand firm as an anvil when it is struck. It is a great athlete who is victorious whilst injured. We should endure everything particularly on behalf of God, so that he may be patient with us for the kingdom. ₂Add further to the eagerness which is already yours. Run with greater energy. Observe the occasions. Be victorious whilst you are here, for here is the course and there are the crowns. Look out for Christ, the Son of God, who, whilst timeless, is in time. Invisible by nature he is visible in flesh. Intangible and impalpable, like one who is bodiless, for our sake he could be handled, and was tangible in a body. Impassible as God he suffered for us as a human being. He endured in every manner on our account

4 ₁Do not let the widows be neglected; you are to be their caregiver, after the Lord. Let nothing be done without your consent, and do nothing yourself without regard to the mind of God, as indeed you do not. Be steadfast. ₂Let gatherings be closer, seek out everyone by name. ₃Do not look down on male or female slaves, yet do not

[2]*Thelema,* possibly a reading brought about through a corruption of *thema* (prize) in Ignatius.

let them become puffed up, but serve all the better for the glory of God, so that, from God, they may obtain a better freedom. And they should have no desire to be set free out of common funds, so that they may not be slaves of passion.

5 ₁Flee the evil arts, rather discuss them. Instruct my sisters to love the Lord and to be satisfied with their spouses in flesh and spirit. Similarly charge my brothers in the name of Jesus Christ to love their spouses as the Lord the church. ₂Anyone who is able to remain in purity for the honor of the flesh of the Lord should do so without boasting. Whoever boasts is destroyed. And if anyone apart from the bishop becomes aware of it, this is corrupted. It is proper for those men and women who are marrying to form their union with the consent of the bishop, so that their marriage may be in accordance with the Lord and not out of desire. Let everything be done for the honor of God.

6 ₁You all should give heed to the bishop, so that God may do so to you. I am a ransom for those who are subject to the bishop, the presbyters, deacons. May my lot be with them in God. Labor together with each other, struggle together, run together, suffer together, lie down together, be raised together as God's stewards, attendants and servants. ₂Be pleasing to the one in whose army you serve, from whom you also receive your wages. None of you should be found a deserter; let your baptism remain as weaponry, faith as a helmet, love as a spear, endurance as armor, your works as a downpayment on your wages, so that you may receive the back-pay worthy of God.[3] Therefore be patient with one another in gentleness, so that God may be with you. May I delight in you at all times.

7 ₁Since the church which is in Antioch in Syria is at peace, as has been made clear to me, through your intercession, I have become more content in a freedom from care which is of God, even should I

[3]See the note in the corresponding section of Ignatius' letter.

attain to God through suffering, so that I may be found to be a disciple in your request.[4] 2Polycarp, most blessed of God, it is fitting to convene a most God-befitting council and to elect somebody, whom you consider most beloved and resolute, who could be called God's runner. He should be held worthy of going to Syria, so that, when he goes to Syria, he may glorify your resolute love in the glory of God. 3A Christian does not have his own authority, but is devoted to God. This deed is God's and yours, when you accomplish it, for I trust in grace that you are ready for the good deeds which please God. Aware of your zeal for the truth I exhort you in a few lines.

8 1Since I have been unable to write to all the churches due my sudden sailing from Troas to Neapolis, as the will directs, you are to write to the churches which lie on this side as one in possession of God's purpose, and so they may do the same. Some will be able to send foot-messengers, others letters through those sent by you, so that you may be glorified by an eternal work, as you are worthy. 2I greet all by name, and the wife of Epitropus, together with her whole household and children. I greet my beloved Attalus. I greet the one who is to be found worthy of going to Syria. Grace will be with him at all times, as with Polycarp who sends him. 3I wish you to fare well at all times in our God Jesus Christ, in whom may you remain in the unity of God and in his oversight. I greet Alce, a name dear to me. Amen. Grace. Fare well in the Lord.

---

[4]Cf. Ignatius "in the resurrection." However, once again, this divergence between ps-Ignatius and Ignatius may be the result of a variant in the ms tradition, as *anastasei* in the original may have been misread as *aitesei*.

Antiochenes

*Like the letters to the Tarsians and to the Philippians, the pseudony-
mous letter to the Antiochenes is fundamentally concerned to set out
the doctrinal position of the forger. Here, in particular, he is concerned
to defend the superiority of the Father as God, even whilst maintaining
the full divinity of the Son. It is this concern which led to the suggestion
that he was an Arian, though Lightfoot rightly points out that such
statements may accord with Nicene orthodoxy,[1] and Funk cites texts
from Athanasius and Gregory Nazianzen to the same effect.[2] It may be
that those who perceive Arianism behind the statements of the forger
are attributing too great subtlety and theological insight to the writer;
the term "semi-Arian" is too imprecise to be useful, in that it navigates
the complex field of the fourth century with reference to Arius and in
that it lumps together a host of distinct positions, but it may, precisely
because of its imprecision, be a fitting label for ps-Ignatius! Alongside
the subordinationist theology, ps-Ignatius has hard words in this letter
for those who declare "that there is one God in order to remove the
divinity from Christ," words which may be seen as expressly opposed to
the position of Eunomius, whose confession, intended as reconciliatory,
starts with the assertion "We believe in the one and only true God," as
such clearly distinct from Christ.[3] More notable yet is the writer's concern to emphasize the Pauline heritage of the Antiochene church and of
Ignatius, as the teaching of Ignatius is found to be simply that of Paul.*

---

[1]Lightfoot, Apostolic Fathers 2.1, 269–70.
[2]Funk, 294.
[3]Eunomius *Confession* 2.

Ignatius to the Antiochenes:

Ignatius, who is also God-carrier, to the church which has received mercy from God, selected by Christ, dwelling in Syria, and first to receive the name of Christ, which is in Antioch, in God the Father and the Lord Jesus Christ, greetings.

1 The Lord has rendered my chains light and easy as I learn that you are at peace, that you are conducting yourself in all fleshly and spiritual concord.[4] I, therefore, a prisoner in the Lord, exhort you to walk in a manner worthy of the calling with which you were called,[5] guarding against those heresies of the evil one which have burst in on us, to the deception and destruction of those who believe in them. Give heed to the teaching of the apostles, and believe both the law and the prophets. Reject every Jewish and Greek error, and do not introduce a multiplicity of gods, nor deny Christ under the pretext of the singleness of God.

2 For Moses, the faithful servant of God, in saying "The Lord your God is one"[6] and thus proclaiming that there was only one God, straightaway confessed our Lord in saying, "The Lord rained fire and brimstone from the Lord upon Sodom and Gomorrah."[7] And again, "And God said, 'Let us make humanity after our image.' And so God made humanity, he made him after the image of God."[8] And further "In the image of God he made humanity."[9] And that he should be made human, he says, "The Lord shall raise up a prophet for you, from among your brothers, one like me."[10]

[4]Beyond the echo of Ignatius' own language here, there is a deliberate echo of a letter from Alexander of Jerusalem to the Antiochenes, preserved by Eusebius at *Ecclesiastical History* 6.11.

[5]Eph 4.1.
[6]Deut 6.4.
[7]Gen 19.24.
[8]Gen 1.26–7.
[9]Gen 5.1.
[10]Deut 18.15.

3 The prophets, speaking as in the person of God, tell of the Father of all: "I am God, the first, and I am also the last, and apart from me there is no God,"[11] also speak of our Lord Jesus Christ. "A son," it says, "has been given to us, whose origin is from above; and his name is called the angel of great counsel, wonderful, counsellor, the mighty God, the powerful one."[12] And concerning his incarnation, "Look, a virgin shall conceive, and will bear a son. And they will call his name Immanuel."[13] And concerning the passion, "He was led as a sheep to the slaughter; and was silent as a lamb before the shearers,"[14] and, "I was like an innocent lamb led to be sacrificed."[15]

4 The evangelists, too, stating that the Father was "the only true God,"[16] did not omit what concerned our Lord, but wrote: "In the beginning was the Word, and the Word was with God, and the Word was God. He was in the beginning with God. All things were made by him, and nothing that was made was made without him."[17] And concerning the incarnation: "The Word," it says, "became flesh, and dwelt among us."[18] And again: "The book of the generation of Jesus Christ, the son of David, the son of Abraham."[19] The apostles, stating that who said "that there is one God,"[20] themselves said "there is one mediator between God and humanity."[21] And they were not ashamed of the embodiment and the passion, for what does it say? "The human being Jesus Christ, who gave himself for the life of the world."[22]

[11]Is 44.6.
[12]Is 9.6.
[13]Is 7.14.
[14]Is 53.7.
[15]Jer 11.19.
[16]Jn 17.3.
[17]Jn 1.1.
[18]Jn 1.14.
[19]Mt 1.1.
[20]1 Cor 8.4, 6.
[21]1 Tim 2.5.
[22]1 Tim 2.5.

5 Whoever, therefore, declares that there is one God in order to remove the divinity from Christ is the son of the devil and an enemy of all righteousness.[23] Whoever confesses Christ, though not as the son of the maker of the world but of another unknown being, distinct from that which the law and prophets proclaimed, is an instrument of the same devil. And whoever rejects the incarnation, and is ashamed of the cross, on account of which I am in chains, is an antichrist. And whoever states that Christ is simply human is accursed, according to the prophet, putting trust "not in God but in a human being."[24] On this account, like the wild myrtle, he is unfruitful.

6 New olive-tree of Christ, I write this to you, not conscious of your having such thoughts, but putting you on your guard in advance, as a father would for his children. Therefore watch out for those who rush to work evil, the enemies of the cross of Christ, whose end is destruction, [whose god is the belly and] whose glory is in their shame." [25] Look out for the dumb dogs, the trailing serpents, the scaly dragons, the snakes, the basilisks, the scorpions. For these are vulpine jackals, apes which imitate humans.

7 You have been disciples of Paul and Peter; do not lose the deposit.[26] Remember Euodius,[27] your worthily-blessed pastor, who was first to have entrusted into his hands, from the apostles, your leadership. Let us not put the Father to shame, let us be legitimate children, and not bastards. You know the manner in which I acted

[23]This statement may be seen as aimed against the extreme Arian position of Eunomius. Diekamp, *Patres apostolici* 2, 216, interestingly observes Eunomius' own comment on the text cited above, Jn 17.3, at his *Apology* 21, that there was no intention to deny the Son's divinity but rather to protect the sovereignty of the Father.

[24]Jer 17.5.

[25]Not all the mss contain the bracketed words within the quotation.

[26]Cf. 2 Tim 1.14.

[27]Euodius, certainly an early Christian leader in Antioch, is claimed as first bishop of Antioch after Peter by Eusebius (*Ecclesiastical History* 3.22). The *Apostolic Constitutions*, interestingly, suggest that Ignatius and Euodius were both bishops of Antioch, Ignatius ordained by Paul and Euodius by Peter.

when I was with you; that which I said to you when I was present I now write to you in my absence. "If anyone does not love the Lord Jesus, let that person be anathema."[28] "Be my imitators."[29] I desire to be your ransom, when I attain to Jesus. "Remember my chains."[30]

8   Presbyters, shepherd the flock which is among you,[31] until God shows who is to rule you. For I am already poured out, so that I may gain Christ. Deacons should know the nature of their dignity, and let them strive to be blameless, so that they may be imitators of Christ. The people should be subject to the presbyters and the deacons. The virgins should know the one to whom they have consecrated themselves.

9   Husbands, be content with your spouses, recalling that, at the creation, one woman was given to one man, not many women to one man. Wives should honor their husbands as their own flesh, nor should they dare address them by their names.[32] They should be temperate, reckoning their spouses, to whom they are united in God's will, as their only menfolk. Parents, train your children with sacred training. Children, honor your parents, "so that all be well with you."[33]

10   Masters, do not act arrogantly towards your slaves, remembering what the patient Job said: "If I were to disregard my manservant or my maid when they judged me, what should I do if the Lord takes issue with me?"[34] And you know what follows. Slaves, do not

[28] 1 Cor 16.22.
[29] 1 Cor 4.16.
[30] Col 4.18.
[31] 1 Pet 5.2.
[32] Cf. *Apostolic Constitutions* 6.29: You wives, be subject to your own husbands, and have them in esteem, and serve them with fear and love, as the sainted Sarah honoured Abraham. For she could not endure to call him by his name, but called him lord, when she said, "My lord is old."
[33] Cf. Eph 6.2–3.
[34] Job 31.13–14.

enrage your masters in anything, lest you cause yourselves irreversible evil.

11 Anyone who is idle should not eat, lest he become a runaway and a whoremonger. Drunkenness, anger, envy, shouting, abuse, and blasphemy should not even be mentioned among you.[35] Widows should not live in indulgence, so that they do not misbehave against the word.[36] Be subject to Caesar in anything in which there is no peril in subjection. Do not provoke those who rule to anger, so that you give no occasion to those who seek after it. It is superfluous to write about magic, or pederasty, or murder, when even the Gentiles are forbidden such practices. I am not commanding you this like an apostle,[37] but as your fellow slave I am reminding you.

12 I greet the holy presbytery. I greet the sacred deacons, and that name precious to me whom, in the Holy Spirit, I perceive in my place when I attain to Christ, whose ransom I may be. I greet the subdeacons, readers, singers, doorkeepers, those who labor,[38] exorcists, confessors. I greet the keepers of the holy gates, the deaconesses in Christ.[39] I greet the virgins betrothed to Christ, in whom, in the Lord Jesus, may I delight. I greet the most serious-minded widows. I greet the people of the Lord from the least to the greatest, and all my sisters in the Lord.

13 I greet Cassian, and his spouse, and their most dear children. Polycarp, the bishop, worthy of honor, greets you. He is concerned

[35]Eph 5.3.

[36]Cf. 1 Tim 5.11.

[37]Cf. Ign. *Rom.* 4.3.

[38]This may well be a reference to the gravediggers, known, simply, as "laborers."

[39]Lightfoot, *Apostolic Fathers* 2.1, 264., takes this as meaning that the deaconesses are to act as doorkeepers, pointing out a parallel in *Apostolic Constitutions* 2.57 and 8.28. This is possible, as it is also possible that *Apostolic Constitutions*, which in the first passage it is clear that the deaconesses keep the women's doors, is the source. It is also possible that neither has any experience of a deaconess's ministry.

for you, and to him have I commended you in the Lord. Indeed the whole church of the Smyrneans remembers you in their prayers in the Lord. Onesimus, the pastor of the Ephesians, greets you. Damas, the bishop of Magnesia, greets you. Polybius of the Trallians greets you. Philo and Agathopous, the deacons who are companions to me, greet you. Greet one another with a holy kiss.

14 I write this to you from Philippi. May the one who alone is unbegotten, through the one begotten before the ages, preserve you in spirit and flesh, and may I see you in the kingdom of Christ. I greet the one who is to rule in my place, in whom I delight in Christ. Fare well in God and Christ, as you are illuminated by the Holy Spirit.

To Hero

This letter is addressed to Ignatius' successor in Antioch, the deacon Hero. Whilst largely a patchwork of material from Ignatius' letter to Polycarp combined with material from the Pastoral Epistles, it is of interest nonetheless in that it seems to point to the nature of Antiochene succession, namely that the succession should be from within the city and that the senior deacon, rather than a presbyter or bishop from elsewhere, should properly accede to the episcopal throne. In doing so it also sets out the ideals of orthodoxy, purity, and humility for an Antiochene bishop, against the political realities which marked the experience of the forger.

Ignatius to Hero:

Ignatius, who is also God-carrier, to the God-honored and much missed Christ-carrier and spirit-carrier, my own son in faith and love,[1] Hero, a deacon of Christ, servant of God. Grace, mercy, and peace from God almighty and Jesus Christ our Lord, his only-begotten Son, who gave himself on account of our sins to deliver us from this present world of evil[2] and saves us for his own heavenly kingdom.

1 I exhort you to progress in your course and to vindicate your dignity.[3] Be mindful of harmony with all the saints. Support those who are weaker, so that you fulfil the law of Christ.[4] Devote yourself

[1] Cf. 1 Tim 1.2.
[2] Gal 1.4.
[3] Cf. Ign. *Pol.* 1.2.
[4] Gal 6.2.

to fasting and prayer, but not in an unbalanced manner, so that you undo yourself. Do not abstain altogether from wine and meat, for they are not abominations. For, it says, "Eat the good things of the earth,"[5] and, "You shall eat meat, just as vegetables,"[6] and, "Wine gladdens the human heart and oil cheers it and bread strengthens it."[7] But do this in a measured and orderly fashion, as these are supplied by God. For "who shall eat and who shall drink without him"[8] "because if something is noble, it is of him, and if anything is good, it is of him."[9] Give attention to reading[10] so that you may not only know the laws yourself, but will explain them to others. As God's athlete, be wary.[11] "Nobody who is at war is entangled with the affairs of this life, so that he can please the one who has chosen him as a soldier. And if somebody struggles, he is not crowned, unless he competes in accordance with the laws."[12] I am a prisoner on account of your ransom.[13]

2   Anyone who speaks beyond what is laid down, even if he seems highly trustworthy, even if he fasts, even if he is celibate, even if he performs miracles, even if he prophesies, he should be viewed as a wolf in sheep's clothing,[14] laboring for the destruction of the sheep.[15] If anyone denies the cross and is ashamed of the passion, he should be considered as the adversary. Even if he feeds the poor with his goods, even if he moves mountains, even if he gives his body to be burned, he should be treated as an abomination. If anyone belittles the law or the prophets which Christ came to fulfill, he should be

[5] Is 1.19.
[6] Gen 9.3.
[7] Ps 103 (104).15.
[8] Eccl 2.25.
[9] Zech 9.17. Cf. to all this *Apostolic Constitutions* 7.20. Extreme asceticism might be seen as an indication of heresy.
[10] 1 Tim 4.13.
[11] Ign. *Pol.* 2.3.
[12] 2 Tim 2.4.
[13] Cf. Ign. *Eph.* 21.1.
[14] Mt 7.15.
[15] Cf. Ign. *Pol.* 3.1.

held as the antichrist. If anyone states that the Lord was simply a human being, he is a Christ-killing Jew.

3   Honor those widows who are truly widows,[16] be a supporter of orphans, for God is the father of orphans and the judge of widows.[17] Do nothing without the bishops, for they are priests, and you are the deacon of the priests. They baptize, they offer the sacrifice, they ordain, they lay on hands. You are to serve them, as Saint Stephen in Jerusalem with regard to James and the presbyters. Do not neglect the assemblies. Enquire after everyone by name.[18] Do not allow anyone to look down on your youth, but be an example for the faithful, both in word and in conduct.[19]

4   Do not look down on domestic servants,[20] for we have a common nature with them. Do not consider women abominable, for they gave birth to you and fed you. Therefore it is right that we should love those who brought your birth about, though only in the Lord. A man can have no children without a woman, so therefore we must honor those who co-operated in our begetting. Apart from those first formed, "neither a man without a woman nor a woman without a man."[21] For the body of Adam was derived from the four elements, whereas Eve was from Adam's side. The remarkable birth of the Lord, from the virgin alone, was not because lawful intercourse is abominable, but this was a birth fitting to God. For it was becoming for the Creator not to employ the customary means of generation, but one remarkable and strange, as befits the Creator.

5   Avoid haughtiness, for "the Lord resists the proud."[22] Abhor falsehood, for, "you will destroy all who utter falsehood." Be on your

---

[16]1 Tim 5.3.
[17]Cf. Ps 67 (68).5.
[18]Cf. Ign. *Pol.* 4.2.
[19]1 Tim 4.12.
[20]Cf. Ign. *Pol.* 4.3.
[21] 1 Cor 11.11.
[22]Prov 3.34.

guard against envy, for its originator is the devil and his successor Cain, who envied his brother and out of envy committed murder. Encourage my sisters to love God and to be content with their own husbands. Likewise encourage my brothers to be content with their spouses. Keep guard over the virgins, as Christ's treasures. Be long-suffering, so that you may be great in wisdom.[23] Do not be forgetful of the poor, insofar as you enjoy prosperity. For sins are wiped away through almsgiving and fidelity.

6 Keep yourself pure, as God's habitation. You are the temple of Christ, you are the instrument of the Spirit. You know the manner in which I have raised you. Even though I am the least, be my emulator. Imitate my conduct. I do not boast in the world, but in the Lord. I am encouraging Hero, my child; but whoever boasts should boast in the Lord.[24] May I delight in you, longed-for son. May your guardian be the sole unbegotten God and the Lord Jesus Christ. Do not trust everyone, do not have confidence in everyone, lest anyone overcome you through soft words. The servants of Satan are many, and whoever trusts speedily is slight in heart.[25]

7 Have God in mind, and you shall never sin. Do not be double-minded in your prayer, for whoever does not doubt is blessed. For I believe in the Father of the Lord Jesus Christ and in his only-begotten Son, whom God will show me, Hero, upon my throne. Therefore, progress in your course. I charge you before the God of all things and before Christ, in the presence of the Holy Spirit and the ministering ranks: guard my deposit, which I, and Christ, have entrusted to you, and do not judge yourself unworthy of what has been shown to be by God regarding you. I hand the church of Antioch to you. I have commended you to Polycarp in the Lord Jesus Christ.

[23]Prov 14.29.
[24]1 Cor 1.31; 2 Cor 10.17,
[25]Sir 19.4.

8 Onesimus, Vitus,[26] Damas, Polybius, the bishops, and all those in Philippi, from where I am addressing you, greet you in Christ. Greet the God-worthy presbytery. Greet my sainted fellow-deacons, in whom I delight in Christ, in flesh and in spirit. Greet the people of the Lord by name, from the least to the greatest. I commend them to you, as did Moses to Joshua, who was their leader after him. And do not let what I have said seem burdensome to you, for even if we are not as they were, we may nonetheless pray to become so, since we are also the children of Abraham. Therefore, Hero, be strong, heroic and manful. For henceforth you will lead in and lead out[27] the people of the Lord in Antioch, and the congregation of the Lord shall not be like sheep who have no shepherd.[28]

9 Greet my host, Cassian, and his serious-minded spouse, and their dearest children. May God grant that they find the Lord's mercy in that day[29] because of their service to us. Greet by name all the faithful in Christ who are in Laodicea. Do not neglect those in Tarsus, but keep a careful eye on them, establishing them in the gospel. I salute Maris, bishop in Neapolis near Zarbus. Also speak to the serious-minded Mary, my most learned daughter, and the church which is at her household.[30] May I be a ransom for her, a pattern for pious women. May the Father of Christ, through his only-begotten Son, preserve you in good health, and of good reputation in everything, to a great age for the benefit of the church of God. Fare well in the Lord, and pray that I may be perfected.

[26]Cf. Ign. *Phil.* 14, where the name is given as Vitalius.
[27]Deut 31.7, 23.
[28]Num 27.17. From instructions given to Joshua.
[29]2 Tim 1.18.
[30]On this name, and that of Maris, bishop, preceding, note the pseudonymous correspondence between Ignatius and the same Mary above.

Ephesians

In writing to the Ephesians Ignatius was concerned about false teaching in the Ephesian churches. In the hands of the interpolator these warnings about false teaching, and the positive message which Ignatius gives regarding the nature of Jesus, are strengthened and reinforced, as well as being updated. Particularly noteworthy are the statements about false shepherds, which would resonate in a church in which no fewer than three persons claimed to be bishop.

IGNATIUS TO THE EPHESIANS:

Ignatius, who is also God-carrier, to the church blessed in greatness by the fullness of God the Father, which was foreordained before the ages to possess at all times a glory that is enduring and unchanging, which is united and elected in true suffering, by the will of the Father and of our Lord Jesus Christ, our Savior, the church that is worthy of good fortune, which is in Ephesus of Asia, warmest greetings in a blameless joy.

1   ₁I have received your much-desired name in God, which you have obtained through your just nature, in accordance with the faith and love in Christ Jesus, our Savior. You are imitators of the love of God towards humanity; rekindling in the blood of Christ the task we share, you have brought it to perfection. ₂For when you heard that I was coming, in chains, from Syria on account of Christ, our common hope, and that I trusted, through your intercession, to have the chance to fight wild beasts in Rome, so that through martyrdom I might be able to become a disciple of the one who offered himself

on our account, as an offering and sacrifice to God,[1] you were keen to see me.[2] ₃Since, therefore, I have, in Onesimus, who is in a love beyond telling, your bishop in the flesh, received your fullness in the name of God, I pray, in Jesus Christ, that you love him and that you should all be of his likeness. For blessed is God who has given you the grace, being as you are, to obtain such a bishop in Christ.

2   ₁Now concerning my fellow-slave Burrhus, your deacon in God, blessed in everything. I pray that he should remain spotless for the honor of the church and that of your most blessed bishop. And Crocus also, who is worthy of God and of you, whom I received as an embodiment of your love. He has revived me in every way, and so may the Father of Jesus Christ refresh him, as well as Onesimus and Burrhus and Euplus and Fronto, through whom I saw all of you, in accordance with love. ₂May I delight in you at all times, should I be worthy. Thus it is proper for you to give glory to Jesus Christ in every way, as he glorified you, so that you may be in a single subjection, "made complete in the same mind and the same opinion, and that you may all speak the same thing concerning him,"[3] being subject to the bishop and to the presbytery, so being hallowed in every way.

3   ₁I do not direct you as though I were a somebody. For even though I am in chains on account of the name, I have not yet been perfected in Jesus Christ. Only now am I at the beginning of my instruction, and I address you as my fellow-slaves. I am in need of your admonition with faith, with instruction, with patience, with longsuffering. ₂But since love does not permit me to be silent concerning you, I have determined to exhort you, that you should run together in union with the mind of God. For Jesus Christ does everything in accordance with the Father's mind, as he himself says

[1]The Latin version renders "an offering and sacrifice to God" as "an offering and sacrifice to God of sweet fragrance," so conforming the phrase to Eph 5.2.

[2]This phrase is supplied from Ignatius as it is lacking in the mss of the long recension.

[3]1 Cor 1.10.

somewhere: "I always do what is pleasing to him."[4] Therefore we should always live in accordance with the mind of God in Jesus Christ, and emulate him, as did Paul. For he says: "Be my imitators, as I am Christ's."[5]

4 ₁It is thus fitting that you should run together in accordance with the mind of your bishop, who is your shepherd in accordance with God, as indeed you do of yourselves, being given wisdom by the Spirit. For your justly renowned presbytery, being worthy of God, is so attuned to the bishop as the strings are to the harp, being bound together in concord and harmonious love, whose leader and guardian is Jesus Christ. ₂And each of you should join the single chorus, so that in a harmonious concord, and taking up God's connection in unity, you become one in harmony with God the Father and his beloved Son, Jesus Christ our Lord. For he says, "Grant, holy Father, that they should be one in us, as I and you are one."[6] It is profitable, therefore, that you should enjoy blameless unity, joined together with God as imitators of Christ, whose members you are.

5 ₁For since, in such a short space of time, I obtained such an intimate acquaintance with your bishop, which was not human but spiritual, how much more do I reckon you fortunate to be enmeshed with him, as the church is with the Lord Jesus and as is the Lord with his Father, so that everything may be harmonious in unity. ₂Let nobody be deceived. Anyone who is not within the sanctuary lacks the bread of God. For if the intercession of one or two has such power that Christ is standing among them, how much more is the intercession of the bishop and the entire church, ascending in harmony to God, supplying all their requests made in Christ. ₃Therefore anyone who separates himself from such as these and does not join the company of sacrifices, and the church of the firstborn whose names are

[4] Jn 8.29.
[5] 1 Cor 11.1.
[6] Jn 17.11, 12.

written in heaven, is a wolf in sheep's clothing, presenting a civilized appearance. Beloved, be anxious to be subject to the bishop and to the presbyters and to the deacons; whoever is subject to them is obedient to Christ who has appointed them. Whoever refuses compliance to them is refusing compliance to Christ Jesus. "Whoever refuses compliance to the Son shall not see life, but the wrath of God shall remain on him."[7] Whoever does not yield to his superiors is self-willed, quarrelsome, and supercilious. For it says: "God opposes the supercilious, and gives grace to the humble,"[8] and, "The supercilious have transgressed greatly." And the Lord says to the priests: "Anyone who listens to you listens to me, and whoever listens to me listens to the Father who sent me. Whoever despises you despises me, and whoever despises me despises the one who sent me."[9]

6 ₁Thus insofar as you see the bishop being silent you should fear him all the more. For we should receive anyone whom the Master sends to look after his household as though he were the sender. That we should look upon the bishop as the Lord himself is thus clear, as he stands before the Lord. For "a man who is watchful and sharp in his affairs should stand before kings, and not stand before slothful people."[10] ₂However, Onesimus himself highly praises your good order in God, because you all live in accordance with the truth and because there is no heresy dwelling among you. Rather you will not even listen to anyone apart from Jesus Christ alone, our true shepherd and teacher. Indeed, as Paul wrote to you, you are "one body and one spirit," so that you are "in one hope of your calling" in faith. Indeed there is "one Lord, one faith, one baptism, one God and Father of all who is above all and through all and in all."[11] Thus you are like them, having been trained by such instructors, Paul the Christ-carrier and Timothy the most faithful.

[7]Jn 3.36.
[8]Prov 3.34 etc.
[9]Cf. Luke 10.16.
[10]Prov 22.29.
[11]Eph 4.4–6.

7 ₁Some disgusting people are accustomed to bearing the name in wicked deceit, whilst acting in a manner unworthy of God, and holding opinions contrary to the teaching of Christ, to the destruction of themselves and of those who put their trust in them. You should shun them like wild animals. For "the righteous person who shuns them is saved for ever; but the destruction of the ungodly is sudden, and a cause of rejoicing."[12] For "they are dumb dogs, that cannot bark,"[13] raving, who bite in secret, against whom you should be on your guard, since they labor under an incurable disease. ₂Our physician is the one true God, who is unbegotten and unapproachable, the Lord of all, the Father and begetter of the only-begotten one. We also have as a physician the Lord our God, Jesus the Christ, before the ages the only-begotten Son and Word, who afterwards became also man, of Mary the virgin. For "the Word was made flesh," the disembodied was in a body, the impassible was in body capable of suffering, the immortal one was in a mortal body, life was in decay, that he might free us from death and decay and heal our souls, and might heal those who were diseased with ungodliness and wicked lusts.

8 ₁Let nobody fool you, as indeed you are not fooled, as you are entirely God's. For when there is no desire in you which might defile you or lead you into trouble, then indeed you are living in accordance with God, and belong to Christ, your expiation, and that of the most consecrated church of the Ephesians, which is celebrated and much-lauded into eternity. ₂The fleshly cannot perform anything spiritual, nor can spiritual people perform anything fleshly, as neither can faith do anything faithless, nor faithlessness do anything faithful. You, who are filled with the Holy Spirit, do nothing fleshly but perform everything which is spiritual. You are being perfected in Jesus Christ who is the "Savior of all people, and especially of the faithful."[14]

[12]Prov 10.35; Prov 11.3.
[13]Is 56.10.
[14]1 Tim 4.10.

9 ₁I know that some have passed in by you who hold the wicked teaching of a foreign and evil spirit. You did not allow them an entry to sow their tares, but stopped your ears so that you would not receive the deceit which was being proclaimed by them as you believed that the spirit which deceives the people does not speak what is of Christ, but what is of itself, for it speaks falsely. The Holy Spirit does not speak what is of himself, but of Christ, and not from himself, but from the Lord, just as the Lord announced to us what he had of the Father. For he says, "The word which you hear is not mine, but that of the Father who sent me."[15] And of the Holy Spirit he says, "He shall not speak of himself, but whatever he will hear from me."[16] And to the Father he says of himself: "I have glorified you on the earth. I have finished the work which you gave me, I have made your name manifest to people."[17] And of the Holy Spirit, "He shall glorify me, for he receives what is mine."[18] But the deceitful spirit proclaims itself, and speaks what is its own, for it is self-pleasing and glorifies itself, for it is full of arrogance. It is a speaker of falsehood, deceitful, fawning, flattering, hollow, absurd, babbling, dissonant, verbose, timorous. Jesus Christ, who has founded you, as chosen stones, fitting for the building of God the Father, upon the rock, will rescue you from its power. You are lifted to the heights by Christ, who was crucified for you, employing the Holy Spirit as a rope. You are borne up by faith, and exalted from earth to heaven by love, even as you journey together blamelessly. For it says, "Blessed are they who are blameless in the way, those who proceed in the law of the Lord."[19] Now the way is without error, namely Jesus Christ, for he says "I am the way and the life." And this way leads towards the Father for, he says, "nobody comes towards

[15]Jn 14.24.

[16]Jn 16.13.

[17]Jn 17.4, 6.

[18]The Latin version adds here: "Thus each glorifies the one from whom each receives, and each proclaims him, and announces whatever words are received." Diekamp, *Patres apostolici* 2, 244–5, is strongly of the opinion that these words should be received into the Greek text.

[19]Ps 109.1.

the Father unless through me."[20] 2 Therefore you are blessed, who are God-carriers, Spirit-carriers, temple-carriers, carriers of holiness, decorated entirely with the commandments of Jesus Christ, "a royal priesthood, a holy race, a people set apart,"[21] through whom I exult, having been found worthy of conversing, in this letter, with the saints who are in Ephesus, who are faithful in Christ Jesus."[22] Thus I rejoice in you, because you have not given in to vanity, nor do you love in accordance with the flesh but in accordance with God.

10 1 And intercede for others without ceasing, for there is hope for their repentance, that they may attain to God. For "can the one who falls not arise again, and the one who goes astray not return?"[23] Therefore permit them to be instructed by you, be agents of God and a mouth of Christ. For the Lord says, "If you remove the valuable from what is unworthy you shall be as my mouth."[24] 2 Be humble in response to their anger, set your earnest prayers against their blasphemies. While they are going astray, stand firm in the faith. Conquer their wild manners in gentleness, their wrath in meekness. For "blessed are the meek,"[25] and "Moses was meek above all people,"[26] and David was very meek.[27] So Paul encourages us: "The servant of the Lord should not be belligerent, but should be tender to all, apt to teach, patient, in meekness educating those who oppose themselves."[28] Do not be anxious to revenge yourselves on those who do you injustice for it says: "If I have returned evil to those who returned evil to me."[29] 3 In our reasonableness let us make brothers

[20]Jn 14.6.
[21]1 Pet 2.9.
[22]Eph 1.1.
[23]Jer 8.4.
[24]Jer 15.19.
[25]Mt 5.4.
[26]Num 12.3
[27]Ps 131.2. Moses and David are also found as types of meekness at *Apostolic Constitutions* 7.7.3, expanding the direction of the *Didache*.
[28]2 Tim 2.24, 25.
[29]Ps 7.4.

of them. To those who hate you say: "You are our brothers," so that the name of the Lord may be glorified. And let us imitate the Lord who, "when he was reviled did not revile in return."[30] When he was crucified, he did not answer, "When he suffered he did not make threats,"[31] but interceded for his enemies, "Father, forgive them; they do not know what they are doing."[32] Anyone who receives a greater injustice, displaying the more patience, is blessed. Anyone who is defrauded, anyone who is despised through the name of the Lord, is truly Christ's.

Be careful lest any plant of the devil be found in you. For it is bitter, and salty. "Be vigilant, be sober,"[33] in Christ Jesus.

11   ₁The last times are come upon us. Let us be shamed, let us fear God's long-suffering, lest we despise the riches of His goodness and forbearance.[34] For we should either be fearful of the wrath that is to come or else love the gracious gift which is now present to us, in living now. As long as we obtain true living in Jesus Christ.

₂Apart from him you should never desire even to breathe. For he is my hope, he is my boast, he is my never-failing wealth. In him I am carrying around chains from Syria to Rome, spiritual pearls, in which it may be granted that I should be perfected, through your intercession, and become a sharer of the sufferings of Christ, and a participant in his death, as of his resurrection from the dead and his never-failing life. May I attain to this, so that I may be found among the lot of the Ephesian Christians, who have always been in agreement with the apostles in the power of Jesus Christ, with Paul, John, and the most faithful Timothy.

12   ₁I know who I am, and those to whom I write. I am the very insignificant Ignatius, and I am like those in danger and under

---

[30]1 Pet 2.23.
[31]1 Pet 2.23.
[32]Lk 23.34.
[33]1 Pet 4.7.
[34]Rom 2.4.

judgement; you are those who have received mercy and are safe in Christ. ₂You are a passageway[35] for those being carried away on Christ's account, "from the blood of Abel, the righteous"[36] up to the blood of Ignatius, the least significant. You are fellow-initiates with Paul who was sanctified, martyred, because he was a "chosen vessel."[37] May I be found in his footsteps, as of those of the rest of the saints, when I attain to Jesus Christ. He always makes mention of you in his petitions.

13 ₁Seek, therefore, to come together more closely to give thanks to God and to glorify him. For when you are each together tightly the powers of Satan are cast down, and his "flaming arrows,"[38] which goad to sin, turn away, ineffective. For your concord and your harmonious faith are his destruction, and the torment of his attendants. ₂Nothing is better than the peace of Christ, in which every war, of the spirits of the air and of the earth, is undone. "For our struggle is not with blood and flesh, but with the powers and the authorities and the rulers of the darkness of this world, against spiritual beings of wickedness in the heavenly places."[39]

14 ₁Therefore none of the devil's devices shall escape your notice if, like Paul, you have perfect faith in Jesus Christ, and love, as these are the cause and end of life. The cause of life is faith, and the end is love. When the two are brought together the man of God is made complete and everything else that is noble and good follows on. ₂Nobody who professes faith should sin, nor does anyone who has obtained love hate a brother. For the one who said "you shall love the Lord your God" said "and your neighbor as yourself."[40] Those who profess

---

[35]The text is very corrupt here. The mss of the long recension read "I am handed over." *Parados* (passageway) has become read as *paradotheis* (handed over).

[36]Mt 23.35.

[37]Acts 9.15.

[38]Eph 6.16.

[39]Eph 6.12.

[40]Lk 10.27.

themselves as Christ's are known not only from what they say, but from what they do, "for it is by the fruit that the tree is known."[41]

15 ₁To be silent and to be authentic is better than to speak whilst being inauthentic. "The kingdom of God is not in word, but in power."[42] Belief is in the heart, confession is with the mouth, with one for righteousness, with the other for salvation.[43] Teaching is good if the one who teaches is acting. For "whoever acts and also teaches is great in the kingdom."[44] ₂Our Lord and God, Jesus Christ, the Son of the living God, first acted, and then taught,[45] as Luke "whose praise is in the gospel through all the Churches"[46] bears witness.

₃Nothing is hidden from the Lord, but even what we have hidden is close to him. Therefore everything we do should be done as though he were dwelling in us, so that we may be his temples and he may be God in us. Let Christ speak in us, as he did in Paul. Let the Holy Spirit teach us to speak of Christ in companionship with him.

16 ₁Do not be deceived, my brothers. Those who corrupt their households shall not inherit the kingdom of God. ₂And if those who corrupt simply human households are condemned to death, how much more so they who attempt to spoil the church of Christ for which the Lord Jesus, the only-begotten Son of God, endured the cross and death, suffer eternal punishment. Anyone who sets his teaching at nought, having grown fat and gross,[47] shall go to Gehenna. In the same way, everyone who has received from God the ability to make discernment, who follows an unskilled shepherd, and accepts as truth a false opinion, shall be punished. "What has light in

[41]Mt 12.33.
[42]1 Cor 4.20.
[43]Cf. Rom 10.10.
[44]Mt 5.19.
[45]So likewise *Apostolic Constitutions* 2.6.6.
[46]2 Cor 8.18. As Diekamp, *Patres Apostolici* 2, 252–3, notes, ps-Ignatius is not alone in this period in identifying this unnamed figure with Luke.
[47]Deut 32.15.

common with darkness, or Christ with Beliar? Or what share does faith have with infidelity, or the temple of God with idols?"[48] And I also say, what has truth in common with falsehood, or righteousness with unrighteousness, or true teaching with falsehood?

17   ₁The Lord received ointment on his head for this reason, that he should breathe incorruption upon the church. For it says: "Your name is ointment poured out. Therefore the maidens have loved you, they have drawn you. We shall run onward to the odor of your ointments."[49] Do not be anointed with the foul smell of the teaching of this age. Do not let the holy church of God be taken prisoner by his wiles like the first woman. ₂Being rational, why are we not sensible? Since we have planted in us, by Christ, the ability to make judgement regarding God, why do we carelessly fall into ignorance? In ignorance of the gracious gift which we have received we perish in stupidity.

18   ₁The cross of Christ is an offense to the unbelieving, but to those who are believing it is salvation and eternal life. Where is the wise one? Where is the debater? Where is the boasting of those who are termed powerful? ₂For the Son of God, begotten before the ages, charged with everything according to the will of the Father, was himself conceived by Mary, in accordance with the plan, of the seed of David and the Holy Spirit. For it says, "Look, the virgin has conceived in the womb and will bear a son, and he will be called 'Immanuel.'"[50] He was born and was baptized by John, so that he might affirm the arrangement committed to the prophet.

19   ₁The virginity of Mary and her giving birth, and likewise the death of the Lord, elude the ruler of this world. Three mysteries of crying out were performed in the quietness of God, which have

[48]2 Cor 6.14–16.
[49]Song 1.3–4.
[50]Is 7.14; Mt 1.23.

been revealed to us. ₂A star shone in heaven brighter than all that were before, and its light was indescribable, and its newness brought amazement to those who saw it. All the other stars, with the sun and the moon, formed a chorus to the star. It was surpassing them in brightness. There was agitation regarding its origin, as it was newly appeared.

₃Hence worldly wisdom was turned into foolishness, wizardry was nonsense and sorcery laughable. Every law[51] of evil was brought to nothing, the darkness of ignorance was dispelled, and tyrannical authority destroyed, as God appeared as a man and as a man operated as God. Yet the first was not simply imagination, nor the second unimportance. But one was absolute truth, the second the plan.[52] What had been prepared by God received its beginning, as from then on everything was in turmoil as the destruction of death came about.

20   ₁Stand fast, brothers, firm in the faith of Jesus Christ, and in his love, in His passion and resurrection. ₂Come together, by grace, in common, one by one, in the single faith of God the Father and of Jesus Christ, his only begotten Son and "first-born of all creation,"[53] of the race of David in the flesh, being guided by the Paraclete. You are to be obedient to the bishop and the presbytery, in an undisturbed conscience, breaking a single bread, which is the medicine of immortality, an antidote which prevents death, yet enables us to live in God through Jesus Christ, a remedy which drives away evil.

21   ₁May I be your ransom, and for those whom you sent to Smyrna for the honor of God. I am writing to you from there, giving thanks

[51]Reading *thesmos*, though this may be a corruption of *desmos*, bond or chain, as in Ignatius.

[52]Ps-Ignatius' language is very allusive here. He is saying that when God appeared as man, and a man acted as God, that there was no matter of this simply being an appearance, nor a matter of the activity of the man being simply human activity, but that the God in Christ was truly God, and that the human element was in accordance with the divine plan.

[53]Col 1.15.

to the Lord and loving Polycarp as I love you. Remember me, as Jesus Christ, blessed for ever, remembers you.

₂Intercede for the church which is in Antioch in Syria, whence I am taken to Rome in chains, though I am the least of those who are believers there, as I have been found worthy of honoring God by wearing these fetters. Fare well in God the Father and the Lord Jesus Christ, our common hope, in the Holy Spirit. Fare well. Amen. Grace.

Romans

The long recension of the letter to the Romans is not greatly different from the original, the expansions chiefly consisting of some further doctrinal clarification.

IGNATIUS TO THE ROMANS:

Ignatius, who is also God-carrier, to the church that has obtained mercy, through the majesty of the most high God the Father, and of Jesus Christ, his only-begotten Son, a church hallowed and enlightened by the will of God, who made all that is, in accordance with the faith and love of Jesus Christ, our God and Savior, that presides in the place of the region of the Romans, and which is worthy of God, worthy of honor, worthy of blessedness, worthy of praise, worthy of success, worthy of sanctification, presiding out of love, named after Christ,[1] named after the Father, Spirit-carrier, whom I also greet in the name of God the Almighty, and of Jesus Christ his Son; to those who are united both in flesh and spirit to every one of his commandments, who are filled unwaveringly with every grace of God, and are purified from every strange taint: many greetings, blamelessly, in God the Father and our Lord Jesus Christ.

1 ₁Since I have been able to perceive your God-worthy faces through prayer to God, I have asked to receive more yet. For chained in Christ Jesus I hope to greet you, should this be the will of the one who has made me worthy to continue to the end. ₂For the beginning

[1] *Christonumos.* Possibly, "keeping the law of Christ" (*christonomos*), as in the middle recension.

is well-arranged, yet to attain grace I have to obtain my lot unhindered to the last. For I fear your love, lest it do me harm. For it is easy for you to do what you wish but it is hard for me to attain to God, if you spare me not by showing fleshly affection.

2 ₁For I do not wish that you should be people-pleasers but that you please God, as you already do. For I shall have no further opportunity such as this to attain to God, nor shall you, if you keep silent, be enrolled in a better task. For if you keep silent about me, I shall become God's, but if you are deeply concerned about my flesh I shall still be running.

₂Do not allow me anything other than being poured out for God, whilst there is an altar still prepared, so that forming a chorus in love you may sing out to the Father in Jesus Christ, because God has made the bishop from Syria worthy of being found at the setting of the sun, after being sent from where it rises to bear witness to his sufferings.[2] It is good to be released from the world, towards God, so that I may rise up to him.

3 ₁You have never envied anyone; you have taught others. I now wish that what you have enjoined should be secure, as you teach them.

₂For myself, ask simply that I should have the power both inwardly and outwardly, that I do not simply say so but that I actually desire not only to be called a Christian but to be found to be one. For if I be found to be so, I shall be able both to speak and then to be faithful, when I am no longer apparent to the world.

₃Nothing visible is eternal; "For whatever is seen is temporary, whatever is not seen is eternal."[3] The matter is not a work of persuasion, but Christianity is majesty. When it is hated by the world it is beloved of God. For he says: "If you were of this world, the world

[2]Although the text is confused here, apparently making Ignatius a personal witness of the passion, Lightfoot, *Apostolic Fathers* 2.3, 268, demonstrates that the confusions can be settled with reference to the Latin version.

[3]2 Cor 4.18.

would love its own. Now you are not of this world, but I have chosen you. Remain with me."[4]

4 [1]I am writing to all the churches and I am instructing everyone that I am willingly dying for God, unless you prevent me. I beseech you, do not become an unseasonable kindness for me. Leave me to be food for the beasts, through which I may attain to God. I am God's wheat and through the beasts' teeth I shall be found to be pure bread for God.

[2]Rather encourage the beasts, so that they may be my tomb and nothing be left over of my body, so that I be found to be no burden to anyone when I am dead. Then shall I be a true disciple of Jesus Christ, when the world does not see even my body. Beseech Jesus Christ on my behalf, so that I may be found a sacrifice for God through these instruments.

[3]I am not directing you like Peter and Paul. They were apostles of Jesus Christ, I am the least. They were free, as slaves of God, I am still a slave. But if I should suffer I shall become a freedman of Jesus Christ, and I shall rise up free in him. And now I am learning, whilst chained, to be desirous of nothing worldly or vain.

5 [1]I am fighting wild beasts from Syria to Rome, through earth and sea, day and night. I am guarded by ten leopards, which is a military unit, who become worse by being well-treated. In their injustices I am becoming more of a disciple, "but I am not made just on this account."[5] [2]May I delight in the beasts prepared for me, and I pray they may be found ready for me. I shall encourage them to devour me speedily, unlike those of whom they take fright and will not touch. So even if they do not wish to do so, I shall force them.

[3]Grant me this: I know what is right for me. Now I am beginning to be a disciple. May nothing, visible or invisible, show jealousy towards me, only let me attain to Jesus Christ. Fire and cross, packs of wild beasts, cuttings, rendings, the scattering of bones, the chopping

[4]Jn 15.19.
[5]1 Cor 4.4.

up of limbs, the grinding of the whole body, the evil torments of the devil can come upon me, only let me attain to Jesus Christ.

6 ₁Neither the ends of the world nor the kingdoms of this age profit me anything. It is better for me to die in Jesus Christ than to reign over the ends of the earth. For, "What does it profit anyone who obtains the whole world, only to lose his own life?"⁶ I long for the Lord, the Son of the true God and Father, Jesus Christ. Him I seek, the one who died and rose up for us.

₂Grant me this, brothers. Do not hinder me in obtaining life, for Jesus is the life of all who believe. Do not wish that I should die, for life without Christ is death. Do not give the world the one who wishes to be God's. Allow me to receive the pure light. When I have arrived there I will truly be a man of God.

₃Allow me to be an imitator of the passion of my God. Anyone who has understanding within would know what I desire and would sympathize with me, knowing what restrains me.

7 ₁The ruler of this age wishes to snatch me and desires to corrupt my understanding of God. Let none of those with you help him! Rather be on my side, that is to say, on God's. Do not speak of Jesus Christ whilst giving preference to the world.

₂Envy should find no place among you. Even if, when I arrive, I beseech you otherwise, be persuaded by me, rather be persuaded by this which I am writing to you. For while I live I am writing to you, anxious to die. My desire is crucified, and there is no burning love for anything in me. There is living water welling up in me, saying to me, within, "Come to the Father."

₃I have no pleasure in corruptible food nor in the pleasures of this life; I desire the bread of God, heavenly bread, bread of life, which is the flesh of Jesus Christ the Son of God, who subsequently became of the seed of David and Abraham, and I desire his blood for my drink, which is incorruptible love and endless life.

⁶Mt 16.26 and par.

8 ₁No longer do I wish to live in a human manner. This will come about if you wish it. "I am crucified with Christ, I live no longer." Nevertheless "Christ lives in me."[7] ₂I ask you in a few letters: do not refuse me. Believe me, that I love Jesus who was betrayed for me. "What return shall I make to the Lord on account of all he has bestowed on me?"[8] God the Father himself and the Lord Jesus Christ shall make plain to you that I speak the truth.

₃And you should pray alongside me, that I may attain the mark in the Holy Spirit. I am not writing to you in accordance with the flesh, but in accordance with the mind of God. If I suffer, you have loved me. If I am rejected, you have despised me.

9 ₁In your prayer remember the church in Syria, which employs the Lord as its shepherd, who says, "I am the good shepherd." And he alone will watch over it, as well as your love for him.

₂And I am ashamed to be called one of them, for I am unworthy, being the least of them and untimely born. But through mercy I gain authenticity, should I attain to God.

₃My spirit greets you, as does the love of the churches which have received me in the name of Jesus Christ, and not as a wayfarer. For those who did not lie on my route preceded me city by city.

10 ₁I am writing this to you from Smyrna, through the Ephesians who are worthily blessed. Along with many others, Crocus is with me, whose name is longed for. ₂I trust that you are aware of those who have gone ahead of me from Syria to Rome for the glory of God. Inform them that I am nearby, for they are all worthy of God, as of yourselves. It is right that you should refresh them in every way. ₃I am writing this to you on the ninth before the kalends of September.[9] Fare well to the last in the endurance of Jesus Christ.

[7]Gal 2.20.
[8]Ps 116.12.
[9]24 August.

Other Antiochene material relating to Ignatius

Given that we have placed the long recension of Ignatius' letters within an Antiochene context it seems appropriate to include some other material relating to Ignatius also deriving from the Antiochene context.

First is an account of Ignatius' martyrdom. There are a number of such accounts, though according to Lightfoot three of these are conflations of the first two, which he terms the "Antiochene" and the "Roman" acts, since the interest of each author is invested in those respective cities. He argues persuasively that the Antiochene acts derive from that city, and suggests that their genesis lay in the translation of Ignatius' supposed relics during the fifth century. The Roman acts are later, and probably not Antiochene in origin. Whereas they are of no historical worth the Antiochene acts serve to demonstrate the growth of the *cultus* of Ignatius in his native city.

It is for the same reason that a translation is offered of John Chrysostom's panegyric of Ignatius, here reprinted, with the permission of the translator and the Press, from Wendy Mayer with Bronwen Neil, trans., *St John Chrysostom: The Cult of the Saints,* Popular Patristics Series no. 31 (Crestwood NY: St Vladimir's Seminary Press, 2006), 101–117.

THE "ANTIOCHENE" ACTS OF THE
MARTYRDOM OF SAINT IGNATIUS

1   As Trajan succeeded to the Empire of the Romans, Ignatius, the disciple of the apostle John, a man of apostolic character in every way, governed the church of the Antiochenes. Already he had, with difficulty, passed through the storms of the many persecutions under Domitian, and, like a good pilot, had withstood the squall of the power of the adversary by the tiller of prayer and fasting, by the constancy of his teaching, and by his spiritual rigor. Yet fearful of losing any of the faint-hearted or of the very simple, whilst, as the persecution relented for a brief period, he rejoiced at the tranquility of the church, he was displeased with himself, that he had not yet achieved a true love for Christ, or the perfection of the rank of a disciple. For he considered that a confession made in martyrdom might connect him more intimately with the Lord. Whilst he remained with the church a few more years, illuminating the understanding of each through his interpretation of the Scriptures, like a divine lamp, he obtained his desire.

2   Later on, when Trajan was in the ninth year of his reign, threatening to recommence persecution, he was determined to oblige all those who were living devoutly either to offer sacrifice or to die. For he was elated with his victory over the Scythians and Dacians, and many other nations, yet considered that the devout society of the Christians meant that his domination was incomplete, unless they chose to submit to the worship of demons alongside all the nations. Thus, fearful for the church of the Antiochenes the brave soldier of Christ willingly went to Trajan, who was staying at that time in Antioch campaigning against Armenia and the Parthians. He stood before the face of Trajan (the emperor): "Who are you, you devilish lowlife, so prepared to transgress our commandments and persuade others to do the same so that they are sadly lost?"

Ignatius said: "Nobody calls the God-carrier devilish, for devils keep far away from the servants of God. But I agree with you if you are calling me a lowlife towards devils, because I am troublesome to them. For I confound their devices, having Christ as a heavenly king."

Trajan said: "What is a god-carrier?"

Ignatius replied: "Anyone who has Christ within."

Trajan said: "Do you not think that we have gods within us, since we use them as allies against our enemies?"

Ignatius said: "You are deceived when you refer to the devils of the nations as gods. For there is one God, who made the heavens and the earth and the sea and all that is in them, and one Christ Jesus, his only-begotten Son in whose friendship I delight."

Trajan said: "Do you mean the one who was crucified under Pontius Pilate?"

Ignatius said: "The one who nailed sin, and its originator, to the cross, and sentenced demonic evil to be trampled under the feet of those who carry him in their heart."

Trajan said: "So you carry Christ in your heart?"

Ignatius said: "Yes. For it is written, 'I will dwell in them, and walk about within them.'"[1]

Trajan pronounced sentence: "We direct that Ignatius, who says that he carries the crucified one around in himself, is to be chained by soldiers to be led to mighty Rome, there to be made food for wild beasts, as a spectacle and for the entertainment of the people."

The sainted martyr, on hearing this sentence, cried out with joy: "I thank you master that you have held me worthy to be honored through the perfection of my love for you; you have chained me in iron bonds to your apostle Paul."

When he had said this, putting on his chains with rejoicing, praying over the church and commending it with tears to the Lord, he was hustled away by the beastly brutality of the soldiers like a prize ram, to be carried off to Rome as food for bloodthirsty beasts.

[1] 2 Cor 6.16; cf. Lev 26.12.

3   And so, with great eagerness and joy, desirous of suffering, going down from Antioch to Seleucia he there took ship. Putting in at the city of the Smyrneans, after terrible weather, he disembarked with great rejoicing, hastening to see the sainted Polycarp, bishop of the Smyrneans, his fellow student (for long before they had been disciples of John). He was received by him, and he communicated to him his spiritual gifts of grace, and gloried in his bonds. He besought co-operation in his purpose from every church in common (for the churches and cities of Asia received the saint through their bishops and presbyters and deacons, all flocking to him to receive some portion of his spiritual gifts of grace), but especially from the sainted Polycarp, that by means of the wild beasts he might quickly disappear from the world so as to appear before the face of Christ.

4   All this he said, and so bore witness, so straining his love for Christ as though he would take heaven by storm by his good confession and by the enthusiasm of those who prayed with him regarding his combat. At the same time he rewarded those churches which stood alongside him in the persons of their rulers, sending out letters of thanks to them, spilling forth spiritual grace with prayer and encouragement. When he saw that all were kindly disposed towards him, fearful lest the affection of the brotherhood might distract his zeal for the Lord, even as a goodly door of martyrdom was opened for him, he sent the following, now subjoined, to the church of the Romans:

[*The text of the Ignatian letter to the Romans (see pp. 66–74) is found here.*]

5   Quietening by his letter those brothers in Rome who were opposed, as he desired, so he set out from Smyrna (for the Christ-carrier was being hustled by the soldiers to reach the sports in the great city, so that being handed over to wild beasts as a spectacle for the Roman people he could obtain the crown of righteousness by competing in this way). From there he set out for Neapolis and passing through Philippi he travelled by land across Macedonia and the part of Epirus which is near Epidamnos. He took ship there, by the coast, and sailed across the Adriatic Sea, so entering the Tyrrhenian, passing islands and cities. When Puteoli came into view the saint was eager to disembark himself, as he wished to tread in the footsteps of the apostle, but a stiff breeze would not allow it as the ship was being driven from a wind to the stern. So he blessed the love of the brothers in that place as he sailed past. So in one single day and night, meeting with favorable winds, we were unwillingly driven forward, grieving the separation which would soon come between ourselves and this righteous man, while he was granted his wish more speedily to quit the world to be close to the Lord whom he loved. Thus as we sailed into the harbor of the Romans, just as the impure games were reaching their conclusion, the soldiers were displeased at the delay while the bishop gladly obeyed them as they hustled him on.

6 Departing early from the place called Portus we met with brothers who were filled with awe and joy, as the news of the sainted martyr had already been noised abroad. With joy because they had the opportunity to meet the God-carrier, with fear since such a man was being led to death. Some he instructed to be quiet, when in fervor they said that they would stop the people from seeking the destruction of the righteous man. He knew them in the spirit straightaway, and greeted all of them, and asked them for genuine love, discussing with them at greater length than in his letter, and persuading them not to begrudge somebody who was hurrying to meet his Lord. As the brothers all fell on their knees he besought the Son of God for the churches, that the persecution should be stayed and that the brothers should have love for each other. He was led away to the amphitheatre with haste in accordance with the prior instruction of the emperor, just as the games were coming to their conclusion, for it was a holiday (as they thought) which in the Roman language is called the thirteenth, on which they would eagerly gather.[2] So he was thrown to the savage beasts by the ungodly. The desire of the sainted martyr Ignatius was thereupon fulfilled, as it is written, "the desire of the righteous is acceptable,"[3] that none of the brothers should be put to trouble through the collection of his remains, just as he had previously, in his epistle, desired that his own end should be. Only the tougher of his sacred remains were left back, which were returned to Antioch and laid in a coffin, a priceless treasure left to the sacred church, through the gracious gift which was within the martyr.

7   This happened on the thirteenth before the kalends of January, when Sura and Senecio, for the second time, were consuls among the Romans.[4] With our own eyes we saw all this with tears. We watched all night in the house, repeatedly beseeching the Lord on our knees, begging, that we might be strengthened, weak as we were, after what had occurred. When we had briefly fallen asleep, suddenly some of us beheld the blessed Ignatius standing by and embracing us, while he was seen by others praying over us, and by others dripping with sweat, as though after a hard struggle, standing beside the Lord with great boldness and ineffable glory. Filled with joy at seeing this, and comparing the visions of our dreams, we sang hymns to God the giver of all that is good, and blessed the holy man. We mark for you the day and the time so that on the occasion of the martyrdom we may gather together and have communion with the athlete and valiant martyr of Christ, who trampled the devil, and completed the race of his Christ-loving desire, in Christ Jesus our Lord, through whom and with whom be the glory and the might, to the Father with the Holy Spirit for ever. Amen.

---

[2]This is the feast of the *sigillaria*, which was part of the extended feast of the *Saturnalia*.

[3]Prov 10.24.

[4]December 20, 107. December 20 is kept as Ignatius' feast in Chalcedonian Orthodox churches.

JOHN CHRYSOSTOM'S SERMON

On the very holy martyr Ignatius who was a God-bearing archbishop of Antioch the Great and had been taken away to Rome and martyred there, and in turn brought back from there to Antioch[1]

1   Among those who host banquets, the biggest spenders and the most status-conscious hold banquets thick and fast, at one and the same time showing off their own wealth and letting their benevolence towards their dependents be seen. So too the grace of the Spirit, providing for us a demonstration of its own power and showing off a great deal of benevolence towards God's friends, is furnishing martyrs' tables for us without a break one after the other. Recently, at least, a quite young and unmarried girl, the blessed martyr Pelagia, had us to dinner with a great deal of festivity. Today again this blessed and noble martyr Ignatius succeeds her festival. Their persons are different, but the table one and the same. The wrestling matches are completely different, but the crown one and the same. Their contests are varied, but the prize the same. My point is that in the outside games, since the labors involve bodies, it is with reason that only men are admitted. But here, since the entire contest involves the soul, the stadium is open to each sex, the spectators consist of each kind. And neither did just men strip off, so that the women, taking resort in the weakness of their gender, mightn't seem to have a plausible defense; nor did just women act like men, so that the male gender wouldn't be put to shame. Instead many people from both this and that [gender] were heralded and crowned, so that you might learn in practice that "in Christ Jesus there is no male, no female" (Gal 3.28), that neither gender nor physical weakness nor age nor anything else of the sort could impede those running the race of piety, if noble

[1]Translated from PG 50.587–596, and found in Wendy Mayer with Bronwen Neil, translators, St John Chrysostom: The Cult of the Saints, Popular Patristics Series no. 31 (Crestwood NY: St Vladimir's Seminary Press, 2006), 101–117; quoted with permission.

enthusiasm and an alert mind and fervent and passionate fear of God were rooted in our souls. For this reason both young girls, and women, and men, and young and old, and slaves and free, and every status, and every age, and each sex stripped off for these contests, and nothing of any kind disadvantaged them, since they brought a noble inclination to these wrestling matches.

2 And so the time [of year] calls us now to relate the good works of this blessed man. But my argument is confused and in turmoil, without a grasp of what to say first, what second, what third. So great a crowd of speeches of praise flows around us from all sides. Indeed our experience is the same as if someone on entering a meadow and seeing a large number of roses, a large number of irises, so great a number of lilies, and other spring flowers of varied and diverse forms, were at a loss what to view first, what second, since each of the items they view is calling their eyes to itself. For truly, we too, on entering this spiritual meadow of Ignatius' good works and view-ing not spring flowers but the very fruit of the Spirit, of varied and diverse forms, in this man's soul, are in turmoil and at a loss, without a grasp of where we should direct our argument first, since each item we view draws us away from its neighbors and invites the soul's eyes to view its own particular attractiveness. For consider! He governed the Church in our community nobly and with as much precision as Christ wishes. For that limit and rule of oversight which he (sc. Christ) said was greatest, he (sc. Ignatius) displayed in practice. Truly, when he heard Christ saying: "The good shepherd lays down his life for his sheep" (Jn 10.11), he gave it up for his sheep with every ounce of courage.

3 He was genuinely in the company of the apostles and enjoyed their spiritual streams. What kind of person is he likely to have been, then, seeing that he was raised alongside them and was in their company everywhere, and shared with them experiences both well-known and secret, and, in their opinion, deserved so great an office? Once again there occurred a time that required courage and a soul that despises everything to do with the present, and bubbles over with divine passion, and values things unseen over things seen. And he shed his flesh with as much ease as a person might take off a piece of clothing. What, then, shall we mention first? The apostles' teaching, which he demonstrated in everything, or his disdain for the present life, or the scrupulous virtue with which he administered his role as head of the Church? Whom shall we praise in song first? The martyr, or the bishop, or the apostle? For the Spirit's grace wove a triple crown and in this way wreathed that holy head. No, rather, it was multi-layered. For if a person were to unwind each of the crowns precisely, they would discover that they were shooting forth other crowns for us too.

4   And if you like, let's go first to praising the bishop. This doesn't seem to be just a single crown. Come, then, let's unwind it in our sermon, and you will see two or three or more being born for us out of it. My point is, I don't marvel at the man just because he was considered deserving of so great an office, but because he was entrusted with this office by those saints, and the hands of the blessed apostles touched his holy head. For this is no small subject for a speech of praise: not because he attracted more abundant grace from above, nor because they caused the Spirit's action to descend upon him more generously alone; but because in him they witnessed every possible human virtue. In what way, let me explain. Paul was writing to Titus at the time—when I say Paul, I don't mean just him, but also Peter and James and John and their whole company. For just as in a single lyre the strings are different, but they make a single harmonious sound, so too in the company of apostles the persons were different but the teaching one and the same, since there was also a single artist, the Holy Spirit, who was setting their souls in motion. And this Paul made clear when he said: "Whether it is they, then, or it is I, so we proclaim [the gospel]" (1 Cor 15.11). So then, he was writing to Titus and showing what kind of person the bishop should be, and he said: "As God's steward, the bishop should be without reproach, not stubborn, not quick-tempered, not an excessive drinker, not given to brawls, not greedy for gain, but hospitable, a lover of goodness, of sober character, upright, devout, self-disciplined, a person who sticks closely to the trustworthy word in accord with what was taught, so that he is capable both of advising others with sound doctrine and of refuting those who argue against it" (Tit 1.7–9). And again when he was writing to Timothy on the same issue he spoke more or less as follows: "If anyone puts up his hand for episcopal office, he desires a fine task. The bishop should therefore be blameless, a husband of one wife, sober, self-controlled, well-behaved, hospitable, instructive, not given to brawls, not an excessive drinker, but mild, peace-loving, not interested in money" (1 Tim 3.1–3).

5 Did you see how much precision in respect of virtue is required of the bishop? For just as a master painter mixes various colors and so renders with absolute precision whatever picture he is about to produce as an archetype of the imperial form, so that all those who copy it and paint from it have an image that is portrayed accurately in every detail, so too indeed blessed Paul, as if painting an imperial image and producing its exemplar, has mixed the various colors of virtue and sketched for us in complete form the distinctive features of the episcopal office, so that each person ascending to this office, by looking at it (sc. the image or exemplar), might administer every aspect of themselves with as much precision. With confidence, therefore, I would say that with precision blessed Ignatius impressed every aspect of this image on his own soul, and was blameless and without reproach and neither stubborn nor quick-tempered, nor an excessive drinker, nor given to brawling, but peace-loving, uninterested in money, upright, devout, disciplined, a person who stuck close to the trustworthy word in accord with what was taught, sober, self-controlled,[2] well-behaved, and the rest that Paul required.

---

[2]Corrected from the published translation's reading, "a teetoaler, of sober character."—Ed.

"What's the proof of this?;' you ask. The same men who made these statements ordained him, and those who were advising others so precisely to subject to scrutiny those about to ascend to the throne of this office would themselves not have done this cursorily. On the contrary, if they hadn't seen all of this virtue planted in this martyr's soul, they wouldn't have entrusted this office to him.

6   My point is that they knew precisely how much danger there is in store for those who perform such ordinations carelessly and at random. Indeed again making this same point clear Paul, in writing to the same Timothy, said: "Lay hands on no one swiftly, nor join in the sins of others" (1 Tim 5.22). What do you mean? Another person sins, and I share the charges and the punishment? "Yes;' he says, "since you placed your authority at the service of impropriety." Indeed, just as when a person entrusts a sharpened sword to someone who is raving and out of their wits, whatever murder the insane person commits, that person who handed over the sword takes on the responsibility, so too a person who places the authority that stems from this office at the service of a person engaged in impropriety draws all the fire for that person's sins and enterprises on their own head. For the person who supplies the root is responsible in every way for what grows out of it. Did you see how it is meanwhile clear to us that the crown of the episcopal office was two-fold, and the status of the men who ordained him made the office more brilliant, in that they gave witness to every proof of virtue in him?

7   Would you like me to reveal to you yet another crown that shot forth from this very thing? Let us give consideration to the time at which he was entrusted with this office. For it is not the same to administer a church now as it was then, just as to travel in the steps of numerous travelers a road that's compacted and well constructed is not the same as [to travel] one that's right on the point of being cut for the first time and has chasms and rocks and is full of wild animals and hasn't yet received a single traveler. My point is that at present by God's grace there is no danger for bishops, but instead profound peace everywhere, and we all enjoy calm and the word of piety has extended itself to the ends of the world and those who rule over us keep a close and precise watch over the faith. But at that time there were none of these things. Instead, wherever one looked, [there were] cliffs and pits and wars and battles and dangers; and governors and emperors and peoples and cities and races—both domestic and foreign—were plotting against the believers. And it wasn't just this that was terrible, but that many of the believers themselves too, in that they had just for the first time tasted strange teachings, were in need of considerable accommodation, and were still rather weak and were often caught out. And it was this that grieved the teachers no less than the external wars; rather it [grieved them] far more. For while the external battles and plots actually provided them with much pleasure because of the expectation of the rewards stored up— truly, this is why the apostles turned away from facing the council, rejoicing that they had been whipped (cf. Acts 5.40–41), and why Paul proclaims: "I rejoice in my sufferings" (Col 1.24) and everywhere boasts in his afflictions—the wounds of their own people and the lapses of their brothers and sisters didn't allow them to catch a breath, but instead like an extremely heavy yoke unrelentingly compressed and dragged down their souls' necks.

8   At any rate listen to how Paul, who so rejoices in his [own] sufferings, bitterly grieves over them. "Who is weak," he says, "and I am not weak? Who is made to stumble and I don't burn?" (2 Cor 11.29). And again: "I am pretty much afraid that, if I come, I won't find you in the state that I wish and that I too will be found by you to not be as you wish" (2 Cor 12.20). And a little later: "[I fear] that when I come again God will humble me before you, and I will mourn for many who have sinned beforehand, and won't repent of their uncleanliness and sexual immorality and licentiousness they have practiced" (2 Cor 12.21). And in every situation you always see him in tears and in mourning because of his own people, and afraid and trembling over those who believed. And so, just as we marvel at a captain not when he is able to save the passengers when the sea is calm and the ship is being carried along by a fair wind, but when he is able to set the vessel to rights with complete safety when the sea is raging, the waves are towering, the marines on board are mutinying, a great storm is besieging the passengers from without and within; so too should we be struck with far greater amazement and wonder at those entrusted with the Church at that time than at those who govern it now—[a time] when there was much warring without and within, when the shoot of faith was still rather tender and in need of considerable care, when like a new-born babe the bulk of the Church required considerable forethought and some extremely wise soul to next look after it.

9   Indeed so that you may learn more clearly how many crowns those who were then entrusted with the Church deserved, and how much effort and danger it was to take on the matter in the opening moments and at the start and to come to it first off the rank, I produce as a witness for you Christ, who puts his vote behind these statements and confirms the opinion we've expressed. For on seeing many people coming to him, and desiring to show the apostles that the prophets expended much greater effort than they, he said: "Others have put in the hard work and you have come in on their hard work" (Jn 4.38). And yet the apostles expended much greater effort than the prophets. But since the latter were the first to sow the word of piety and drew people's uninstructed souls toward the truth, he attributed the bulk of the hard work to them. My point is that it is not, absolutely not, the same for a person who comes after many other teachers to teach and for that person to sow the seeds for the first time. For what has already been practiced and has become a habit for many, is easily taken on board. But what is now being heard for the first time confuses the mind of the audience and throws up many issues for those doing the teaching. At any rate this even confused those among the Athenians who were listening, and because of this they turned away Paul, with the accusation: "You're introducing something foreign to our ears" (Acts 17.20). My point is, if being at the head of the Church at present provides hard work and considerable effort for those who steer it, consider how the effort was at that time double, or triple, or many times more, when there were dangers and battles, and plots, and constant fear. It isn't, it absolutely isn't possible to come close in theory to the unpleasantness which those saints endured at that time. Rather that person alone will know it, who has had actual experience.

10   Let me mention a fourth crown too, which emerges for us from this episcopal office. So, what is it? That he was assigned our country. I mean, it is labor intensive to be at the head of just a hundred or five hundred men. But to be entrusted with so large a city and a population stretching into the 200,000s, of how much virtue and wisdom do you imagine that to be proof? For truly, just as in the case of armies the more experienced generals are entrusted with the praetorian legions with their larger body count, so too in the case of cities the more capable magistrates are assigned the larger, heavily populated ones. And, in any case, this city was of considerable interest to God, as he in fact revealed through his actions. At least, [God] ordered Peter, the commander-in-chief of the entire world, to whom he entrusted the keys of heaven, to whom he assigned control of everything, to spend a considerable length of time here. To him our city was thus the equivalent of the entire world. When I recalled Peter, I saw a fifth crown being woven from it too. It was he (sc. Ignatius) who succeeded to this office after him. For just as, if a person removes a large stone from foundations, they for sure hurry to insert in its place a second [stone] equivalent to it, lest they be a step away from shaking the entire building and making it less sound; so too, when Peter was about to move away from there, the grace of the Spirit inserted in his place a second teacher equivalent to Peter, so that the construction that was already there wouldn't become less sound through the poor quality of his successor.

11   And so we have counted up five crowns: from the magnitude of the office, from the status of those who ordained him, from the unpleasant nature of the time, from the proportions of the city, from the virtue of the person who handed the episcopal office on to him. After weaving all of these I could have mentioned a sixth or a seventh or more than these. But, so that we don't waste the whole time on a discussion of his episcopacy and so be deprived of the tales about the martyr, come, for the rest let's move to that contest.

12   A cruel war was once stirred up against the Churches and, just as if an utterly cruel tyrant had got hold of the earth, everyone was snatched away from the midst of the marketplace, accused of nothing out of the ordinary, except that, free of error, they raced towards piety, that they resisted the worship of demons, that they recognized the true God and adored his only-begotten Son. And, on account of those [virtues] for which they should have been crowned and marveled at and honored, on their account everyone who had taken on the faith was punished and overwhelmed with countless tortures, but the heads of the Churches to a far greater degree. For the Devil, being a criminal and clever at devising such plots, anticipated that if he removed the shepherds, he would easily be able to scatter the flocks. But the one who catches the clever in their trickery allowed this to happen, with the intention of showing him that it is not humans who steer his Churches, but he himself who in every instance shepherds those who believe in him. [He did this] so that whenever [the Devil] saw the matters of piety not diminishing, despite [the shepherds'] removal, nor the word of the message being extinguished, but rather growing, he might learn through experience—both he himself and all who serve him in these matters—that our affairs are not human, but that the basis of our teaching has its root above in heaven, and it is God who guides the Churches in every respect, and that it isn't possible for the individual who fights God to ever overcome him.

13   It's not just this piece of chicanery that the Devil put into effect, but also a second of no less magnitude than this. For he didn't allow the bishops to be killed in the cities which they headed, but first escorted them to a foreign country and then did away with them. He did this simultaneously out of a haste to get them stripped of necessities, and from the hope of rendering them weaker from the hardship of the journey, which is precisely what he did in the case of this blessed man. For he summoned him from our city to Rome, imposing upon him longer laps of the race, in anticipation that he (sc. the Devil) would depress his (sc. Ignatius') spirits both through the [sheer] length of the road and the vast number of days [involved], not knowing that on so long a journey [Ignatius] had Jesus as a fellow merchant and migrant. Instead, [Ignatius] became stronger, and provided ample proof of the power that was with him, and trained up the Churches in a major way. I mean that the cities along the road raced together from all directions[3] and anointed[4] the athlete and sent him on his way with a large quantity of supplies, offering him assistance through their prayers and intercessions. And they (sc. the cities) received no ordinary comfort when they saw the martyr running to meet death with as great an enthusiasm as was fitting for a person summoned to the royal palace in heaven. And they learnt from experience, from the enthusiasm and brilliance of that noble man, that it was not death toward which he ran, but a migration and translation, and ascent to heaven. After teaching these things in every city through what he said, through what he did, he would take his leave.

14   And what happened in the case of the Jews when, in shackling Paul and dispatching him to Rome, they thought they were sending him off to his death, but in fact sent him as a teacher to the Jews who lived there, this very thing happened in the case of Ignatius too with

[3]From Ignatius' letters it is evident that at the very least he passed through Philadelphia, Sardis, Smyrna, Troas, Neapolis, and Philippi, while representatives of the cities of Ephesus, Tralles, and Magnesia came to meet him in Smyrna.

[4]I.e., helped to get him ready, encouraged him, spurred him on.

a certain abundance. For he went away as a marvelous teacher for not just those who inhabit Rome, but also for all the cities lying in between, persuading them to despise the present life and consider as nothing what can be seen, and to love the future, and look towards heaven, and pay heed to none of the disasters in the present life. He traveled, in practice teaching them these [virtues] and more than these like a sun rising from the east and running its course towards the west. Rather, he was even more brilliant than that. I mean that while this [sun] runs its course above, bringing perceptible light, Ignatius shone from below, sending an intelligible light of instruction into their souls. And while when that [sun] goes off to the regions of the west, it is hidden and at once introduces night, when this [sun] went off irlto the regions of the west, it rose more brilliantly from there, and benefited everyone along the road in the greatest possible way. And when he reached the city (sc. Rome), he taught her to practice philosophy too. Truly, it is for this reason that God agreed that he lose his life there: so that his death would be an instruction in piety for all who inhabit Rome.

15 My point is that, while by God's grace you are no longer in need of any proof, since you were firmly rooted in the faith, the inhabitants of Rome, in that at the time there was a great deal of impiety there, needed greater assistance. It's for this reason that both Peter and Paul and this man after them were all sacrificed there. This [occurred] on the one hand so that they might purify with their own blood the city stained with the blood of idols, on the other, so that they might provide practical proof of the resurrection of the crucified Christ, by persuading the inhabitants of Rome that they wouldn't have despised the present life with such great pleasure if they themselves had not been utterly convinced that they were about to ascend to the crucified Jesus and see him in heaven. For this is truly a substantial proof of the resurrection, that the murdered Christ exhibited such great power after death that he convinced living human beings to ignore their country and household and friends and relatives and life itself for the sake of confessing him, and to choose whips and dangers and death instead of the pleasures of the present. My point is, these deeds were not those of a dead person nor a person still in the tomb, but of one risen from the dead and alive. After all, how could one account for the fact that when he was alive all the apostles in his company became weaker from fear and betrayed their teacher and fled away, but when he died, not just Peter and Paul but also Ignatius, who hadn't even set eyes on him nor enjoyed his company, displayed such great enthusiasm for him that they even laid down their very life for him?

16   So then, so that all the inhabitants of Rome might learn these things in practice, God allowed the saint to end his life there. And that this is the reason, I'll guarantee from the way he died itself. For he didn't receive the condemning vote outside the walls in a pit, or in a court of law, or in some corner. Instead, in the middle of the theater, with the whole city seated in the stands,[5] he endured the way of martyrdom via wild animals dispatched against him, so that by erecting his trophy against the Devil under everyone's gaze, he might make all the spectators enthusiasts of his own struggles, not just through dying so nobly, but also through dying with enjoyment. For he viewed the wild animals irreverently in this way—not as someone about to be torn away from life, but as someone summoned to a better and more spiritual life. What makes this clear? The words that he spoke when he was about to die. For when he heard that this type of torture awaited him, he said: "Bless those wild animals!"[6] Of such quality are those who passionately love. Whatever they suffer for their loved ones, they accept with pleasure and seem to be full of passion precisely whenever what is happening is far more cruel; which is what happened, then, too in the case of this man. For he

[5]Lit. "above."

[6]The Roman martyrdom of Ignatius (section 10; Lightfoot II.2, p. 533 ll. 20–21) records Ignatius as saying: "I am God's grain and I am ground by the teeth of wild animals, so that I might become pure bread." Both traditions express the idea that Ignatius embraced the manner of his death.

strove to emulate the apostles not just in his death but also in his enthusiasm. And on hearing that they had been whipped and yet departed with joy (cf. Acts 5.41), he too wanted to imitate his teachers not just in his death but also in his joy. It's for this reason he said: "Bless the wild animals!" Indeed he thought that their mouths[7] would be much more gentle than the tyrant's tongue. And rightly so. For while the latter called him to hell,[8] their mouths sent him off to the kingdom [of heaven].

17   Well then, when he lost his life there—no rather, when he ascended to heaven—from that moment he returned crowned as victor. Truly this was a feature of God's management: to bring him back to us and distribute the martyr between the cities. For while she (sc. Rome) received his dripping blood, you were honored with his relics. You enjoyed his episcopacy; they enjoyed his martyrdom. They saw him competing and winning and being crowned; you have him perpetually. God removed him from you for a short time and happily gave him [back] to you with greater glory. And, just as those who borrow money pay back whatever they receive with interest, so too God, after using this valuable treasure among you for a short time and showing it to that city, gave it back to you with greater brilliance. My point is that you sent away a bishop, and received a martyr. You sent [him] away with prayers, and received [him] with crowns. And not just you, but also all the cities in between. For how do you think they felt when they saw the remains being escorted back? How much pleasure did they reap? How much did they rejoice? With how many acclamations did they bombard the crowned victor from every direction? For just as the spectators immediately welcome a noble athlete who has wrestled down all his competitors and exited the arena with magnificent glory, and don't allow him to set foot on the ground but escort him home in a litter

---

[7]Reading *stomata* (mouths) for the Greek *tomata*, which appears to be a misprint in the edition.

[8]Lit. "Gehenna."

and bombard him with countless words of praise, so at that time too in succession the cities welcomed that saint from Rome, and carrying him on their shoulders sent him along as far as this city, praising the crowned victor, praising in song the President of the games,[9] mocking the Devil, because his trick backfired with opposite effect, and what he thought he was doing to the martyr's detriment happened in his own case. And whereas at the time he (sc. the martyr) benefited and uplifted all those cities, from that time even up to the present day he continues to enrich your city. And, just like a perpetual warehouse that is drained day after day and does not run dry, and makes all who share in it more prosperous, so indeed too this blessed Ignatius sends back home full of blessings, confidence, noble thoughts, and a great deal of courage those who come to him.

18 Let's, then, not walk to him just today, but also every day, and reap spiritual fruit from him. For it's possible, absolutely possible, for the person who's present here with faith to harvest great blessings. My point is that not just the bodies but the saints' coffins themselves, too, are full of spiritual grace. For if this happened in the case of Elisha and a corpse that touched his coffin shattered the bonds of death and came back to life (4 Kgs 13.21), it is even far more possible now, when grace is more generous, when the Spirits' energy is more abundant, for a person who touches a coffin to draw from there a great deal of power. Indeed, it is for this reason that God allowed us [to have] the saints' relics, out of a desire to guide us towards the same enthusiasm as them and to provide a harbor and a secure consolation for the evils that constantly beset us. For this reason, I encourage all of you, whether a person is depressed or ill or suffering abuse, or is in some other condition of life, or deep in sin, let them be present here with

[9]I.e., Christ. The image of Christ as the president of the games in which the martyrs compete against the Devil and win is a common one in martyr homilies of this period. See J. Leemans, "Gregory of Nyssa and the Agonothetes: An Exploration of an Agonistic Image to speak about God and Christ," in E. Moutsoulas, ed., *Jesus Christ in the Theology of Gregory of Nyssa: Minutes of the Ninth Conference on St. Gregory of Nyssa (Athens, 7–12 September 2000)* (Athens: University of Athens, 2005), 529–556.

faith, and they will put aside all those [troubles] and come back with much pleasure, having rendered their conscience lighter from the sight alone. Rather, it isn't essential for only those who are in trouble to be present here; no, even if a person is in cheerful spirits, even if they're in glory, even if they're in power, even if they address God with a great deal of boldness, let that person not despise the benefit. For on coming here and seeing this saint, they will render the good things [in their life] unchanging, persuaded by the memory of his good works to moderate their soul and not allowing their conscience to be aroused to any swell-headedness by the good things they do. It is no small thing for those doing well not to become puffed up over their happy state of existence, but to know how to bear doing well in a measured way. In consequence for everyone the warehouse is useful, the inn convenient—for those who have stumbled, so that they may be free of temptations; for those in a happy state, so that the good things might stay secure for them; for those who are sick, so that they may return to health, for those who are healthy, so that they won't fall sick. On taking all these factors into consideration, let's value spending time here above every enjoyment, every pleasure, so that at one and the same time rejoicing and profiting we may be enabled through the prayers of the saints themselves to become housemates of these saints and share their lifestyle, through the grace and loving kindness of our Lord Jesus Christ, with whom to the Father be glory, together with the Holy Spirit, now and always, and forever and ever. Amen.

APPENDIX 2

The additional Latin letters
of the long recension

In the introduction to the long recension reference was made to the correspondence between Ignatius, the apostle John, and the Mother of God. These are found only in Latin manuscripts, and would seem to be a western mediaeval forgery. It is of no historical value except as an example of learned piety within the west, nor of any discernible theological merit, but a translation is given here in view of its appearance in the manuscript tradition, and since it receives mention elsewhere in this volume.

IGNATIUS, AND THE BROTHERS WHO ARE WITH HIM, TO JOHN THE SAINTED ELDER

We are greatly saddened that you have delayed in strengthening us by your addresses and consolations. Many of us will be disappointed if your absence is extended. Therefore hurry yourself to come, because we believe it will be useful.

There are also many of our women here who desire to see Mary (mother) of Jesus, and each day desire to escape us to come to you so that they may meet her and touch those breasts which nourished the Lord Jesus and may enquire of her regarding certain secret matters. But Salome, whom you love, the daughter of Anna, staying with her five months in Jerusalem, reports that she is full of all graces and fruitful with all virtues, as do certain other well-known people. They also say that she is cheerful amidst persecutions and afflictions, uncomplaining amidst poverty and neediness, grateful amidst injury, and rejoicing when troubled. She sympathizes with the downtrodden and afflicted as one herself undergoing affliction, and does not delay in coming to their aid. She shines forth in contending against the harmful assaults of vice in the struggle of faith. She is mistress of our new religion, and ministers among the faithful in all acts of piety. She is truly devoted to the humble, and she humbles herself more devotedly than the devoted and is wonderfully magnified by all, even while being detracted by the Scribes and Pharisees. Beyond this many people report a great deal about her. We do not dare put our faith in everything reported by anyone, nor report them all to you. But, as is told us from those who are worthy of belief, in Mary of Jesus a natural angelic sanctity is allied with human nature. Such reports as these excite our emotions and excite a great desire to catch sight of this amazing and most sacred marvel, if it is lawful so to speak. However, do accede to our request speedily. Farewell. Amen.

His own Ignatius to John, the sainted elder:

If you should grant me leave I should like to go up to Jerusalem and see the faithful and holy ones who are there, especially Mary, (mother) of Jesus, who is, they say, admired and loved by everyone. For which friend of our faith and religion would not want to see and speak with her who bore the true God of gods? And likewise the venerable James, who is surnamed "the Just." They report that he is very like Jesus Christ in his life and mode of conduct as though he were a twin brother from the same womb. They say that if I see him I will see the bodily features of Jesus himself. And there are the other sainted men and women. Alas, what is the delay? Why am I detained? Good instructor, make haste to give me cause for gladness, and fare well.

Amen.

Her own Ignatius to Mary the Christ-bearer

You should have comforted and consoled me. I am a neophyte and a disciple of your (beloved) John. For I have heard wonderful things to say of your (son) Jesus, and am astonished when I hear them. However, I desire with my whole heart to learn more about what I have heard, from you who were always close to him and familiar, and aware of his secrets. I did write to you before to ask about the same matters. Farewell, and may your neophytes, who are with me, be comforted from you and through you and in you.

The humble handmaid of the Lord to her beloved Ignatius:

What you have heard and learned from John regarding Jesus is true. You are to believe them, cling to them, and hold more firmly the profession of that Christianity which you have embraced, and are to conform your conduct and your life to that profession. I shall come with John to see you, and those who are with you. Stand firm and bravely in the faith, and do not let the ferocity of persecution unsettle you, but may your spirit be strong and rejoice in God your salvation. Amen.

Further reading

The texts employed are as follow:

For Ignatius, that printed is J.B. Lightfoot, *The Apostolic Fathers* 2.1 (London: MacMillan, 1889), though I have frequently been guided by Pierre Thomas Camelot, *Ignace d'Antioche, Polycarpe de Smyrne: Lettres, Martyre de Polycarpe* (4th edition, corrected; Paris: Cerf, 1998).

For ps-Ignatius I have had an eye to the texts both of J.B. Lightfoot, *The Apostolic Fathers* 2.3 (London Macmillan, 1889) and F. Diekamp, *Patres apostolici: editionem Funkianem novis curis in lucem emisit* 2 (Tübigen: Laupp, 1913), though I have followed neither exclusively.

Those interested in the authentic Ignatius would do well by starting with Allen Brent, *Ignatius of Antioch, a Martyr Bishop and the Origin of Episcopacy* (London: Continuum, 2007), through which further studies may be set in context and accessed. Thomas A. Robinson, *Ignatius of Antioch and the Parting of the Ways: Early Jewish-Christian Relations* (Peabody MA: Hendrickson, 2009) is written in a lively style, and presents an interesting, neo-conservative, reading of Ignatius. Beyond this the reader might consult the commentary by W.R. Schoedel, *Ignatius of Antioch* (Philadelphia: Fortress, 1985).

Unfortunately there is no readily accessible work on ps-Ignatius in English, although there have been some dissertations, and a number of recent major works on the fourth century context. In getting an idea of the context the reader might start with John Behr, *The Nicene faith* (two parts) (Crestwood NY: St Vladimir's Seminary Press, 2004). There are a number of substantial works which treat ps-Ignatius among other topics, namely Theodor Zahn, *Ignatius von Antiochien* (Gotha: Perthes, 1873), J.B. Lightfoot, *The*

Apostolic Fathers 2 (three parts) (London: MacMillan, 1889) and F.X. Funk, *Die apostolischen Konstitutionen: eine litterar-historische Untersuchung* (Rottenburg: Wilhelm Bader, 1891), as well as the work of Arnold Amelungk, *Untersuchungen über Pseudo-Ignatius: ein Beitrag zur Geschichte einer litterarischen Fälschung* (Marburg: G. Otto, 1899). All, however, are products of the nineteenth century. For readers with Latin the notes and introductory material in Diekamp's edition, noted above, certainly repay study.

POPULAR PATRISTICS SERIES

ST VLADIMIR'S SEMINARY PRESS
1-800-204-2665 • www.svspress.com